Wild About Birds

The DNR Bird Feeding Guide

by Carrol L. Henderson

*Minnesota DNR
Nongame Wildlife
Supervisor*

about the author/photographer

Carrol L. Henderson received a bachelor of science degree in zoology from Iowa State University in 1968 and a master of forest resources from the University of Georgia in 1970. He did his graduate studies on the fish and wildlife resources of Costa Rica.

Henderson joined the Minnesota DNR in 1974 when he was selected as the assistant manager for the Lac qui Parle Wildlife Management Area near Milan. In 1977 he became the supervisor of the Minnesota DNR's Nongame Wildlife Program and has continued in that role to the present. During the past 18 years, Henderson has developed a statewide program for the conservation of the state's nongame wildlife species and has had responsibility for planning and developing projects to help bring back bluebirds, bald eagles, peregrine falcons, river otters and trumpeter swans. He has also provided guidance to many other states in the development of their nongame wildlife programs.

In recognition for his conservation achievements, Henderson received the William R. Miles Environmental Educator of the Year Award in 1987 from the Minnesota Environmental Education Board, the Dr. Robert Green Environmental Award from the Minneapolis Jaycees in 1988, the national Chevron Conservation Award in 1990, the 1992 Chuck Yaeger Conservation Award from the National Fish and Wildlife Foundation, the 1993 Minnesota Award from the Minnesota Chapter of The Wildlife Society, and the 1994 Thomas Sadler Roberts Memorial Award from the Minnesota Ornithologist's Union for outstanding contributions to Minnesota ornithology.

Henderson has served as president of the Nongame Wildlife Association of North America, the Minnesota Chapter of The Wildlife Society and the Minnesota Fish and Wildlife Employee's Association. His writings include the first two books in this series, *Woodworking for Wildlife* and *Landscaping for Wildlife.* He is also the primary photographer for the book *Galapagos Islands - Wonders of the World* which was published in 1995.

acknowledgements

This publication was made possible by the generous Minnesota citizens who donated to the Nongame Wildlife Checkoff on their state tax forms and by the Reinvest in Minnesota Critical Habitat Matching Fund through the use of Environmental Trust Fund allocations from the Legislative Commission on Minnesota Resources.

I extend my sincere appreciation to the following people and organizations who have graciously allowed me to visit their homes and grounds to view their bird feeding arrangements and to photograph the birds and other wildlife at their feeders:

Jan and Dave Ahlgren, Stillwater, Minnesota • Steve and Josephine Blanich, Deerwood, Minnesota • Lyle and Carol Bradley, Anoka,

Minnesota • Walter and Dorothy Breckenridge, Minneapolis, Minnesota • Peggy Callahan and Mark Beckel, Wildlife Science Center, Forest Lake, Minnesota • Luis and Zoila Diego Cruz C., San Jose, Costa Rica • Joe Deden, Manager, Forest Resource Center, Lanesboro, Minnesota • Pat and Rose Deutz, Marshall, Minnesota • Michael K. Fresvik, White Bear Lake, Minnesota • Peter Getman, Minneapolis, Minnesota • Ches and Patti Gevings, Blaine, Minnesota • Judy Gibbs and Kathy Hermes, Duluth, Minnesota • Ann and Jack Goodwin, Milltown, Wisconsin • Don Handley, Circle Pines, Minnesota • Norma Haugen and Grace Mayta, Thief River Falls, Minnesota • Art and Betty Hawkins, Hugo, Minnesota • Don and Pam Henderson, Zearing, Iowa • Leona Henderson, Nevada, Iowa • Linda Janilla, Stillwater, Minnesota • Earl Johnson, DNR Area Wildlife Manager, Detroit Lakes, Minnesota • Peggy Jones, Wyoming, Minnesota • Maggie Kuusisto, Shafer, Minnesota • William and Dorothy Longley, Forest Lake, Minnesota • Gerald and Shirley Maertens, Bemidji, Minnesota • Richard and Tam McGehee, Roseville, Minnesota • Bob and Luz Elena Meyer, Lynd, Minnesota • Vici Nass, East Bethel, Minnesota • Northland Arboretum, Brainerd, Minnesota • Bob and Carolyn Papke, Farmington, Minnesota • Pam and Ken Perry, Brainerd, Minnesota • Powder Valley Nature Center, Kirkwood, Missouri • Orwin Rustad, Faribault, Minnesota • San Diego Zoo, San Diego, California • LeRoy and Donna Sellman, Blaine, Minnesota • Keith and Shelly Steva, Thief River Falls, Minnesota • John and Colette Thorsnes, Arlington, Virginia • Ray and Debbie Whitney, Dellwood, Minnesota • Wild River State Park, Center City, Minnesota • Jean and Herb Wilson, Nevada, Iowa • Bill and Mary Wyatt, Detroit Lakes, Minnesota.

Appreciation is extended to the following for the art and photographs for this book: Dr. Walter Breckenridge, Chip Clark, Art Craigmile, Janet C. Green, Don Henderson, Ethelle Henderson, Dawn Hetrick, Thomas W. Keenan III, Rolf Lidberg, Mary McGee, Dave Maslowski, Stephen Maxson, Warren Nelson, Dr. Lynn Oliphant, Jan Orr, Myrna Pearman, Dick Peterson, Dr. George Rysgaard, Edward Shinabarger, John Thorsnes, Trudy Vrieze-Hofstrand, Donald Waite, and Ron Winch. All other photos are by the author.

Holly Welch deserves credit for the final editing, graphic design, diagrams, layout, and for bringing the book to camera-ready condition. Arturo Leyva assisted with design of the feeder diagrams.
Adele Smith, head of the graphics unit of the Minnesota DNR Bureau of Information and Education, coordinated work on bird feeder design and on the layout, design and color separations. Janice Orr assisted in typing and correcting the manuscript and Erin Carlin Schauer edited. The following people helped edit the text and/or bird feeder designs: Dave and Jan Ahlgren, John Barnum, Kathy Beaulieu, Margaret Dexter, Don Handley, Katherine Haws, Robert Janssen, Dr. Doug and Julie Keran, William L. Longley, Judy Melander, Jack Mooty, Brooks Pennington, Pam Perry, Dr. Noble Proctor, John Schladweiler, Peter Stephano, Kent Solberg, George Steever and Jeanie Vesall.

table of contents

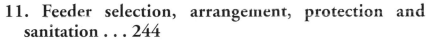

preface

This is the third in my conservation trilogy, a series of books written for the Minnesota Department of Natural Resources (DNR) about attracting wildlife to your property.

Woodworking for Wildlife, the first book in the series, deals specifically with nest structures that accommodate forty-eight different species of wildlife. The second book, *Landscaping for Wildlife,* covers landscaping and planting techniques that can be used to improve wildlife habitats in the Midwest.

Wild About Birds culminates a two-year effort bringing together a wide variety of information about the increasingly popular hobby of feeding birds. By the time I completed this book, I had doubled the number of bird species at my own feeders. I think you can do the same.

This book goes beyond the basics of simply feeding birds. I used this project as an opportunity to share some of the knowledge that I had gained about birds in my work with the Minnesota DNR and to include interesting facts, stories and photos that friends from the birding community have shared with me.

This book is an educational tool to teach both adults and children about birds and their migration, plumage, feeding habits, seasonal adaptation to different climates, habitat relationships and nesting details. Using bird feeding activities as the focus for bird study makes bird feeding even more rewarding.

I have attempted to make this book the most comprehensive reference on bird feeding available. With 68 bird species described and photographed, *Wild About Birds* provides comprehensive species coverage for most states east of the Rocky Mountains and for provinces of central and eastern Canada. For most species both the male and female plumage is shown. Unusual plumage and immature birds are also shown for some species.

I photographed as many of the birds as possible during visits to about three dozen Midwestern families who were especially successful in attracting birds. I typically set up two cameras on tripods and pre-focused them on bird feeder perches at the homes I visited. I attached 50-foot cable releases to the cameras so I could extend the cords back into the homes. Then I could take photos as I visited with the host families about their bird feeding techniques.

In the winter of 1993-1994, however, the temperatures plunged to 25 degrees below zero when I was scheduled to take photos at several homes. Although cameras could only function for about 2 hours before freezing, my photos of evening grosbeaks and redpolls bring back fond but chilly memories of those winter adventures.

Bird feeding can evolve from simple encounters with birds as in this artwork by Rolf Lidberg . . .

. . . to a hobby that has evolved into intricate feeder designs and arrangements.

As my project drew to a close, I also solicited photos from other photographers so I could include species that I was unable to photograph during the last two years.

Where high quality close-up photos were unavailable, I used the services of two of the Midwest's most talented taxidermists: Don Henderson and Peter Getman. Don mounted the rooster pheasant shown in the species account and Peter mounted the European starling, red-headed woodpecker, purple martin and several other songbirds that had been found dead by the public and turned in to the Minnesota DNR. The birds provided an opportunity to portray the closeup, intricate beauty that is not visible at a normal viewing distance.

I also wanted to include at least two dozen bird feeding designs that could be cut out and assembled using simple plans and standard woodshop equipment. Dave Ahlgren of Stillwater was the skilled woodworker who provided me with most of the designs and concepts.

After drafting the plans, I assembled the feeders in the Minnesota DNR's Carlos Avery woodshop so I could refine the dimensions and try them out before recommending them. Minnesota DNR employees Steve Kittelson, Margaret Dexter and Mark Eslinger all assisted in this effort. Peter Stephano, the Features senior editor for *Wood Magazine* also reviewed the woodworking section of this book to ensure its technical accuracy.

This project grew and grew. I had fed birds before, but it was a casual activity that resulted in a very modest response from the birds. Once I gained a better understanding of different foods and feeders, I began to attract birds that I hadn't previously seen in my yard. I was able to take many bird photos in my own yard as I diversified the bird foods and increased the number of feeders.

Feeding birds can provide happiness for people of all ages. You can attract many birds throughout the year and enjoy the beauty of their color, form and song. But bird feeding must be done in a holistic context that includes landscaping your property to provide a good habitat as well as placing nest boxes to attract birds.

And don't forget the plight of the many declining neotropical migrant birds that don't visit backyards or bird feeders. No amount of sunflower seeds will help those species. They need funding directed toward state wildlife agencies to help preserve and manage our northern forests, wetlands and grasslands. Then we will always be able to enjoy birds in our lives, whether they are at our feeders or in the wildlands beyond our backyards.

Feeding birds can attract wildlife throughout the year. It gives you the opportunity to enjoy the natural beauty of every season. This female cardinal was pausing on the handle of an old hand cultivator before flying to a mealworm feeder.

bird feeding as a hobby

1

bird feeding as a hobby

Bird feeding traditions began with people scattering table scraps outside. This drawing was printed in Harper's Weekly in 1886.

Feed the birds.

It sounds like a simple task. But for millions of people, feeding the birds grows from a task to a hobby, and from a hobby to a passion, as they discover nature's beauty and variety at their doorstep.

Unfortunately, many children don't grow up in settings where they can enjoy wildlife abundance. Modern clean farms with monoculture-type fields usually have much less wildlife than the diversified farms of 40 years ago. And most people now live in urban or suburban settings with low wildlife diversity.

Luckily, many wildlife species are adaptable. If we improve our backyard habitats, these adaptable species will live there and provide countless hours of viewing enjoyment. The opportunity to watch robins raise their young, to see chickadees visiting a bird feeder and to hear cardinals sing in the treetops can brighten any day.

Bird feeding as a hobby had modest origins. People discarded table scraps outside their homes for "the birds." The people who threw out table scraps weren't particular about which birds showed up, as long as they cleaned up the food.

Slowly there was a change from table scraps to striped sunflower seeds and chunks of suet. The development of black oil sunflower seeds revolutionized bird feeding. These seeds had thinner coats, making them easier for smaller birds to break open with their bills and reach the nutritious "sunflower hearts" inside. People eventually discovered that sunflower seeds could attract many interesting birds during the summer.

Many people now enhance their backyard theater of seasons by adding specialty foods and feeders that attract a wide variety of birds. In the summer, for example, sugar water attracts hummingbirds and white proso millet attracts indigo buntings. Grape jelly brings in northern orioles and catbirds, orange

Many people enjoy sketching the birds at their feeders.

Don't underestimate the importance of involving children in bird feeding activities. It could help them develop a lifelong interest in wildlife.

These children are intently watching a downy woodpecker at a bird feeder.

halves attract red-bellied and red-headed woodpeckers, apples attract robins and blue jays, and mealworms lure bluebirds and chipping sparrows.

White proso millet can be used in the spring and fall to entice white-throated sparrows, white-crowned sparrows, dark-eyed juncos and fox sparrows. A mixture of sunflower seeds and white proso millet attracts evening grosbeaks, redpolls, pine siskins and purple finches during the winter. Niger thistle attracts those friendly goldfinches all year long.

There are more than 65 different kinds of wild birds that visit bird feeders in the Midwest. You might want to buy a bird identification guide and a notebook so you can record the birds that visit your yard. You should also consider investing in a good pair of binoculars so you can see the birds better.

Bird watching at feeders is a hobby that can grow on you. First you learn to identify the birds and distinguish males from females. You begin to understand their food habits, songs, habitat needs and migratory traditions. The bird feeder becomes an outdoor classroom where you can learn about nature, ecology, predation, natural selection, territorial phenomena, camouflage, coloration and pecking orders among birds. You can also learn more than you ever wanted to know about squirrels and raccoons. The window to your yard becomes a window to nature, filled with action as birds and small animals, and perhaps an occasional bear, feed while competing to survive and raise their families.

The next step in your birdwatching might be visits to natural areas beyond your yard. County and state parks, nature centers, state

Bird feeding can provide some excellent opportunities for wildlife photography.

Bird feeding can also lead to a wider interest in birds: looking in areas besides your backyard for birds that do not visit feeders.

wildlife management areas, national wildlife refuges and private reserves are available for viewing wild birds. Local bird clubs, nature centers and the state ornithologists' union regularly sponsor birding hikes and excursions to see interesting and spectacular wildlife habitats. These activities reinforce a love of nature and challenge you to learn about the diversity of wildlife habitats preserved through private, state and federal wildlife conservation efforts.

Birds can also be an effective hook for teaching children about nature, so it is very important to let them participate in the bird feeding experience. Let children help assemble and fill simple bird feeders. Point out the different birds visiting the feeders and explain what they are doing. Teach kids different birds' names, and use the birds to teach colors to young children. Use birds' migratory destinations to teach kids geography and directions. Wood ducks, you can tell the neighborhood children, go to southeastern states like Mississippi, Alabama and Georgia. Purple martins fly south to Brazil in the winter.

Children can learn to identify birds by their songs with the help of commercially-made audiotapes. They can sketch birds at the feeders to stimulate an interest in art. Children can take photos or videos of birds at feeders to develop their photography skills, or they can learn to use woodworking tools as they assemble feeders. They can also learn to reuse common items like two-liter pop bottles and scraps of wood as bird feeder parts, and they can give these feeders to friends as gifts.

Never underestimate the impact of providing and maintaining bird feeders at your local hospital or retirement home. Wild bird feeding can become a point of interest and conversation if the main lounge or community room has several bird feeders right outside the window. Many people who can no longer go outdoors or get around easily find much more joy watching the birds at their window than watching television.

Feeding the birds provides an enchanting opportunity to enjoy wildlife in your own yard. Every species that visits your feeders will have its own interesting life story, and every individual bird provides a learning opportunity about our natural world.

Good luck and good birding.

Children at the Environmental Learning Center near Isabella, Minnesota hand feed a chickadee. The children put a dummy in a chair and regularly filled its glove with sunflower seeds. The chickadees grew accustomed to this and would soon eat out of the children's hands if they sat in the dummy's lap. Photo by Trudy Vrieze-Hofstrand.

2
bird feeding as a
farm-related industry

bird feeding as a farm-related industry

According to the U.S. Fish and Wildlife Service, the amount of money spent for bird feeding in the United States increased dramatically between 1986 and 1994.

In 1984 it was estimated that U.S. citizens spent about $500 million each year for bird food and another $54 million for bird feeders. Only eight years later the national expenditures for bird feeding were estimated at over $2 billion per year, with another $468 million spent on bird feeders and nest boxes. There are about 65 million people involved with bird feeding across the nation.

There is no evidence that this dramatic increase in wild bird recreation has slowed. The volume of bird food sales increases at about 20 or 30 percent each year.

Bird feeding statistics are equally impressive at the state level. In Minnesota, for example, the U.S. Fish and Wildlife Service estimated that 1.6 million people fed birds in 1991, and that they spent over $65 million for bird feed. Another $16 million was spent on bird feeders, bird baths and nest boxes.

With an estimated 20 percent annual growth rate in sales volume, it appears that the sale of bird food in Minnesota now exceeds $100 million per year.

The Robbinsdale Farm and Garden Store in Minneapolis, Minnesota sold 4 million pounds of bird feed in 1993. Another local company sold 10 million pounds of bird feed that same year. According to a 1991 Minnesota Department of Agriculture study, as many as 75,367,820 pounds of wild bird food were sold in Minnesota during that year, a total that does not include unmixed sunflower seeds or bags weighing under ten pounds. There could be as much as 300 million pounds of bird food sold annually in Minnesota alone!

The bird feeding boom has been good for small businesses across the nation. Wild Birds Unlimited®, founded in 1981, has

Most people who feed birds use from one hundred to two hundred pounds of bird food per year, but some enthusiasts use more than four hundred pounds per year! These two are stocking up for the winter.

8

become a national chain of over 180 stores, grossing $35 million in 1993. Wild Bird Centers of America® , founded in 1989, now has more than 60 stores across the country.

Bird feeding is strongly tied to the Red River valley of northwestern Minnesota and eastern North Dakota. The region is a major producer of sunflower seeds, the single most popular bird feed component. About 15 percent of the sunflower seeds sold by Red River Commodities in Fargo, North Dakota is used as bird feed.

Farmers can grow approximately 1,200 to 1,600 pounds of sunflower seeds per acre. At the rate that bird feed is presently sold and used, about 7,000 acres of land are needed to produce the sunflower seeds used by Minnesota bird lovers each year.

References: Patterson 1993, U.S. Department of Interior 1984, 1993a and 1993b, Walsh 1994.

Black oil sunflowers are an important crop in the Red River Valley of North Dakota and Minnesota. The wild bird feeding industry provides an important and increasing market for the use of this home-grown agricultural crop.

The Bird Feeder store in Cross Lake, Minnesota is one of many stores specializing in wild bird-related foods and products.

There is an amazing variety of products available to attract wildlife to your yard. Visit your local wild bird store for new ideas.

3

birds that come to Midwestern feeders

birds that come to Midwestern feeders

There are at least sixty-five species of birds that visit feeders in the Midwest, providing a kaleidoscope of color and activity throughout the year. Birds can generally be divided into five different migration groups: Canadian (boreal) migrants, permanent residents, short distance migrants, Central American migrants and South American migrants.

CANADIAN (BOREAL) MIGRANTS

Canadian migrants are birds of the northern forests extending from Alaska and the Northwest Territories across Canada, south into states like Idaho and Minnesota and eastward to Nova Scotia. These areas are collectively known as boreal forests. Spruce, hemlock, fir, cedar, red pine, white pine and tamarack forests provide summer nesting habitats for many Canadian migrants.

Many species of the boreal forest, including grosbeaks, redpolls, pine siskins and crossbills, go through a variable ten-year cycle of abundance. Sometimes they exhibit smaller waves of abundance and decline within the ten-year cycles. Coniferous trees produce different amounts of seeds each year, causing great changes in the number and distribution of songbirds.

This boom-and-bust lifestyle of northern wildlife causes some species with nomadic patterns of existence to migrate south during winters when food is scarce. Fewer birds migrate when there is enough food to go around.

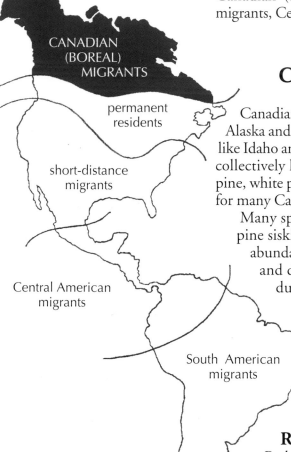

CANADIAN (BOREAL) MIGRANTS

permanent residents

short-distance migrants

Central American migrants

South American migrants

This map shows the approximate nesting range of boreal migrants. Boreal migrants that migrate South usually winter in the area marked "permanent residents."

Red-breasted nuthatch

Red-breasted nuthatches may be small, but their quick movements and extreme fearlessness in the presence of people make them feeder favorites.

A red-breasted nuthatch is only four and a half inches long. It has a blue-gray back like a white-breasted nuthatch, but it also has a black stripe through its eye and a rufous or rusty-colored breast. The top of its head is dark blue-gray.

Red-breasted nuthatches inhabit coniferous forests, while white-breasted nuthatches are associated with hardwood forests. In some years, however, large numbers of red-breasted nuthatches migrate through the Midwest to residential backyards, farmsteads and woodlands that have conifers. They have been seen at feeders from central and southern Minnesota to Oklahoma, Arkansas and Tennessee.

Red-breasted nuthatches nest in shallow tree cavities or former woodpecker nests. They smear conifer pitch, or resin, around their nest entrances to discourage predators from entering. Other birds or mammals don't like getting the sticky pitch in their feathers or fur.

These birds lay between four and seven eggs that hatch after about 12 days. Their young require a longer fledging period than most comparable-size birds: they fly after three weeks of parental care.

Food: Seeds of spruce, fir and maple; ragweed, sour dock and other seeds of weeds exposed above snow drifts; also sap, insects, spiders, larvae, suet, sunflower seeds, peanut butter, cantaloupe seeds, doughnuts, nut meats and exposed fatty deposits on dead animals like deer.

Feeding habits: Red-breasted nuthatches store, or cache, many seeds for later consumption by sticking them in holes and crevices in tree bark. They plug these holes with pieces of bark to conceal the seeds from other birds.

References: Davison 1967, Mahnken 1983, Janssen 1987, Roberts 1932, Tessaglia and Rosenberg 1994, Waldon 1991 and Warton 1990.

The sprightly red-breasted nuthatch has a slightly upturned bill that is adapted for probing under the bark of trees. These birds are quite unafraid of people and will sometimes fly to a feeder while you are filling it.

Golden-crowned kinglet and ruby-crowned kinglet

The sprightly golden-crowned kinglet is one of the smallest birds to visit backyard feeders—only three and a half inches long. Kinglets are in constant motion, hovering and flitting from branch to branch as they seek small insects among spruce cones and needles. They are rare visitors at feeders.

A golden-crowned kinglet's body is olive-green on top and light gray below, with two white wing bars. It has white spots above its eyes. A male kinglet's head is highlighted by a black crown around distinctive yellow and orange patches. A female kinglet has a yellow patch on her head.

Golden-crowned kinglets migrate from early September through early December. They winter anywhere between southern Minnesota and the Gulf Coast states and between the Great Plains and the East Coast.

They return early, from mid-March through mid-May, feeding primarily on small insects that live in spruce trees. They may visit suet feeders as they move north.

Golden-crowned kinglets nest in the northeastern third of Minnesota and boreal forests of Canada. They suspend their nests of mosses and lichens from horizontal limbs of spruce, fir, hemlock or red cedar trees. A typical nest will contain eight or nine eggs that hatch after an incubation period of 14 or 15 days.

Ruby-crowned kinglets are slightly larger than golden-crowned kinglets, measuring about four inches long. Their bodies have similar markings, but ruby-crowned kinglets have white eye rings instead of the white spots. A male ruby-crowned kinglet has a red crown without the black edging found on golden-crowned kinglets. A female will not have this red crown. Ruby-crowned kinglets' songs are much stronger and more musical than those of their golden-crowned counterparts.

Spruce or fir trees are popular places for ruby-crowned kinglets to build their moss and lichen nests. They lay between seven and ten eggs, their incubation period lasts about 12 days, and their young fledge after 12 days.

Food: Small insects, cracked nuts, peanuts, some plant seeds and fruit.

Feeding habits: Ruby-crowned kinglets feed by hovering over pine and spruce cones and capturing the small insects inside.

They may use birdbaths during their migration, and they may visit suet feeders. If you fill your hummingbird feeder in early May before the hummingbirds return, you may be treated to the sight of a kinglet taking nectar.

Golden-crowned kinglets are infrequent visitors during the spring as they migrate to boreal forest nesting areas in the northern states and Canada.

References: Davison 1967, Janssen 1987, Roberts 1932 and Waldon 1991.

American tree sparrow

Among the faithful visitors to winter bird feeders are American tree sparrows—native sparrows that nest in northern Canada, the Northwest Territories and Alaska.

Tree sparrows' rusty caps suggest the familiar chipping sparrows that are present in the summer. A tree sparrow, however, has a distinctive "tie tack" mark in the center of its whitish-gray breast. Lark sparrows, birds in the summer resident category, have similar breast markings but lack the rusty cap. Song sparrows, also summer breeding residents, have central breast spots, but theirs are surrounded by heavy streaking.

Stunted, scrubby thickets and scattered woodlands that include willow, birch, alder and spruce trees make up American tree sparrows' summer nesting habitats. Their nests are often on or near the ground in hummocks of grass at the base of small trees or shrubs. They lay about five eggs with an incubation period of 12 to 13 days. The young fledge after only eight or ten days, and they fly at 14 days.

American tree sparrows arrive at their wintering areas in October and November and remain there until March or early April, eating seeds directly from tree and shrub branches.

Food: They primarily eat millet that has been thrown on the ground or fallen from hanging feeders. When there's no millet around, American tree sparrows will eat sunflower seeds, corn, bread and suet.

Feeding habits: American tree sparrows hover over plants when the ground is snow-covered, allowing their wings to strike the seed heads. Then they fly to the ground to eat the newly fallen seeds. They will also hop up from the ground to reach seed heads just above them.

References: Davison 1967, Janssen 1987, Naugler 1993, Stokes 1987 and Warton 1990.

The American tree sparrow, a winter visitor, feeds on small seeds like white proso millet that have been scattered on the ground.

Fox sparrow

Native sparrows are often seen as a rather drab-looking group of birds. This negative attitude toward sparrows may have come from the undesirable qualities of exotic house sparrows, which are not actually sparrows at all but members of the weaver finch family.

Fox sparrows are extraordinary birds that command attention whenever they show up at a feeder. They are huge by sparrow standards: about 6 1/4 inches long, compared to American tree sparrows and white-throated sparrows that measure 5 1/4 inches long. Their bright rusty color, reminiscent of a red fox, gives rise to the name fox sparrow.

The large size and bright rusty markings of the fox sparrow make it stand out among the birds seen during spring and fall migrations. Fox sparrows feed on the ground.

A fox sparrow often has a tie-tack mark in the center of its heavily streaked and spotted breast. While these markings are similar to the markings on song sparrows, a fox sparrow's large size and rusty color prevent it from being mistaken for that species. Fox sparrows also have a beautiful song, a welcome sound in springtime woodlands.

Fox sparrows nest in the same far northern boreal regions as white-crowned sparrows, with a range extending from British Columbia southward along the Rocky Mountains to Colorado and Utah. These birds do not nest in the boreal forests of Minnesota. Fox sparrows nest on or near the ground, and a normal clutch is three to five eggs.

Food: Barley, blackberries, bristle grass, canary grass, cracked corn, wild grape, millet, oats, peanuts, ragweed, raspberry, smartweed, sorghum, wheat, euonymus, cedar, birch, alder, bread scraps and suet. During the summer they also eat beetles and millipedes.

Feeding habits: When fox sparrows feed, they jump forward and then quickly jump backward, tossing assorted leaves and ground litter to expose the seeds and small invertebrates that comprise their diet.

At ground feeders they eat millet, black oil sunflower seeds and cracked corn. The best time to maintain ground feeders for fox sparrows is from September through November and March through mid-May.

References: Davison 1967, Janssen 1987, Robbins, Bruun, and Zim 1983, Roberts 1932 and Stokes 1987.

White-throated sparrow

A white-throated sparrow can provide one of the most welcome sounds in our northern woodlands: a clear whistled call that sounds like "old Sam Peabody-Peabody-Peabody..." It is a pleasant call frequently associated with the drumming of ruffed grouse and the "teacher-teacher-teacher" calls of ovenbirds.

A white-throated sparrow often has, as its name implies, a white throat patch. It also has a white stripe above its eyes and a yellow spot next to its bill, or beak. Some of these sparrows, however, have brownish-white throat patches and tan stripes instead of white markings. Sparrows of either coloring are still considered the same species.

Similar white-crowned sparrows also have white stripes above their eyes, but are missing the yellow spot and the white throat. These sparrows have brown backs and medium gray breasts and bellies. Young birds have tan and brown striped heads with white throat patches.

White-throated sparrows nest in the coniferous forests of Canada and the northern parts of states bordering Canada. They build their nests on or near the ground in low shrubs or among the branches of fallen trees. Four or five eggs hatch after an incubation period of 12 to 14 days. The young fledge after ten days.

Food: Small insects, seeds, fallen fruits, amaranth (pigweed), barnyard grass, blackberry, blueberry, bristle grass, canary grass, crabgrass, dandelion, American elderberry, wild hemp, millet, ragweed, smartweed, sorghum, switchgrass, dogwood, American mountain ash and viburnum.

Their diets change from 90 percent plant matter in the winter to 50 percent in the summer, and they eat invertebrates like ants, beetles, bugs, caterpillars, flies, snails and spiders.

Feeding habits: You can attract white-throated sparrows by scattering white proso millet or cracked corn on the bare ground during the migratory periods: September through November and again from March through April. Once the birds are attracted to a feeding site they will also use tray feeders and fly-through feeders.

Look closely at large flocks of white-throated sparrows; you may discover a white-crowned sparrow or fox sparrow among them.

References: Davison 1967, Janssen 1987, Roberts 1932, Stokes 1987 and Warton 1990.

A few white-throated sparrows may try to winter in northern areas but they are not very winter hardy. This sparrow survived for a while, but eventually succumbed to the cold. Notice how it's sitting rather than standing, and how its head droops.

In its darker phase, the white-throated sparrow's throat patch is more indistinct. You can see sparrows in both color phases feeding together during migrations.

The distinctive white-throated sparrow has two color phases. In this phase you can see the yellow spot above its eye and the distinctive white throat patch.

17

White-crowned sparrow

At a glance, adult white-crowned sparrows look just like white-throated sparrows. Closer inspection reveals black and white stripes on top of the white-crowned sparrows' heads.

A white-crowned sparrow has one broad white stripe down the center of its head and a black stripe on each side of the white stripe. Narrower white and black stripes extend from the back of the sparrow's eyes to the back of its head. A white-crowned sparrow doesn't have the yellow spots over its eyes like a white-throated sparrow, but it does have a distinct pink bill. Other sparrows' bills are usually gray. Immature white-crowns look much like swamp sparrows.

White-crowned sparrows are characteristic of northern boreal regions of Canada and Alaska, and their breeding range extends south along the Rocky Mountains to Colorado. They are one of the few species of Canadian migrants that do not nest in the boreal forests of northeastern Minnesota.

White-crowned sparrows are much less common than white-throated sparrows during spring and fall migration. A few birds may overwinter in northern states, but most of them migrate to states from Missouri southward. They can be seen in the company of dark-eyed juncos and white-throated sparrows.

These sparrows make their nests on or near the ground in thick, shrubby habitats. The four or five white-crowned sparrow eggs hatch after 12 days, and the young fledge ten days later.

Food: Mainly small seeds from shrubs and weedy annuals, including amaranth, bluegrass, bristle grass, dandelion, goose-foot, wild hemp, ragweed, smartweed, grain sorghum, sunflower seeds and walnut meats. About 35 percent of their summer diet is comprised of ants, beetles, bugs, caterpillars, grasshoppers, spiders and wasps.

Feeding habits: White-crowned sparrows will feed on millet, sunflower seeds and cracked corn that has been scattered on the ground during the spring and fall migration.

The white-crowned sparrow is less common than the white-throated sparrow during the migration period. Look for the alternating black and white stripes on their heads.

This immature white-crowned sparrow has alternating brown and buff stripes on the top of its head.

References: Culver 1991, Davison 1967, Janssen 1987, Roberts 1932 and Warton 1990.

Dark-eyed junco

Dark-eyed juncos are grayish, sparrow-sized birds commonly seen hopping, scratching and feeding on the ground under hanging bird feeders during the fall, winter and spring. These birds were once called slate-colored juncos because of the beautiful slate-gray coloring on their backs and sides, but now they and three other races of juncos are grouped into a single species known as the dark-eyed junco.

Females have clay brown or brown-gray coloring, and males are slate gray with white bellies. Their outer tail feathers are white so that they create a conspicuous flash when they flush. This helps warn other juncos that a predator may be approaching, the same way the flash of a deer's raised white tail alerts other deer that danger lurks in the vicinity.

Boreal coniferous forests provide nesting habitats for dark-eyed juncos. Their range extends from Alaska across Canada to the Atlantic Ocean, and down to the southern extent of boreal forests like those in northern Minnesota.

Dark-eyed junco nests are made of grasses, rootlets and moss, and concealed on the ground. Juncos lay three to five eggs which take 11 or 12 days to hatch, and the young fledge in 9 to 13 days. After nesting, juncos migrate to wintering areas from central Minnesota to the southern states and northern Mexico.

Male dark-eyed juncos winter farther north than females, so there is frequently a disproportionate number of males at winter feeding stations in northern states. Among a flock of juncos you may notice a pecking order. Some males dominate selected feeder sites by chasing away other males. Males normally dominate the smaller females, and adult males and females both dominate the younger birds.

Food: Amaranth, crabgrass, barnyard grass, bristle grass, canary grass, dropseed, goosefoot, wild hemp, millet, oats, petunia, ragweed, grain sorghum, Sudan grass, switchgrass, wheat, pigeon grass, lamb's quarters, chickweed, purslane, wild sunflower and pine seeds; weevils, small beetles, flies, moths, caterpillars, grasshoppers, ants and spiders; wheat bread, corn bread, doughnuts, oatmeal, peanuts, pie crusts, pumpkin seeds, walnut meats, and peanut butter.

A female dark-eyed junco is pictured on the left. A male is pictured on the right. The female's body is lighter gray and her back and sides are buff or brown. The male junco has a medium gray color over his body, a buff tinge on his back feathers, a white belly and a light bill.

Male pine grosbeak.
Photo by Stephen Maxson.

Immature male pine grosbeak.
Photo by Warren Nelson.

Feeding habits: At feeders, dark-eyed juncos will eat white proso millet, black oil sunflower seeds, cracked corn, grain sorghum, peanuts, old bakery goods, broken walnuts, wheat or suet. They will eat out of tray, screen or self feeders, but they usually feed on the ground. They are often seen feeding with American tree sparrows, fox sparrows, white-throated sparrows and white-crowned sparrows.

References: Culver 1991, Davison 1967, Janssen 1987, Roberts 1932, Stokes 1987 and Warton 1990.

Pine grosbeak

The large size and tame nature of pine grosbeaks make them imposing visitors at bird feeders. About the size of a robin, adult male pine grosbeaks are rosy-pink with two white to pink wing bars. Females are gray with a brassy yellow tinge on the tops of their heads and rumps. One-year-old males are gray with a rusty tinge on top of their heads and rumps.

Pine grosbeaks do not nest in the Midwest but are rare and beautiful winter visitors in northern Minnesota. In some years they are found as far south as the Minnesota/Iowa border. Pine grosbeaks travel in small flocks that wander into northern states from Canadian boreal forest nesting areas.

Food: Pine grosbeaks are attracted to tree and shrub plantings where they eat seeds, buds and fruits of apple, white ash, bittersweet, blackberry, boxelder and cherry trees. They also eat crabapple seeds (not the pulp), mountain ash fruits, dogwood fruits, and the seeds of balsam fir, sumac, jack pine, red cedar and Norway spruce.

Feeding habits: Pine grosbeaks may visit feeding stations for sunflower seeds. In the winter they eat fruits of American highbush cranberry by mashing them so they can swallow the seeds and drop the pulp and skin to the ground.

References: Davison 1967, Janssen 1987, Roberts 1932 and Waldon 1991.

Female pine grosbeak.

White-winged crossbills have conspicuous white wing bars. Their wings are dark brown and their bodies are a dull pink or rose red.
Photo by Warren Nelson.

Female white-winged crossbills are olive-colored and have conspicuous yellow markings on their rumps and white wing bars.
Photo by Warren Nelson.

Red crossbill and white-winged crossbill

Adult male white-winged crossbills are a dull rose red, with dark brown wings and conspicuous white wing bars. Females are olive green with yellow on their rumps.

These crossbills breed across most of the boreal region of North America, from Alaska to Nova Scotia. Their populations can fluctuate greatly from one year to another. Since their food items are very limited and seed production can vary greatly from one region to another, they have a nomadic lifestyle adapted for moving to where food is abundant.

Breeding takes place wherever there are adequate coniferous forest habitats and good crops of tamarack cones. Crossbills normally travel in flocks, and large movements may occur in October and November as the birds seek heavy crops of cones for food.

Food: This species has a distinctive crossed bill specialized for

Red crossbills stop at a feeder during the 1988 crossbill invasion. Photo by G. N. Rysgaard.

Male red crossbill.
Photo by Dave Maslowski/
Maslowski Wildlife Productions.

feeding on tamarack cone seeds. They are so adept at plucking seeds from the cones that they may eat up to three thousand per day. They do not usually visit bird feeders, but they do have an affinity for salt that can bring them to salt blocks placed for deer. They may also be seen along roadsides where salt accumulates.

Red crossbills are conspicuous but extremely erratic northern visitors to the Midwest. Males are dull red with brownish wings and tails. Females are olive green with yellow rumps. Second-year (non-breeding) males are similar to females, but they are splotched with reddish feathers.

Like white-winged crossbills, red crossbills have crossed mandibles. They don't, however, have wing bars, and their bills are sturdier.

Red crossbills nest in low numbers in the boreal forests of northern Minnesota and into the boreal forests of Canada, northern Europe and northern Asia. They experience cyclical changes in abundance that can result in winter invasions of these interesting birds in coniferous plantings well south of their typical boreal forest habitats.

The last great red crossbill invasion in the Midwest was in 1988. Bill Longley, a licensed bird bander in Forest Lake, Minnesota, trapped and banded fifty-two in his yard that year, but has seen none since then.

Feeding habits: Red crossbills are infrequent visitors at feeders where they will eat sunflower seeds and salt. They are also known to visit thistle feeders and to feed on seeds of tough pine and spruce cones.

References: Benkman 1992, Davison 1967, Janssen 1987, Roberts 1932 and Waldon 1991.

Common redpoll and hoary redpoll

Redpolls are small winter visitors characterized by tiny bodies, soft grayish striping and beautiful rose-colored highlights. Redpolls don't travel in small numbers; they're likely to swarm in by the dozens. Usually they sit quietly in the top of a nearby tree, watching the feeding station. When all seems well, they come fluttering out of the treetops like falling leaves.

A female redpoll has a black chin spot and a dark reddish patch on the top of her head. A male has a reddish cap, but is best known for the stunning rose-red marking on his breast. Male house finches are slightly larger than redpolls and have more of an orange-red breast coloring. Male purple finches are much larger than redpolls and have red-purple coloring.

Redpolls are split into two species: common redpolls and hoary redpolls. Hoary redpolls are much whiter than common red-polls, with pure white or rosy-white rumps that don't have streaking or striping.

Redpolls nest in the birch forests, low thickets and shrub-lands of arctic and subarctic regions of Canada, the Northwest Territories and Alaska.

Most redpolls only migrate to southern Canada and are uncommon in the United States. Sometimes, however, redpolls appear at Midwestern winter feeding stations. In some years they show up as early as October.

Redpolls may be extremely common during some winters and uncommon in other years. Redpolls are named for the red caps on their heads. This male is distinguished by the rose-red markings on his upper breast.

In other years, they show up in mid-January and stay through early April. This unpredictability is characteristic of many boreal birds whose numbers fluctuate with the cyclical changes in abundance of natural foods.

Food: Seeds of tamarack, alder, elm, birch and other trees. They eat the seeds of "weeds" like evening primrose, ragweed, pigweed, smartweed, lamb's quarters, goosefoot and foxtail. They also eat tiny insects, insect larvae and insect eggs.

Feeding habits: A redpoll's tiny bill is well-suited to feeding at cylindrical feeders. If you wish to attract these birds, mix Niger thistle seed with peanut hearts and sunflower chips in a cylindrical thistle feeder, cylindrical self feeder or hanging pop bottle feeder. The feeder should have small feeder holes that are no more than 1/4 inch in diameter.

When many redpolls are present, try spreading Niger thistle on the ground under thistle feeders or on top of black oil sunflower seeds in tray feeders. This provides more room for the swarm of little birds.

This female redpoll has found a homemade finch mix made from Niger thistle and sunflower chips.

References: Davison 1967, Janssen 1987, Proctor, pers. comm. and Roberts 1932.

Pine siskin

The tiny pine siskin is one of those "little brown birds" that adds variety and interest to an assemblage of winter species. They can get extremely thick on a feeder. Pine siskins are another boreal species showing erratic changes from year to year.

A pine siskin has a brown, heavily-streaked body with a conical but sharply pointed bill, a deeply forked tail with a yellow base, a distinct yellow edge on its wing primaries and a yellow patch on its wings. The yellow highlights distinguish pine siskins from other small birds like redpolls, house finches and purple finches.

Pine siskins are summer nesting residents in boreal forests of Canada and throughout much of the northern half of Minnesota where coniferous forests abound, although they nest sporadically in other regions where conifers grow in groves or plantations.

The yellow highlights on a pine siskin's primary wing feathers make it an easy bird to recognize.

Food: Seeds like pine, hemlock, spruce, northern white cedar and tamarack; seeds of birch, elm, alder and willow; common annual and perennial plant seeds like chickweed, dandelion and sunflower; small insects, including aphids. They will also eat salt when they find it along roadsides. Pine siskins sometimes feed on the tender shoots of young vegetables in gardens.

Feeding habits: At feeders, pine siskins prefer small seeds like Niger thistle, hulled sunflower, nut meats, white proso millet and sunflower chips. They often feed with redpolls and goldfinches because they have similar food preferences. Pine siskins' bills are small enough so they can use commercial thistle feeders that dispense Niger thistle.

Reference: Davison 1967, Janssen 1987 and Roberts 1932.

Evening grosbeak

Evening grosbeaks are stunning birds that are sometimes called northwoods parrots because of their stocky build and noisy, gregarious behavior. Their color is almost too rich to be accurately captured on film.

Measuring about eight inches long, an evening grosbeak is one of the largest members of the finch family. A male has bright yellow eyebrow markings, a chocolate-yellow breast and a chocolate-brown head and shoulder area. His primary feathers are black, with contrasting white wing coverts. One of the most conspicuous characteristics of an evening grosbeak is its huge conical bill that allows it to eat large seeds. In springtime this bill changes from yellow to green.

Evening grosbeaks are a resident breeding species in the boreal forests of the northern United States and Canada. They nest from the

While a female evening grosbeak is not as colorful as a male, her yellow highlights are still quite bright. Notice her thick, conical bill adapted for feeding on a variety of larger seeds and fruits.

Pacific Northwest and the Rocky Mountains south into Mexico. They also nest in northeastern Minnesota. There is some range expansion underway to the west and to the south.

Grosbeaks are regular winter visitors at feeders in the northeastern third of Minnesota, sometimes visiting in flocks of over a hundred. During some winters they may also wander south to the Minnesota/Iowa border. Farther south, evening grosbeaks are nomadic and erratic in their travels.

This boreal species nests in habitats like spruce and northern white cedar swamps. They frequently make their nests in fir, maple, pine or spruce. Evening grosbeaks lay three to five eggs that will hatch after 12 to 14 days of incubation. The young fledge when they are two weeks old.

The only problem with evening grosbeaks is that, even though they are extremely beautiful birds and their calls can revive a cold and lifeless winter landscape, they can be real "pigs" at the bird feeder! A large flock can go through many hundreds of pounds of sunflower seeds during the winter. Some people enjoy grosbeaks at first, only to realize that they cannot keep up with the birds' voracious appetites.

Food: Seeds of boxelder, maple, ash, mountain ash, dogwood, sumac, juniper, apple, elderberry, fir, pine, red cedar, serviceberry, spruce and wild cherry. In the summer about one-fifth of their diet includes caterpillars, beetles, spiders, and other invertebrates.

They also eat spruce budworm caterpillars, so they often nest in higher concentrations in the vicinity of spruce budworm outbreaks. This provides them with more food for their young. Higher fledging success is likely during years with higher populations of spruce budworms.

Feeding habits: At feeders evening grosbeaks will eat black oil sunflower seeds, peanuts and safflower seeds. While most any feeder will serve the purpose, some people will use a very large surface like a picnic table or a sheet of plywood as a feeding tray to accommodate many grosbeaks. Otherwise a large tray feeder, large screen feeder or Perry extra large screen feeder would be an excellent choice.

References: Davison 1967, Janssen 1987, Manry 1993, Roberts 1932, Stokes 1987 and Warton 1990.

Male evening grosbeak.

Evening grosbeaks usually land in treetops near a feeder and announce their arrival with a chorus of musical calls. This male grosbeak visits a feeder.

Evening grosbeaks provide a spectacular addition to bird feeding sites because of their bright colors and group feeding behavior.

PERMANENT RESIDENTS

Permanent residents are birds that live in the same state or region throughout the year. Gallinaceous, or ground nesting, birds like ring-necked pheasants and northern bobwhites that do not migrate, hardy backyard birds like black-capped chickadees and downy woodpeckers, and some birds that undergo short migratory shifts within the same state or to nearby states like American crows all qualify as permanent residents.

In northern regions there are some permanent residents like boreal chickadees and gray jays that live only within their northern boreal forest habitats. Other permanent residents of the Midwest include tufted titmice, year-long residents in hardwood forests like those of extreme southeastern Minnesota.

Each permanent resident has a significant strategy it uses to endure cold weather and to find food during the winter. Some birds that usually eat insects, for example, might switch to eating seeds during the winter. Many permanent residents eat seeds or dried fruits like sumac, bittersweet, crabapple, mountain ash or American highbush cranberry that remain available throughout the winter. Cardinals and purple finches eat a variety of tree seeds. Smaller birds like goldfinches and northern bobwhites eat weed seeds that are on or near the ground. Pheasants forage for waste grain left in agricultural fields.

While most insect-eating birds migrate south when their food is not available, woodpeckers and nuthatches survive by searching for insect larvae concealed under the bark or in the wood of trees. This allows them to obtain protein during the winter. Black-billed magpies, crows and ravens scavenge for meat and fat on dead animals. Carcasses of deer and moose provide food for them and for chickadees, nuthatches and woodpeckers. Gray jays, nuthatches and blue jays cache nuts, acorns, seeds and even insects in late summer and fall for retrieval during the winter months when food items are scarce.

Physical adaptations also help small birds survive in the winter. A chickadee's body temperature drops at night to lower its metabolic needs. This reduces the amount of nutrients that must be burned to keep it warm at night. Many birds roost in tree cavities at night to reduce the effects of wind chill.

As you enjoy these hardy permanent residents, take the time to notice their specialized food habits and the survival strategies that allow them to live in the challenging and constantly changing weather conditions of the upper Midwest.

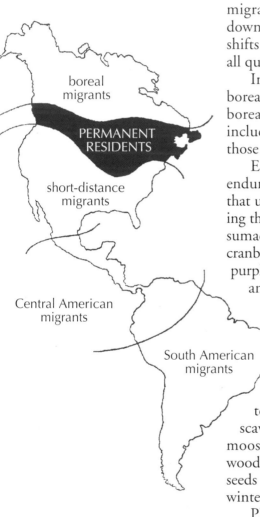

From a Midwestern perspective, the general range for permanent residents includes northern states and southern portions of Canadian provinces.

26

Ring-necked pheasant

One distinctive sound reverberating across midwestern farmlands in springtime is the crow of the ring-necked pheasant. These big, beautiful birds are exotic, or imported from another region. Originally from China, ring-necked pheasants were successfully introduced to the United States in 1881 and became one of the few exotic birds successfully established in our wilds. Gray partridges, rock doves, European starlings and house sparrows are other exotic species that evolved in another country and have been successfully established in the United States.

Ring-necked pheasants are excellent game birds, but their natural aggressiveness helped speed the decline of native prairie chickens. Pheasants lay eggs in the nests of other ground-nesting birds, like prairie chickens, in addition to laying a clutch of eggs that they incubate themselves. Remaining populations of prairie chickens in Minnesota are north of the zone inhabited by pheasants.

Adult rooster pheasants are nearly three feet long, including a tail that may exceed 20 inches. They have iridescent greenish-purple heads, white neck bands and iridescent chestnut chests and shoulders. Their backs are buff to golden, orange, brown and black, and their tails are brown, banded with black. Their faces and wattles are mostly bare and bright red. Smaller than the roosters, hens are tan or buff with a mottling of brown to provide camouflage while incubating eggs.

Pheasant habitats consist of mixed meadows, grasslands, pastures, woodlots and marshes. They don't do well on modern clean farms that are plowed from one end to another. They can thrive if they are provided with undisturbed or unmowed summer grassy nesting cover (often road ditches or Conservation Reserve Program lands).

Ring-necked pheasant roosters, like this one, have tail feathers over 20 inches long.

They also need secure winter cover in the form of marshes, grasslands and woodlots, and food plots of corn, sudex, buckwheat or sorghum.

Pheasants lay between six and twelve olive to buff-colored eggs in a ground nest lined with grass. The young hatch after an incubation period of about 24 days. Young pheasants are called precocial because they are able to leave their nests with the hen within one day of hatching.

Food: Blackberries, wild plums, cherries, chokeberries, grapes,

27

apples, raspberries, dogwood, strawberries, sunflowers, buckwheat, corn, soybeans, barley, sorghum, wheat, alfalfa, crabapples, millet, safflowers, smartweed and sumac make up 85 percent of pheasants' summer diet and 99 percent of their winter diet.

During the summer and fall they eat beetles, caterpillars, crickets, earthworms, ants, spiders and grasshoppers. Forty-seven grasshoppers were once counted in the crop, or gullet, of a rooster pheasant taken during an early November hunting trip!

Feeding habits: Pheasants will eat ear corn and shelled corn from feeders during the winter. Feeders like those shown on pages 205-207 are excellent for feeding pheasants. These feeders should be placed adjacent to good wintering cover in a sheltered location that will not drift over with snow. A lean-to feeder as shown on page 236 also works well for feeding pheasants in winter.

Pheasants are normally considered birds of farmland areas, but they will also live in urbanized areas where there is adequate open space, marshland and undisturbed grassy habitat for nesting.

References: Culver 1991, Davison 1967, Harrison 1978 and Roberts 1932.

Wild turkey

Once you're accustomed to the presence of chickadees and hummingbirds at your bird feeder, the arrival of a wild turkey is a startling experience. They're wily and outstanding game birds, but they can also provide a thrill when they cautiously stalk up to a bird feeder to scratch for grain.

Wild turkeys are the largest game birds in North America, with adult toms weighing over 25 pounds. They may stand 30 inches high. A tom's body is black with metallic highlights, his wing feathers are barred with white, and his bare head ranges from blue to pink to red depending on his mood. He has a fleshy "snood" that hangs down along the side of the bill. A tom has a black, hairy beard that hangs from the front of his breast and brown-black tail feathers that are tipped with buff. Domestic turkeys have white tips on their tail feathers. Hens are smaller than the toms and usually do not have a beard.

The thrill of seeing and hearing a wild turkey gobbler is a highlight in springtime woodlands.

The return of truly wild turkeys (not game farm birds that have been released) is an American conservation success story. Once rare throughout the Midwest, wild turkeys have staged a comeback that rivals that of the wood duck. Wild turkeys were extirpated from southern Minnesota by 1900, and releases of game farm birds in the mid-1920s failed. From 1964 to 1968 a total of 39 wild turkeys were taken from wild populations in Nebraska, South Dakota and Arkansas and released in Winona County, Minnesota. Between 1971 and 1973 another 29 wild turkeys were captured in Missouri and released in Houston County, Minnesota. By 1994 the turkey population had increased to between 22,000 and 24,000 birds, and additional releases are still being made in eastern, central and western Minnesota.

Wild turkeys have benefited from releases all over the United States. The subspecies found in the Midwest is the eastern wild turkey, but different subspecies are also found in the southwest and western states.

Habitats for wild turkeys vary from hardwood forests, where turkeys depend on the production of seeds like acorns, to agricultural regions interspersed with wooded ridges, valleys, farmsteads and woodlots.

Turkeys usually lay between ten and fifteen large, lightly speckled eggs in a shallow depression on the ground. Their eggs hatch after 28 days and the precocious young leave the nest shortly after hatching.

Food: Corn, buckwheat, millet, acorns, oats, peanuts, pine seeds, grain sorghum, soybeans, wheat and sunflowers; fruits like blackberries, blueberries, dewberries, dogwood berries, gooseberries, grapes, mulberries, strawberries, cherries, chokeberries, Virginia creeper and elderberries; animal food like ants, bees, beetles, centipedes, cicadas, crayfish, crickets, flies, grasshoppers, salamanders, snails, spiders and wasps.

Wild turkeys eat 85 percent plant food and 15 percent animal food.

Feeding habits: Wild turkeys are rare visitors at bird feeders. They may show up where houses or cabins are adjacent to woodlands. They will pick up corn, wheat or sunflower seeds that have been scattered on the ground specifically for ground-feeding birds, or they will forage for seeds that have fallen from hanging bird feeders. Wild turkeys will probably take corn from Olson deer feeders or ear-corn feeder cribs like the ones shown on pages 205 and 206.

Wild turkeys shouldn't, however, be encouraged to visit a feeder that is also visited by domestic poultry. Wild turkeys are very vulnerable to the diseases carried by domestic chickens, ducks and turkeys.

This wild turkey hen was photographed at the Powder Valley Nature Center near Kirkwood, Missouri.

References: Culver 1991, Davison 1967, Harrison 1978 and the Minnesota DNR 1991.

Northern bobwhite

"Bob-white!" This clear, piercing whistle of the northern bobwhite is one of the distinct and memorable calls in the bird world. Bobwhite quail are categorized as gallinaceous birds because they live by scratching on the ground for food.

A bobwhite quail has stocky, rounded body contours with a reddish-brown mottled back and a white belly highlighted with dark scalloped feather edges. About ten inches long, a male has a white throat and white lines above his eyes. A female has a buff throat and eye stripes.

Like pheasants and wild turkeys, bobwhite quail may visit feeders adjacent to their habitat areas. This male bobwhite has a white stripe above his eye and a white chin marking. Female bobwhites have buff-colored markings.

The behavior of a group of quail, called a covey, helps protect them from predators. When approached, the covey will sit motionless and become nearly impossible to see. When it is approached too closely, the covey flushes in all directions, confusing the predator and making it difficult to concentrate on capturing a single quail. At night the quail form a circle facing outward, with their bodies touching. This facilitates a quick escape if a predator attacks them.

Bobwhite quail are found throughout the eastern and southeastern United States, the Midwest, and the Great Plains south to Texas. The northern border of their range extends to the southeastern tip of Minnesota, including Houston and Fillmore counties. Historically they have nested as far north as Pine and Benton counties in Minnesota, but their range has diminished in recent decades. This is perhaps due to their vulnerability to severe winter weather. They might also have lost some of their natural winter hardiness when well-meaning conservationists, who did not understand the genetic problems that can go hand in hand with restocking wildlife, released southern-origin quail in the cold climate of Minnesota.

Quail live in mixed agricultural, grassland and woodland habitats. They do well in areas with thickets, hedge rows, and patchworks of small fields and woodlots.

According to Dr. T. S. Roberts, author of *The Birds of Minnesota*, the bobwhite quail, "when unmolested, is a gentle, friendly creature, coming confidingly about farms and dwellings and into the environs of cities and towns. It builds its nest beside the path or in the fence corner and not infrequently in the shrubbery of city yards and parks."

Bobwhite nests are usually made in relatively open areas near paths, trails or field edges. A clutch of eggs may range from 7 to 28, with an average of 14. The eggs hatch after 23 or 24 days. Quail do not fledge from the nest after a couple weeks of parental care like most birds do; the entire quail family leaves the nest after the young hatch. Bobwhite chicks can fly short distances by two weeks of age and can flush with the parents by three weeks of age. One brood is raised each year.

Food: Small seeds and berries that have fallen to the ground: canary grass, bristlegrass, clover, chickweed, corn, dogwood berries, lespedeza, lupine, millet, mulberries, acorns, oats, ragweed, sorghum, sunflower, Sudan grass, strawberries, switchgrass, raspberries and soybeans. They also eat invertebrates like beetles, bugs, caterpillars, centipedes, crickets, spiders, leafhoppers and grasshoppers.

Bobwhites use bird baths on the ground for drinking, and, since most other wildlife will not compete with quail for lespedeza seeds, they benefit from small food plots of lespedeza.

Feeding habits: Quail will use large to medium-sized self feeders, lean-to feeders and fly-through feeders if they're placed near thickets and heavy cover in their home range. Self-feeders and fly-through feeders can be placed on top of fence posts to keep them from being covered by deep snow in winter.

References: Davison 1967, Martin et. al. 1951 and Roberts 1932.

Rock dove

Anyone who has fed pigeons in a city park knows how well common rock doves, or pigeons, take advantage of a free lunch.

Rock doves are not native to North America; they were brought to North America in the early 1600s by colonists from Europe. These adaptable birds are now permanent residents throughout southern Canada, the lower forty-eight states, Mexico and Latin America.

Pigeons may be black, tan, gray or white, or spotted with any combination of these colors. Measuring about 14 inches long, they are only slightly smaller than crows. They have a strong flight pattern and can achieve speeds of up to 82 miles per hour. They also exhibit agile aerial maneuvers, originally used to escape from their primary natural predator, the peregrine falcon. The average life expectancy for rock doves is less than two and a half years.

Rock doves are very prolific. They hardly ever stop raising young, even in winter. A pigeon will lay two large white eggs on whatever ledge or shelter it can find and incubate the eggs for 16 to 19 days. The young, called squabs, fledge after 25 or 26 days of parental care. The squabs eat a nutritious material called pigeon's milk that is produced from the linings of their parents' crops. A pair of pigeons may raise six to seven broods of young per year, according to a study in Kansas.

Rock doves find a variety of human structures suitable for nesting, including barns, sheds, bridges and warehouses, as well as protected eaves and sheltered nooks on older houses. Originally they nested on cliffs.

This species can carry aspergillosis, coccidiosis, equine encephalitis, Newcastle disease and histoplasmosis. For that reason, large concentrations of rock doves should not be tolerated or encouraged.

Food: Rock doves eat many kinds of seeds and grains. They quickly learn to visit feeders stocked with shelled corn, wheat and sunflower seeds.

Feeding habits: Feeding rock doves may not be a high priority for most people, but in some inner city areas they may be among the few birds to respond to feeding. Because of their rapid rate of reproduction, rock doves at feeders can eventually increase to such numbers that they create a nuisance. They are not protected by state or federal law, and their numbers may need to be occasionally reduced using humane techniques for trapping and removal.

References: Culver 1991, Davison 1967, Johnston 1992, Roberts 1932, Warton 1990.

Rock doves are extremely common in urban and farmland areas. The one shown here is a homing pigeon.

Red-bellied woodpecker

You can always tell a red-bellied woodpecker not by the red on its belly, but by the red on the back of its head. Only if you see this woodpecker at the right angle in perfect sunlight will you be able to see a slight crimson wash to its belly—but even then, don't count on it.

These are beautiful woodpeckers. A red-bellied woodpecker has a striped black and white back, a light clay-brown belly and cheeks and a crimson red head.

A female has red on the back of her head while a male has a red patch extending from the back of his head down over his face to the base of his bill.

Red-bellied woodpeckers are found in eastern hardwood forests and they have extended their North American range into Minnesota within the last hundred years. This pattern of expansion is similar to that of the northern cardinal.

The first report of red-bellied woodpeckers in Minnesota was recorded in 1892, and the first nesting record was in 1903. Since then, these birds have expanded their range to cover the southern half of Minnesota and South Dakota. They readily adapt from forest habitats to woodlots, cities, orchards, gardens and backyards.

If you can't see the red belly on this red-bellied woodpecker, you are not alone. Female red-bellied woodpeckers have red markings only on the backs of their heads. This male also has red markings from his bill over the top of his head.

32

Nest cavities created by red-bellied woodpeckers may be from 5 to 70 feet above the ground. Their nests contain four or five eggs that are incubated for two weeks. The young fledge after 24 or 25 days.

Food: Wood-boring beetles, crickets, ants, grasshoppers, insect larvae, acorns, shelled corn, suet, juice from orange halves, apples, blackberries, blueberries, bread, cherries, dogwood berries, elderberries, grapes, Virginia creeper berries, hazelnuts, hickory nuts, mulberries, peanuts, peanut butter and sunflowers.

Feeding habits: At feeders they eat cracked corn, shelled corn, ear corn, suet, bread, peanuts, orange halves, peanut butter and cracked walnuts.

References: Davison 1967, Janssen 1987, Martin et. al. 1951, Roberts 1932, Stokes 1987 and Warton 1990.

Downy woodpecker

Downy woodpeckers are the most common small woodpeckers in the Midwest. They can be found across most of the United States and Canada in both boreal and hardwood forest habitats as well as in cities, farmsteads and small woodlots.

Downy woodpeckers are only about seven inches long. Their black backs are speckled with white, their bellies are white, and they have white stripes extending back from their chins and above their eyes. Adult males have red spots on the backs of their heads and young males have red spots on top of their heads. Females have no red on their heads.

Downy woodpeckers are almost identical to the slightly larger hairy woodpeckers, but their bills are only about half an inch long. This is shorter in proportion to the size of their heads than a hairy woodpecker's bill, which is an inch long. Sometimes you can see both woodpeckers near each other at suet feeders, so you can get a better idea of the relative size of their bodies and length of their bills.

Downy woodpeckers establish a nesting territory by drumming on dry, resonant branches or buildings with their bills. This drumming sound is different from the irregular tapping associated with pecking on wood in search of food.

The woodpeckers excavate a hole in a tree trunk between 8 and 18 inches deep to make a nest cavity, where they lay from four to six eggs. The eggs hatch after an incubation period of 12 days and the young fledge after about three weeks.

Food: Eighty percent of downy woodpeckers' high-protein summer diet and 70 percent of their winter diet consists of insects, insect caterpillars and larvae, and animal fat. In winter, they may eat exposed fat deposits on the carcasses of dead animals like white-tailed deer. They also eat cherries, Virginia creeper berries, mulberries, poison ivy berries, acorns, broken walnuts, corn, peanuts, sumac seeds and sunflowers.

Feeding habits: Downy woodpeckers peck into soft rotting wood or under the bark of trees to spear hidden insects and insect larvae with their long, barbed tongues. They also peck into goldenrod galls to eat the grubs inside.

An immature male downy woodpecker has a red spot on the top of his head.

An adult male downy woodpecker can be identified by the red marking on the back, not the top, of his head.

Although their markings are similar, you can tell downy and hairy woodpeckers apart by their bills: the larger hairy woodpecker's bill is longer. A female hairy woodpecker is pictured on the left and a female downy woodpecker is pictured on the right.

The bases of downy woodpeckers' tongues are inserted along their skulls around to the tops of their heads, providing a greater length for probing in the wood.

Downy woodpeckers are easily attracted to chunks of suet placed in the feeders shown on pages 210, 211 or 213. They come to feeders for meat scraps, suet, cracked pecans, peanut butter, cheese or fruit. You can also attract them by providing a peanut feeder or a section of deer ribs on a tree trunk.

References: Culver 1991, Davison 1967, Dennis 1994, Longley (pers. comm.), Mahnken 1983, Roberts 1932, Stokes 1987 and Warton 1990.

Hairy woodpecker

Hairy woodpeckers are one of the most common woodpeckers in the United States. Extremely adaptable, their range extends from Alaska to Mexico and from New Brunswick to Florida. These medium-sized black and white woodpeckers are about nine inches long.

The main difference between hairy woodpeckers and similar downy woodpeckers is that hairy woodpeckers are larger, stronger and more powerful when using their bills to chip away bark and wood in dead trees. They can reach insects and larvae that are inaccessible to the smaller downy woodpeckers.

Hairy woodpeckers' tongues also show a remarkable adaptation for reaching larvae deep in the recesses of dead trees: the tip resembles a rigid, barbed spear. Their tongues extend under their chins, coil around the backs and tops of their heads forward to the front of their eyes and around to the back of their eye sockets. Their tongues are actually much longer than their bills.

Two of the hairy woodpecker's toes, like the toes of most woodpeckers, point forward. The other two point backward, allowing them the grip necessary to climb up tree trunks. Most birds that are adapted for standing on branches or on the ground have three toes pointing forward and one toe pointing backward.

Hairy woodpeckers inhabit hardwood and coniferous forests, urban areas and agricultural regions. They nest in trees with decayed heartwood by creating 10- to 12-inch deep cavities that are between 5 and 30 feet above the ground. Their four to six eggs require about 12 days to hatch. The young are cared for in the nest cavity for about a month.

Food: Ants, aphids, beetles, caterpillars, millipedes, insect larvae, spiders and fat deposits on dead animals; cherries, dogwood, mulberries, serviceberries, apples, blackberries, chokecherries and poison ivy berries; seeds like corn, hazel nuts, acorns, broken walnuts, peanuts and sunflowers.

Feeding habits: Hairy woodpeckers are easy to attract with suet feeders, deer rib cages or peanut feeders. They will take hummingbird nectar solutions (four parts water to one part sugar) and other foods like suet and peanut butter.

References: Davison 1967, Janssen 1987, Roberts 1932, Waldon 1991 and Warton 1990.

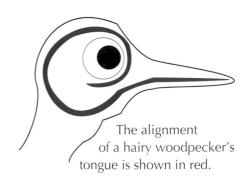

The alignment of a hairy woodpecker's tongue is shown in red.

A pileated woodpecker visits a suet feeder.

Pileated woodpecker

Pileated woodpeckers are the most impressive of all North American woodpeckers. About the size of a crow, they are stunning birds with white and red head and neck markings that contrast with their large black bodies. The males' "mustache marks" are red, while the females' are black. In flight, pileated woodpeckers have a distinctive flapping and gliding pattern that can be identified at a considerable distance.

Often regarded as rare, pileated woodpeckers are actually rather common wherever there are stands of mature hardwood forest, groves of large hardwood trees or mature riparian forests, forests lining river or lake edges, in agricultural regions.

Pileated woodpeckers leave

35

conspicuous evidence of their foraging activities. They chip out large sections of punky, rotten or soft wood in trees as they search for carpenter ants and insect larvae. Pileated woodpeckers create nest cavities in live or dead trees. They lay three to five eggs which hatch after 18 days of incubation. The cavities created by pileated woodpeckers may subsequently be used by other birds and mammals for nesting and roosting.

This species nests in mature trees that are at least 16 inches in diameter. They may have one nesting tree and at least two other trees with cavities that provide alternate sleeping chambers.

Feeding habits: More than a few people have stood wide-eyed in amazement when a pileated woodpecker appeared at their backyard suet feeder for lunch. Obviously, they can go through lots of suet. They are, however, exciting visitors to watch. They respond better to suet feeders firmly attached to a post or base than to hanging feeders. Pileated woodpeckers are also attracted to deer rib cages and deer carcasses.

References: Culver 1991, Davison 1967, Janssen 1987 and Roberts 1932.

Gray jay

Gray jays are popular members of the crow family and permanent residents of the boreal forests from Alaska south to northern Midwestern states and eastward to Nova Scotia. Unlike most boreal songbirds, these birds do not migrate south for the winter, probably

A female pileated woodpecker is pictured on the left and a male pileated woodpecker on the right. Left photo by Stephen Maxson.

because they have an unusual technique for caching nutritious food for use throughout the winter. They use their extremely sticky saliva like glue to fasten food items to trees for later use.

Gray jays have also been called Canada jays or whiskey jacks. About the size of a blue jay, a gray jay has white on its breast and face, dark gray on the back of its neck and head and medium gray over its back and tail. Overall, gray jays have a rather fluffy appearance, and those that have learned to panhandle for food at northern campsites can be quite fearless of people.

Nesting for gray jays begins in March and April, earlier than most other birds, possibly because of the protein they gain from their stored food items. Gray jays construct nests in black spruce, white spruce or balsam firs. Their clutches include between two and five eggs, hatching 18 days after the last one was laid. Incubation occurs in frigid conditions that can be as cold as 30 degrees below zero. The young fledge after 23 days.

Food: Grasshoppers, beetles, spiders, wasps, butterflies, bugs, flies and centipedes as well as mice, voles, the eggs and nestlings of small birds, blueberries, mushrooms and some seeds. Gray jays will also eat carrion, and they may catch and kill small vertebrates.

Feeding habits: Gray jays have been known to pluck engorged winter ticks from the backs of live moose. In the winter they retrieve and eat food items that they caught and stuck onto trees during the summer and fall. At feeders they will eat suet, carrion, seeds, kitchen scraps, bread, crackers and fruit. Rib cages from deer also work well.

Gray jays live in boreal forests but they do not migrate. They cache food in the summer and fall so they can survive through the winter.
Photo by Stephen Maxson.

References: Dennis 1994, Mahnken 1983, Strickland and Ouellet 1993 and Waldon 1991.

A blue jay's tail feather in the sunlight.

The same blue jay tail feather with the sunlight coming from behind, rather than shining on it. This way the light does not refract and we can see the feather in its true color: gray.

Blue jay

Blue jays are among the most intelligent, colorful and noisy birds to visit Midwestern backyards. Members of the crow family, blue jays are very adept at learning how to exploit whatever food supplies are present.

Dr. T. S. Roberts captured the essence of the "pretty bird, bad bird" reputation that accompanies the blue jay:

"This big, crested bird, arrayed in beautiful blue with trimmings of black and white, vies in beauty with the most radiant of our feathered tribe. Its intelligence and accomplishments also place it in the first rank. It is wise and resourceful, and while its usual utterances may be harsh and unmusical, it is capable of performances, subdued though they may be, so varied and tuneful that it has been compared with the Mockingbird. Its powers of mimicry are said to be almost unlimited, and it can even be taught to whistle for the dog and to call its keeper by name. It is the fashion to speak of it as a rascal and a robber, and it can not be denied that it has its faults, some of them, perhaps, serious. But with a bird that has so much to commend it and that adds an element of beauty and life to the long and dreary winter months, it seems but fair to condone and forget the charges against it."

Blue jays have rich blue coloring on their backs, black and white highlights on their wings, white breasts and bellies, and black stripes on their tails. The blue coloring is a structural color and not a pigment in the feather.

Blue jays are very common songbirds. In a 1980 Anoka County, Minnesota study, a researcher counted 121 blue jay nests in one square mile. They live in hardwood, conifer, urban and rural habitats throughout the eastern half of the United States, the Great Plains and across much of Canada. The northern populations of blue jays migrate down to the Midwest during the winter, but in most other areas these birds are permanent residents.

This species makes bulky stick nests that range from 5 to 50 feet above the ground. Inside the stick, bark and leaf nest is a lining of plant rootlets. Four or five eggs hatch after 17 or 18 days.

Food: Blue jays are omnivorous, which means that they will eat anything, including: blueberries, cherries, elderberries, grapes, mulberries, plums, chokecherries, strawberries, serviceberries, acorns, corn, hazel nuts, peanuts, pine, pumpkin seeds, sorghum, squash seed, buckwheat, sunflower seeds, broken walnuts, wheat, oats, safflower and sumac seeds.

Bread, cornbread, crackers, animal fat, suet, doughnuts, peanut butter, raisins, apples and sugar water solutions; ants, beetles, cater-

Blue jays are common visitors at feeders.

pillars, grasshoppers, fish, frogs, mice, salamanders, snails and the eggs and young of other birds.

Plants make up 90 percent of a blue jay's diet in the summer and 60 percent in winter.

Feeding habits: Blue jays will frequently take one seed at a time and fly to another perch where they pin down the seed with their feet and hammer it with their bill to crack the shell. This is similar to the way black-capped chickadees and tufted titmice eat seeds otherwise too hard for them to crack.

Blue jays also cache large supplies of food, including acorns, during the fall. This provides them with food during the lean winter months. Since they bury some of their acorns in the ground, blue jays actually help plant oak trees if they fail to retrieve their hoarded acorns in the winter.

References: Davison 1967, Janssen 1987, Mahnken 1983, Roberts 1932, Warton 1990.

This blue jay, a partial albino, is speckled with white. A pure albino would be completely white with pink eyes. Both albino and partial albino birds are rare.
Photo by Edward Shinabarger.

Black-billed magpie

For a long time, magpies were infrequent winter visitors from the western states, primarily seen along the western and southern counties of Minnesota. Since the early 1960s magpies have become a regular nesting species in northwestern Minnesota, and during the summer they are now seen regularly in the Floodwood area west of Duluth.

Magpies are extremely attractive birds. A magpie has a black head, breast and shoulders with a white belly. Its wings and tail are an iridescent mix of green, blue and bronze. It has a white patch in the center of its outspread primary wing feathers resembling the wing spots on mockingbirds. These pigeon-sized birds have long tails and measure about 19 inches.

Magpies are extremely intelligent members of the crow family. They are omnivores and scavengers, and they have a very social lifestyle.

Black-billed magpies mate for life and construct enormous globe-shaped nests of sticks that may be three feet in diameter. Their actual nests inside are shaped like cups and made from mud and fibers. Magpies may spend up to 40 or 50 days building their nests. They also weave thorny twigs and branches onto the outside of their nests for protection from predators. Female magpies incubate between five and eight eggs for about 17 days. The young fledge in 25 to 29 days.

Food: Magpies eat almost anything. They frequently scavenge the meat and fat from dead animal carcasses, anything from muskrats to moose. They also eat caterpillars, small rodents, eggs and nestlings of other birds. At bird feeders magpies will remove suet in large chunks.

Black-billed magpies feed on carrion and can be attracted to suet or deer rib cages.

References: Culver 1991, Janssen 1987, Roberts 1932, Svedarsky (pers. comm.), Waldon 1991.

American crow

American crows are common Midwestern birds. From northern coniferous forests to hardwood forests, agricultural regions and inner cities, crows are everywhere. Because they're one of the most intelligent of all bird species, they can adapt to many different foods and habitat types. Their glossy black plumage may not be attractive to some people, but these 17-inch birds do just fine anyway.

Crows usually roost in evergreen groves. They have communal roosts where they concentrate by the hundreds during late summer, fall, and winter. This behavior is probably an adaptation for protection against their major predator: the great horned owl. Owls can kill the sleeping crows.

Rather coarsely-structured nests, usually in tall conifer or hardwood trees, are home for four to six crow eggs in early spring. The eggs hatch in about 18 days, and the young fledge after four or five weeks.

Food: Insects, small mammals, road-killed animals, fruit, vegetables, seeds, garbage, agricultural grain, and eggs and young from other bird nests.

Feeding habits: Crows are scavengers as well as predators of small vertebrates. In early summertime they walk through grassy roadsides searching out the eggs of pheasants and ducks. In backyards, they will fly off with newly-fledged robins or other songbirds in their bills. For this reason they are not very welcome in most backyards.

While crows are normally quite shy and reluctant to approach bird feeders, they may come in to eat sunflower seeds, shelled corn or suet.

This young crow has just fledged.   References: Culver 1991, Davison 1967, Roberts 1932 and Warton 1990.

Common raven

Ravens are among the most intelligent of all birds. Members of the crow family, they are characteristic of the northern boreal and mixed boreal-hardwood forests.

Although ravens are just one type of several all-black birds in the Midwest, they are distinguished from the similar American crow by their larger size, their proportionally more massive bills, their wedge-tip tails, and their deeper and more resonant vocabulary of croaks, squawks and grunts. Their throats also have a shaggy appearance.

Ravens nest in tall conifers and on the rocky ledges of cliffs along the North Shore of Lake Superior and in the Boundary Waters Canoe Area Wilderness. Their nests are made of sticks and lined with fur or animal hair. Ravens mate for life and create a very strong pair bond. They lay between four and seven eggs which take about three weeks to hatch.

Nesting ranges for ravens appear to be expanding westward and southward in Minnesota. During the winter, a few of these birds may be found as far south as the Carlos Avery Wildlife Management Area near Forest Lake in Anoka County.

Food: Like magpies, ravens will eat almost anything. They scavenge carrion and are well known for following timber wolf packs to locate moose and deer kill sites, which they scavenge after the wolves have left. They may even enter the rib cage of dead deer to feed.

Ravens are smart enough to discover where they can scrounge food leftovers from humans: campsites, dumps and city garbage cans.

Feeding habits: Ravens' shy reputation came about primarily because people thought they were a nuisance and regularly shot at them. Where they are well protected they become fearless and tolerant of people. In Thompson, Manitoba, ravens have become urbanized to the point that they often raid garbage cans, spread the garbage around, and subsequently drop bones and other objects into urban neighborhoods from the air.

Obviously not your typical backyard bird, ravens certainly have the potential to become typical with a few more decades of protection in the Midwest.

References: Janssen 1987, Roberts 1932 and Waldon 1991.

Common ravens are larger than crows and have proportionally larger bills. They will feed in some cities but they usually avoid humans.
Photo by Ron Winch.

Black-capped chickadee

Black-capped chickadees were selected as Minnesota's most popular bird in a contest sponsored by the Minnesota DNR and the Minnesota Zoo. They ranked higher than bald eagles, cardinals and loons.

These five-inch birds are able to survive even the most frigid winter weather right in your own backyard. Their presence provides constant entertainment for someone confined to the house by the cold weather.

In addition, their familiar "fee-bee" and "chickadee-dee-dee" calls are comforting and delightful sounds during cold winter days.

Black-capped chickadees have white bellies and cheeks, black caps and chins, and gray backs. Chickadees survive the freezing weather by storing food for later use. They can remember where they have stored seeds for up to eight months, long enough to get them through the coldest of northern winters.

Chickadees also have the ability to lower their body temperature at night and enter a state of controlled hypothermia. This saves energy that would otherwise be necessary to maintain a higher body temperature during the night.

Chickadees are found from southern Alaska across Canada and much of the northern half of the United States. In natural habitats, they nest in tree cavities like old woodpecker holes. Their nest cavities are frequently lined with rabbit fur.

Chickadee nests will contain six to eight eggs which hatch after an incubation period of 12 days. The young fledge at 16 days of age.

Food: Goldenrod, ragweed, hemlock, blueberries, blackberries, wild cherries, poison ivy and bayberries. The summertime chickadee diet consists primarily of animal matter, especially caterpillars.

During the fall and winter, a chickadee's diet is mixed: half seeds and berries and half insects, spiders and fat from dead animals like white-tailed deer.

Feeding habits: Chickadees are easy to please. At feeders, they eat sunflower seeds, suet, peanuts, peanut butter, pumpkin seeds, old bread and doughnuts.

Chickadees seem to take turns visiting feeders, taking one seed at a time. In a wooded neighborhood, there can be a continual procession of chickadees coming and going from a winter feeder.

Chickadees can become extremely tame. At the Environmental Learning Center near Isabella, Minnesota, the naturalists placed a dummy on a chair adjacent to the bird feeder and then regularly placed sunflower seeds on the dummy's glove. Children attending the camp sit on the dummy's lap and have the trusting chickadees eat from their hands. See the photo on page 5.

References: Culver 1991, Davison 1967, Harrison 1978, Martin et. al. 1951, Roberts 1932, Smith 1993, Stokes 1987 and Warton 1990.

Chickadees are easy to feed and provide continual antics at your winter bird feeders.

Boreal chickadee

Boreal chickadees have brown caps, different from the black and gray coloring of black-capped chickadees. They make their animal hair nests in the cavities of dead or broken trees, like old spruce. Chickadees lay six or seven eggs which take about 12 days to hatch. Fledging is estimated at 16 days.

Boreal chickadees are usually only seen in northeastern Minnesota and the boreal forests of Canada. A few boreal chickadees may wander south during the winter, but this is not a regular migratory movement.

Food: Animal food comprises 90 percent of boreal chickadees' summer diet and 50 percent of their winter diet. They eat beetles, bugs, caterpillars, moths, spiders, ants, bees and wasps. They also eat fir, hemlock, pine and spruce seeds.

Feeding habits: Boreal chickadees are uncommon at feeders, but they may come to eat suet, suet mixtures and sunflower seeds.

Boreal chickadees have brown caps. Photo by Myrna Pearman.

References: Davison 1967, Harrison 1978, Janssen 1987 and Roberts 1932.

Tufted titmouse

Tufted titmice are in the same family as black-capped chickadees, and they eat in a similar manner. They take sunflower seeds from a bird feeder one at a time, move to another perch, and hold down the seed with their toes. Then they use their wedge-shaped bills to hammer at the seed until they can pull out the nutritious heart. They eat that part and discard the rest.

Tufted titmice have crests like blue jays, but their color makes them difficult to confuse with other birds. A tufted titmouse has a blue-gray crest and back, rusty sides, a black forehead, and a white breast and belly.

Tufted titmice expanded their range into Minnesota in the 1940s and are now permanent residents in Houston and Fillmore counties. Their range extends eastward to Maine, southeastward to Florida and south to Texas. They are sporadically reported in other counties to the north and to the west.

Titmice live in nest boxes or in tree cavities once inhabited by woodpeckers. They lay between five and seven eggs that will hatch after 13 days, and their young fledge in 15 to 18 days. A family of titmice will stay together all winter.

Food: Butternuts, hazel nuts, hickory nuts, peanuts and broken walnuts; cantaloupe, pine, sunflower and safflower seeds; bread, cookie crumbs, cornbread, peanut butter and pie crusts; caterpillars, wasps, ants, beetles, scale insects, spiders and suet.

Tufted titmice eat 85 percent animal food during the summer and 25 percent animal food during the winter.

Feeding habits: Tufted titmice will come to a variety of tray, fly-through, cylindrical, suet and self feeders. They are easy to attract if you are in a wooded area within the species' range.

Tufted titmice select a single sunflower seed and move from the feeder tray to a branch or board where they can pin the seed down with their toes. Then they pound on the seed with their wedge-shaped bill to break it open and expose the nutritious sunflower heart.

References: Culver 1991, Davison 1967, Grubb and Pravosudov 1994, Janssen 1987, Martin et. al. 1951, Roberts 1932, Stokes 1987 and Warton 1990.

Tufted titmice are related to chickadees and live in the hardwood forests of the eastern United States.

White-breasted nuthatch

White-breasted nuthatches are famous for their characteristic upside-down pose. They're the only birds that feed by hopping down a tree trunk upside down, probing the bark with their bills for small insects and insect larvae.

If you look closely at a white-breasted nuthatch's bill, you will see that it is slightly upcurved. Most birds have bills that are either straight or downcurved.

This distinctly-shaped bill helps the nuthatch reach food items unavailable to other birds. Woodpeckers and brown creepers probe for insects and larvae by moving up a tree trunk, so they are not likely to find the same creatures eaten by white-breasted nuthatches.

A white-breasted nuthatch is about six inches long, with a blue-gray back and, as the name implies, a white breast. Its face and cheeks are also white. A male's cap is black and a female's cap is blue-gray.

These birds are found in the eastern United States, across the Great Plains, in the Rocky Mountain states and in southern portions of several Canadian provinces where there are hardwood or mixed forests. Nuthatches also inhabit farms, backyards and urban areas that have relatively mature trees.

They nest in tree cavities or former woodpecker nests that are 5 to 20 feet above the ground. They lay between five and eight eggs that require 12 days of incubation. The young fledge after two weeks.

Feeding habits: Nuthatches usually feed at suet feeders, but they'll also frequent feeders with sunflower seeds, safflower seeds and peanuts. They take one seed at a time and wedge it into a piece of bark where they can chop or hack it open with their sharp bill. Nuthatches also use nectar feeders that have been placed for orioles.

References: Culver 1991, Janssen 1987, Pravosudov and Grubb 1993, Roberts 1932, Stokes 1987 and Warton 1990.

This female white-breasted nuthatch shows the upside-down feeding posture characteristic of this species. Her blue cap distinguishes her from male nuthatches.

A male white-breasted nuthatch can be distinguished from a female by his black cap. His long, slender bill is slightly upturned to help him probe under bark for insects.

Brown creeper

Brown creepers are small, mouse-sized birds usually noticed only by the most avid of birdwatchers. Their feeding behavior resembles that of a miniature woodpecker. They begin at the base of a tree and hop upward, probing with their slender, slightly-curved bills into the nooks and crannies of the bark for small insects, insect eggs and larvae.

Brown creepers feed in spiral patterns as they ascend tree trunks, fly down to the base of another tree, and repeat the process.

These five-inch birds have brown backs, heads and tails which are heavily streaked with white. Their breasts and bellies are also white. Standing against the bark of a tree, brown creepers are extremely well camouflaged.

Generally speaking, brown creepers are permanent residents in Minnesota, but they do undergo some regional shifts from summer to winter. They nest throughout much of the forested region in the northern half of the state.

Brown creepers search for insects, insect eggs and larvae by working up from the base of a tree. This brown creeper is visiting a peanut butter feeder. Photo by Dave Maslowski/ Maslowski Wildlife Productions.

A few of these birds may winter in the northern counties, but most migrate to southern Minnesota, or perhaps south as far as Illinois. They are sometimes found dead after cold periods of winter weather because they are not as winter-hardy as birds like chickadees.

There are very few nesting records for these birds because they conceal their nests behind loose slabs of bark hanging two or three inches from dead tree trunks. Their nests are made from leaves, twigs, shredded bark, moss and spider webs.

Five to eight eggs laid in brown creeper nests require just over two weeks to hatch. The young fledge after about 15 days of parental care.

Probably the most dramatic and exciting aspect in the life of this tiny and somewhat drab-looking bird comes during the mating season: the male selects a display tree where it does a fast, ascending spiral flight around the tree trunk. A female attracted by this activity will join with the male in his dizzying spiral courtship ritual.

Food: Ants, beetles, bugs, caterpillars, insect eggs, moths, spiders and wasps.

Feeding habits: At feeders brown creepers will eat bread and peanut butter. You can also make a brown creeper suet mix using the recipe on page 151.

Another way to attract brown creepers is by smearing peanut butter onto the bark of a tree. It's important to rub the peanut butter in an upward motion because brown creepers feed by probing the bark from below.

References: Davison 1967, Janssen 1987, Roberts 1932 and Waldon 1991.

European starling

European starlings were introduced to the United States in New York City in 1890. Since that time they have spread across the United States and Canada. The total North American population of European starlings now exceeds 200 million.

These birds are not protected by federal law and can be nuisances when they compete with native birds for nesting cavities. Wood ducks, bluebirds, tree swallows, black-capped chickadees and other native cavity-nesting species have been affected by the starlings' aggressive behavior.

Markings on a starling include iridescent highlights of green and purple on black plumage. When starlings molt in the fall, their new feathers have buff to white pointed tips, giving the bird a speckled appearance. In wintertime the buff feather tips wear off, changing the starling from speckled to iridescent black in time for the spring breeding season. Starlings' bills change from dark gray or black in the fall and winter to golden yellow in the spring.

Adult starlings are about eight inches long and have a rounded, plump appearance accentuated by tails that look very short when compared to red-winged blackbirds or grackles. Young starlings are gray.

Starlings nest in woodpecker holes, hollow trees, or nest boxes set out for wood ducks or other birds. European starlings need entrance holes that are at least one and three-quarters inches in diameter. Eastern bluebird nest boxes typically have entrance holes with smaller dimensions that prevent starlings from entering. Starlings will be evicted by kestrèls if they attempt to compete for a kestrel nest box, but they are able to drive wood ducks from their nest boxes.

Starling nests are usually an odd collection of leaves, grasses, twigs, feathers and other assorted garbage. They lay four or five pale blue-green eggs that require 12 days of incubation. The young fledge at 21 days.

Feeding habits: European starlings are notorious for raiding suet feeders, but that is an easy problem to solve. Provide a feeder like the one shown in Design #17, requiring a bird to hang upside down while pecking at the suet. Since starlings' leg muscles are weak compared to those of nuthatches, chickadees and woodpeckers, they are unable to use such feeders.

References: Cabe 1993, Culver 1991 and Warton 1990.

Northern cardinal

Northern cardinals, one of the most popular and beautiful visitors at Midwest bird feeders, need little introduction. They're a widely-used symbol for the bird food industry, and their year-round presence adds an elegant touch to the natural landscape.

Bright red male cardinals are especially beautiful against frosty, snow-covered trees in winter. The males' clear and distinctive "what-cheer, what-cheer" song is also a welcome symbol of the coming spring.

Cardinals are one of three feeder birds with a crest, a distinction they share with blue jays and tufted titmice. Cedar waxwings and Bohemian waxwings also have crests, but they don't come to feeders.

Less dramatic than her bright red and black male counterpart, a female cardinal has a gray-brown back that fades to a cream-colored breast. She has pink highlights on her wings, tail and crest, and her bill is bright orange-red.

Newly-grown starling feathers are pointed with buff-colored tips.

Cardinals are found throughout most of the eastern United States and from Nebraska south into Mexico. They have been expanding their range northward during the past 120 years. The first recorded cardinal in Minnesota was seen in 1875. By the 1920s and 1930s, cardinals had become a breeding species as far north as Minneapolis and as far west as Owatonna.

Male cardinals have red plumage.

Now the species occupies much of the southern half of the state and is sighted sporadically in north central and northwestern Minnesota and along the North Shore of Lake Superior in the winter. A few pairs nest regularly in the Brainerd area and some are as far north as Moorhead.

Because they're very adaptable, cardinals can be found in a variety of hardwood forest habitats, small rural and urban woodlots, farmsteads and urban backyards. They do best where they can find thick, shrubby growth for nesting and roosting. Shrubs and vines also provide much of this species' natural food.

Cardinals build bulky nests of vines, leaves and twigs in shrubs or small trees. Their nests are usually within ten feet of the ground. They lay three or four

eggs that hatch in about 12 days, and the young fledge when they're only ten to 12 days old.

Food: Arborvitae, blackberries, cherries, dogwood, elderberries, grapes, mulberries, raspberries, black nightshade, plums, serviceberries, strawberries, viburnum, hawthorn and blueberries; barley, bristlegrass, buckwheat, corn, hazelnut, hackberries, hickory nut meats, millet, oats, peanuts, pine, ragweed, rice, safflower, sorghum, sunflower, broken walnuts, wheat, river birch, bittersweet, elm, eastern red cedar fruits and sumac; bread, cantaloupe seeds, cornbread, peanut butter, pumpkin seeds, squash seeds, watermelon seeds, dried apples and raisins; ants, beetles, caterpillars, grasshoppers, scale insects and weevils.

A female northern cardinal has a gray-toned or brown back, cream breast, and pink highlights on her crest, wings and tail.

Plant seeds and fruits comprise 90 percent of cardinals' food in the fall and winter, but only 40 to 50 percent of their food during the summer.

Feeding habits: You can usually attract cardinals to feeders by providing black oil sunflower seeds mixed with other seeds like safflower and peanut pickouts. They will also eat mealworms placed in the feeders shown in Designs #21-23. Cardinals use a wide assortment of feeders including tray feeders, deck railing feeders, cylindrical feeders, self feeders and ground sites.

References: Culver 1991, Davison 1967, Janssen 1987, Roberts 1932 and Warton 1990.

Purple finch

Purple finches add another color to your bird feeder pallet: rich wine or raspberry red, darker than the similar house finch's fire-engine red.

In addition to their attractive colors, purple finches have beautiful warbling songs to delight you in springtime. Waldon quoted writer Chuck Bernstein when he said that "warblers don't warble, but purple finches and goldfinches do."

Look for raspberry-red colors on a male purple finch's head, back, breast and rump. His back is brown and his belly is white. A female purple finch is brown above and white below, with some brown speckles on her breast. She has a conspicuous white stripe extending backwards from just above each eye.

You can find purple finches throughout most of the lower forty-eight states and Canadian provinces, except for the Rocky Mountain region from southern Saskatchewan and Alberta south to New Mexico, Arizona and west Texas.

Purple finches live in Minnesota throughout the year, but they undergo a migratory shift from summer nesting habitats in the boreal regions of northern Minnesota and the coniferous plantings of southern and central Minnesota to wintering areas that vary from central and southern Minnesota to the Gulf Coast states.

Purple finches are quite adaptable because they nest in boreal forest habitats as well as plantations or backyard areas with coniferous trees. Female purple finches build their nests in coniferous trees like pine or spruce, using horizontal limbs between 5 and 60 feet off the ground. They incubate between four and six eggs for 13 or 14 days, and the young fledge after two weeks.

Food: Seeds of ash, birch, boxelder, butternut, corn, elm, fir, hemp, millet, oats, pine, ragweed, red cedar, safflower, spruce, Sudan grass, buckwheat, maple, cotoneaster, poplar, sumac and yellow-poplar plus mulberries, cherries, coralberries and grapes. They will also eat caterpillars, beetles and plant lice.

Feeding habits: At feeders purple finches eat peanuts, pumpkin seeds, safflower, sunflower, cornbread, broken walnuts, squash seeds and peanut butter.

References: Janssen 1987, Roberts 1932, Stokes 1987, Waldon 1991, Warton 1990.

House finch

House finches have made a dramatic appearance in the Midwest since the early 1980s. Originally native to the western United States, some house finches were captured and taken to New York in 1940 for sale in the pet trade. When the State of New York made such trade illegal, the store owners turned the house finches loose to avoid arrest.

Female purple finches and house finches have similar brown coloring, but female purple finches (above) have conspicuous white stripes over their eyes. Female house finches (left) have heavy striping on their chests and bellies but no eye stripes.

Male purple finches, pictured on the left, have purple-red coloring over most of their bodies. Their rumps, backs, shoulders and bellies are red.

Male house finches, right, are usually orange-red in the shoulder, upper chest and facial areas. Their bellies are typically striped with brown.

Birds within the same species still have their differences. They do not all look like the pictures in field guides! This male purple finch is a house finch look-alike. Unlike most purple finches, his red coloring does not extend all the way down his breast. He does not, however, have the brown stripes characteristic of house finches.

The house finches responded by adapting to the urban habitats of Long Island, and have since been spreading westward and southward so that they now occupy most of the eastern United States and Midwestern states from Minnesota south to Mississippi.

While house finches are similar to native purple finches, there are several differences. Male house finches are more fire-engine red in their faces and upper chests, a coloration caused by three types of carotenoid pigments in their feathers. Depending on the relative amount of these pigments in its diet, a house finch's colors can range from pale orange or yellow to bright red.

A male house finch will have more brown streaks on his breast and flanks, an orange-red cast on his head and upper breast, and red markings that do not extend as far back on his shoulders and belly as they do on a purple finch. Female house finches do not have the conspicuous white eyebrow stripes characteristic of female purple finches.

House finches have shown great adaptability to backyards. They frequently nest in hanging begonia baskets and on Christmas wreaths that are accidentally left hanging on front porches until the arrival of the spring nesting season.

Four or five eggs are laid in a nest constructed of fine weeds, twigs, and grass. The eggs hatch after 13 or 14 days of incubation, and the young fledge after 12 to 19 days in the nest. House finches may raise three broods of young during the spring and summer.

Many birders have been concerned about the impact of this new bird on existing populations of native songbirds. Some people think that this bird out-competes house sparrows and causes their populations to decline. If so, that could be seen as a benefit rather than a drawback.

Feeding habits: The biggest problem with house finches is that, out east, their numbers have become so great that they overwhelm feeders and prevent more timid birds from gaining access. This problem has been solved by finch-proof cylindrical commercial feeders which have the perches above the feeding ports rather than below. House finches have weak feet compared to birds like chickadees and they cannot feed successfully in an upside down position.

Another way to discourage house finch use at cylindrical thistle feeders is to cut the perches to five eighths of an inch long.

At feeders, house finches will eat sunflower seeds, millet, cracked corn, suet, peanuts and bread. They may also eat ripe fruit in orchards. Bill Longley of Forest Lake, Minnesota, reported that they eat broccoli flower buds.

Preferences: Culver 1991, Daniel, pers. comm., Hill 1993, Mahnken 1983 and Warton 1990.

American goldfinch

One bird that captures the immediate attention of even casual nature lovers is the beautiful American goldfinch, sometimes known as the wild canary. Like chickadees, goldfinches are hardy enough to provide enjoyment at bird feeders all year long, visiting feeders that provide Niger thistle seeds or fine sunflower chips.

Dr. T. S. Roberts described the beauty and delight provided by goldfinches: "The handsome little Gold-finch is surely one of the most joyous and light-hearted of all our feathered throng. Sociable and genial among its kind, cheery and musical of voice, and gay and happy in demeanor, it goes frolicking through the summertime in little troops or couplets with an abandon and a happy-go-lucky air that suggests that it had never a care nor duty in the whole year round."

The male's beautiful black and yellow pattern makes him unlike any other Midwestern bird. His cap, wings and tail are black while the remainder of his body is bright yellow. As fall progresses, his plumage becomes splotchy and molts into gray winter feathers.

Male and female goldfinches are similar during the winter, except that males' throats are brighter yellow in wintertime and their primary feathers are blacker. The wing covert feathers on male goldfinches' backs are tipped with white, while those on females' backs can be tipped with buff.

With the coming of spring, however, the feathers molt once again, and the males' gray plumage is temporarily speckled with the bright yellow feathers of summer. By May, he has these bright yellow feathers all over his body, along with his characteristic black cap and black wings with white wing bars.

Females become a softer dull yellow and have no black cap during the summer months.

Goldfinches are distinct even in flight: they have a bouncing or undulating flight pattern and a pleasant four-note chirp that sounds like "per-chic-o-ree."

American goldfinches have an extremely large range including all of the lower 48 states, northern Mexico and the southern portions of the Canadian provinces east of British Columbia.

Some goldfinches are present in Minnesota all year long, but others move from the boreal forest regions to more southerly portions of their range in the winter. They are not usually common in northern Minnesota during the winter.

Habitats for this adaptable species include mixed woodland,

Immature purple finches have white eye stripes less distinct than those on an adult female.

The soft yellow area on the edges of this immature house finch's bill is characteristic of young birds.

This male goldfinch is in winter plumage.

meadows, fields, farmland, urban backyards, brushy fence rows and orchards. Goldfinches benefit from soil disturbance that allows wild thistles and sunflowers to grow. Sunflowers provide food for the goldfinches, and thistles provide both food and down lining for their nests.

Compared to other songbirds, the goldfinches' nesting cycle begins very late in the summer. Their mid-July nesting habits coincide with the ripening of thistle seeds, primary food for goldfinch chicks.

Female goldfinches construct tightly-woven nests in the upright fork of a tree or shrub. She'll make her delicate nest 2 to 14 feet above the ground and line it with thistle down, cattail down and other silky plant fibers.

Male goldfinches feed the females during the 12 to 14 days of incubation. The four to six chicks will eat partially-digested seeds during their two weeks of parental care prior to fledging. Most other songbirds feed insects to their chicks. Whenever cowbirds lay their eggs in a goldfinch's nest, the cowbird chicks lack their important protein-rich insect diets and usually don't survive.

Food: Alder, birch, burdock, canarygrass, chickweed, coreopsis, cracked corn, cosmos, dandelion, elm, daisy fleabane, goosefoot, hemlock, hemp, joe-pye-weed, millet, nut meats, oats, peanuts, pine, ragweed, spruce, Sudan grass, sunflower, thistle, turnip, zinnia, coneflower, goldenrod, grain sorghum, sow thistle and trumpet creeper seeds plus mulberries, serviceberries and a few aphids, caterpillars and plant lice.

Dr. T. S. Roberts reported that the stomach of one goldfinch contained 2,210 eggs of a plant louse that infests white birch trees.

Feeding habits: Goldfinches will visit cylindrical feeders that dispense Niger thistle seeds or sunflower hearts and sunflower chips. They will also eat cracked nut meats and millet seeds.

References: Culver 1991, Davison 1967, Middleton 1993, Roberts 1932, Waldon 1991 and Warton 1990.

Female goldfinches are yellow in their summer plumage.

This male goldfinch is in summer breeding plumage.

House sparrow

House sparrows, like European starlings, are exotic English nuisance birds that were introduced into the United States at Brooklyn, New York, in 1851. From New York, the species spread throughout North America and Canada, and south through Mexico and Latin America.

House sparrows show remarkable adaptability to survive in both frigid northern climates and tropical settings. Unlike native North American sparrows and finches, house sparrows are members of the weaver finch family.

Male house sparrows have chestnut necks, gray caps, black bib markings, brown backs, and gray bellies. Females and fledged young look similar but lack the black bib marking.

These six-inch sparrows are unwelcome birds that have caused enormous problems for native songbirds in far greater proportions than their small size would suggest.

As cavity nesters, they aggressively search out tree cavities and nest boxes occupied by house wrens, chickadees, bluebirds and tree swallows. They attack whatever parent or young birds they find there, using their sharp bills against the songbird's head. This leaves both adult and young in the nest boxes with fractured skulls. Since house sparrows are common in urban areas and farmsteads, that is where their effect on songbirds has been particularly severe.

A male house sparrow has a gray breast, black bib marking and a black and brown speckled back.

House sparrows construct rather messy nests comprised of assorted papers, grasses, string and feathers. Their nests are constructed differently than most other common birds: rather than a cup or bowl shape, they create more of an arch or enclosed spherical shape with grasses and plant fibers. The sparrows lay about five or six finely-speckled eggs which hatch after an incubation period of 11 days. The young fledge in two weeks. House sparrows may produce up to four broods of young each breeding season.

House sparrows can reach densities of 1,200 to 1,300 per square kilometer around buildings associated with livestock production. Their general density in rural areas is about 200 per square kilometer.

The highest concentrations of sparrow nests are in barns, cattle sheds, hog houses, corn cribs and chicken houses where there is waste feed and undigested grain in hog and cattle manure.

House sparrows readily come to feeders that have smaller seeds like millet or cracked corn. They also like old bread and doughnuts. You can discourage them from coming to feeders by offering only black oil sunflower seeds and thistle in cylindrical feeders.

The numbers and variety of songbirds using a feeder may be enhanced by live-trapping and humane destruction of excessive house sparrow populations. The Cedar Valley Live Trap® and other similar live traps can be used to capture sparrows in a humane fashion. Trapped sparrows should be humanely euthanized, not transplanted and released somewhere else.

References: Culver 1991, Lowther and Cink 1992, Stokes 1987 and Warton 1990.

53

SHORT-DISTANCE MIGRANTS

Short-distance migrants are birds like American robins, wood ducks, eastern bluebirds and mourning doves that are usually not winter-hardy enough to stay in northern states during the cold winter months.

Typical wintering areas for short-distance migrants range from Iowa down into the northern temperate regions of Mexico. There are always a few robins, bluebirds and mourning doves that attempt to winter in northern states, but they are in the minority. Many perish during extended periods of cold weather.

Some of the short-distance migrants, like wood ducks, are water birds. They need open water in forested wetlands to find their food: emergent aquatic vegetation or aquatic invertebrates, acorns and exposed waste grain in harvested grain fields.

Many songbirds, including bluebirds, gray catbirds and robins, need to go far enough south to find fruiting trees and shrubs that will provide a steady food supply throughout the winter. Birds that scratch on the ground for seeds and small invertebrates, like rufous-sided towhees and brown thrashers, must also travel to forested regions south of the snow belt.

Birds such as mallards and Canada geese are both permanent residents and short-distance migrants. Some of the giant Canada geese that nest in Minnesota also winter in Minnesota. Other giant Canada geese from the Midwest have migratory traditions that take them as far south as Kansas. They were included here because this category more closely follows their original behavior before the winter aeration systems and open water we associate with power plants made it possible for them to winter north of their traditional sites.

Many of the birds mentioned in this category only come to bird feeders in the summer. Others are infrequent visitors at bird feeders.

The varied thrush is included in this section, but its unusual migratory movements are west to east instead of north to south. It frankly does not fit into any of the five migration categories very well. It has been assigned to the short-distance migrant category even though it travels a considerable distance from the Pacific Northwest to the Midwest.

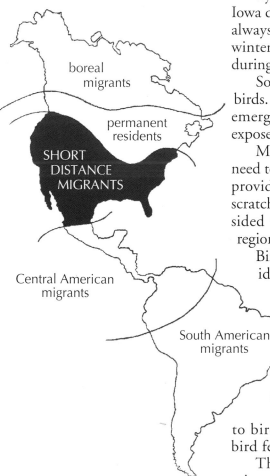

boreal migrants

permanent residents

SHORT DISTANCE MIGRANTS

Central American migrants

South American migrants

The darkened area shows the approximate wintering range for short-distance migrants.

Trumpeter swan

Trumpeter swans are the largest waterfowl species in North America, weighing up to 35 pounds and having a wingspread of seven feet. These magnificent white birds were extirpated from the Midwest, but restoration programs are bringing them back.

Hennepin Parks west of Minneapolis, Minnesota began a swan restoration program in 1966. The Minnesota DNR expanded the program to the state's northwest beginning in 1982 by collecting trumpeter swan eggs in Alaska. The Minnesota DNR transported the eggs to Minnesota for hatching, and released the swans after two years.

A total of 217 trumpeter swans had been released by the Minnesota DNR by the end of 1994, supplementing other releases by Hennepin Parks. The swans have been successfully mating, raising their own young and migrating southward to Missouri, Arkansas, Nebraska, Kansas, Oklahoma and Iowa.

Other Midwestern states, including Wisconsin, Michigan and Iowa, have subsequently begun releasing trumpeter swans. Approximately twelve to fifteen pairs of DNR-reared swans are now nesting in the wild.

This Minnesota DNR trumpeter swan, #98, wintered in style at a country club in Arlington, Virginia. Photo by John H. Thorsnes.

Trumpeter swans select mates in their third year and begin nesting in their fourth year. They usually select remote marshes for mating, where there will be minimal contact with humans. After about 34 days of incubation, the five to seven eggs hatch into young swans, called cygnets. Cygnets are gray in their first year and are easily distinguished from the white adult swans.

These swans migrate as family groups in the late fall to wintering locations anywhere from central Minnesota to Arkansas and Oklahoma. A few swans have migrated to Colorado.

One Minnesota DNR swan, #98, even migrated to Arlington, Virginia, in December 1989. It spent the winter on a tidal bay of the Potomac River by the Woodlawn Country Club. The country club staff built a feeder and fed the swan cracked corn through the winter until it returned to Minnesota in April 1990.

Trumpeter swans are much less afraid of humans at their wintering areas, which may be open stretches of river or open reservoirs. Feeding trumpeter swans is not encouraged until after late December so that the feeding does not stop the swans' migration too far north.

Feeding should not be done on a site where there could be lead shotgun pellets from waterfowl hunting or lots of lead fishing sinkers. Swans are very vulnerable to lead poisoning and can die from accidentally swallowing a single shotgun pellet. Such pellets are normally picked up while the swans are feeding on the bottom for plant roots or eating grit to help them grind up their food.

If trumpeter swans show up at a wintering site along a lake or river, please contact your state DNR or Department of Conservation. They'll want to know about the location of the swans and they'll be able to give you advice about whether or not to feed them.

Swans have been absent from the Midwest for so many years that extra publicity at the wintering grounds is necessary to keep them from being illegally shot by people mistaking them for snow geese. Local radio, television and newspaper publicity should be solicited in wintering areas to publicize the presence of the wintering swans and to emphasize that they are a protected species.

Some swans are marked with yellow or green neck collars printed with black letters and numbers. The swans released by the Minnesota DNR are marked with orange wing tags, on females' left wings and on males' right wings. Swans with orange wing tags can be reported to the Minnesota DNR at 1-800-766-6000.

Food: Swans will readily eat shelled corn and commercial duck maintenance chow pellets. Bread is not a nutritious food for them. Since feeding them tends to make them very tame, they should not be fed in an area that exposes them to being shot by vandals or inexperienced hunters.

Canada goose

Majestic Canada geese made a dramatic recovery in the Midwest since the mid-1960s, both as abundant spring and fall migrants and as a resident breeding species. They have jumped from being a rare species all the way to being a pest in some urban parks, sod farms and golf courses.

Migrant races of Canada geese range from the small, three-pound Richardson's variety to the more common interior sub-species weighing six to eight pounds. Adults of the resident subspecies, known as the giant Canada goose, can reach a weight of 12 to 15 pounds.

These birds have brown-gray backs, silvery white breasts, and black necks and heads highlighted by white cheek patches. Males and females look identical. They begin nesting in early April, and their four to seven young hatch a month later. Geese typically mate for life, but they will take a new mate if their first one dies.

Food: They graze on succulent grasses like bluegrass, but they will also eat corn, soybeans or wheat.

Feeding habits: Canada geese will readily come to a site where food is available to them, and their high numbers can quickly become a nuisance. Some municipalities have made it illegal to feed waterfowl because of the nuisance problems that routinely occur with high concentrations of mallard ducks and Canada geese.

Reference: Culver 1991.

Canada geese readily adapt to feeding in urban areas, but with their large numbers and their droppings they quickly become a nuisance in heavily used sites.

Hen wood ducks have gray bodies, iridescent wing feathers, and white eye patches.

Wood duck

With their iridescent blue, green and purple highlights, trimmed with white stripes, scallops and bright red eyes, wood ducks are the most beautiful waterfowl species in North America. Although hens have more basic brown markings with white eye masks, they are also iridescent and quite beautiful.

Today wood ducks are an abundant species, but at the turn of this century they were essentially endangered. Many years of protection and restrictive hunting regulations helped the wood duck begin its population recovery.

Many people consider male wood ducks the most beautiful of all North American waterfowl. Their feathers have iridescent blue, green and purple highlights.

Thousands of nest boxes placed near and in wetlands have given wood ducks the protected nesting sites they need.

Wood ducks typically return from wintering grounds in the southeastern United States around March. They find mates at the wintering grounds, and the males follow females back to the females' home ground.

Wood ducks average 12 eggs, but they can lay up to 14. Hens have been known to lay their eggs in other duck's nests, and other ducks like hooded mergansers and common goldeneyes have been known to lay their eggs in wood duck nest boxes, a practice that results in mixed-species broods. These clutches may exceed thirty eggs! Wood duck eggs hatch in about 30 days.

Instructions for building and placing wood duck nest boxes can be found in *Woodworking for Wildlife*. In areas where wood duck populations have been augmented by successful nest box programs, the ducks can be encouraged to come ashore and feed where shelled corn is scattered on the ground for them. Former Minnesota DNR commissioner Joe Alexander attracts wood ducks by using a cyclone seeder to scatter wheat or rye on his lawn along Minnehaha Creek in Minneapolis, Minnesota.

Lyle Bradley of Anoka, Minnesota, often has dozens of wood ducks on his lawn every morning during the spring and fall. He lives next to an oxbow marsh of the Rum River, and many wood duck pairs use nest boxes on his property. Since wood ducks do not visit feeders in high numbers, and then only in the early morning, they do not reach the nuisance proportions that mallards and Canada geese do.

Dozens of wood ducks and some mallards breakfast on Lyle Bradley's lawn in Anoka, Minnesota.

Feeding habits: Wood ducks can be attracted by scattering shelled corn on the shores of ponds and in yard areas, especially in late March through early May when they're looking for nest boxes and again in September and early October.

References: Bellrose 1976, Longley (pers. comm).

Mallard

The greenhead mallard is the most common and adaptable duck in North America. These ducks have become a familiar sight on prairie marshes, urban lakes and residential backyards. In recent years mallards have been reported nesting several stories up in large flower pots on apartment building patios, in enclosed elementary school courtyards and along the edges of parking lots at urban shopping malls.

This incredible adaptability has helped mallards sustain their numbers in some areas where continued drainage and pollution of wetlands have reduced the quantity and quality of traditional wetland habitats.

A drake mallard is characterized by his green head, white neck band, brown chest, gray back, black rump, white belly and striking violet-blue speculum, or patch, on the trailing edge of his secondary wing feathers. A hen is mottled brown with less striping on her belly and a dark stripe through her eye. Adult mallards weigh about two and a half pounds.

Mallards frequently mate with other duck species, including domestic ducks, so there are many unusual variations of size and markings that do not correspond to typical mallard markings.

Mallards nest throughout most of North America. Nests are normally on the ground in grassy nesting cover or near the bases of shrubs in grassy areas or in yards. Nesting normally begins between April 10 and April 30. Hens lay one egg per day until the clutch of about nine eggs is complete. After the last egg is laid the hen begins incubation, which lasts 28 days.

Food: Mallard ducks eat a wide variety of aquatic foods, acorns and agricultural grains: smartweed, duckweed, wild millet, bulrush, bur reed, widgeon grass, pondweed, acorns, corn, barley, wheat, sorghum, peas, rice and oats. At feeders they readily eat shelled corn and black oil sunflower seeds. About ten percent of their food in the summer is comprised of aquatic insects, fish and snails.

Feeding habits: Along lakeshore areas mallard ducks and Canada geese readily respond to feeding and usually become a nuisance because of their large numbers. Some municipalities have regulations against feeding ducks.

Some ducks nest in residential areas and are present in low numbers, flying in to land on roofs of houses and descending to backyard feeders for a meal of shelled corn and sunflower seeds.

References: Bellrose 1976, Martin et. al. 1951 and Davison 1967.

As mallard ducks continue to adapt to urban settings, they become more common on city lakes and in residential backyards. Male mallards are easy to recognize by their green heads and white neck bands. Female mallards are mottled brown.

Ring-billed gull

Ring-billed gulls are not usually associated with backyard bird feeders. They fall in the same category as crows: opportunistic scavengers that will go wherever food is free for the taking.

Most of Minnesota's urban ring-billed gulls live in Duluth where they visit backyards and picnic areas as well as the parking lots and the trash containers of fast-food restaurants. In other words, they are very adaptable birds.

One ring-billed gull nest was found in the Duluth harbor in 1974, and now the nesting population exceeds 15,000. There are large gull colonies in Lake of the Woods and smaller colonies at Mille Lacs Lake and Leech Lake in Minnesota. These colonies have increased dramatically in the past 20 years and have created serious competition with common terns and piping plovers for nesting sites.

A ring-billed gull has a white body, light gray back, black-tipped wings, and yellow legs, feet and bill. Its bill has a black ring near the tip, in contrast to the similar but larger herring gull's all-yellow bill.

These birds live on islands, peninsulas and adjacent lands of large inland lakes. They make ground nests in shallow depressions lined with sticks, stones, leaves, grasses and feathers.

Between two and four eggs take about three weeks to hatch. The young take another three weeks to fledge.

Food: About 90 percent of ring-billed gulls' food is comprised of beetles, small birds, fish, crickets, bird eggs, grasshoppers, grubs, mice and mollusks. The balance consists of carrion, garbage, table scraps and plants.

Feeding habits: During migration they visit agricultural areas to feed on small invertebrates exposed by farmers who are plowing or disking their soil. During spring and fall migratory periods, they might also hang out in the parking lots of urban malls and shopping centers to feed on scraps of food.

References: Culver 1991, Janssen 1987 and Roberts 1932.

Although ring-billed gulls are more likely to visit the parking lots of shopping malls and the garbage bins at fast food restaurants than backyards, they have learned where to find food in the urban areas near their nesting colonies.

Mourning dove

Mourning doves are common birds in the United States. In the 1989 U.S. Breeding Bird Survey, mourning doves were found on 1,254 out of 1,344 survey routes, ranking second only to red-winged blackbirds.

Named for their mournful, cooing calls, they are regular backyard residents from late March until the frosts of September. A few doves try to winter in the north, but most migrate to the southern United States, Mexico, and Central America in early September.

Mourning doves are about a foot long and have gray bodies and long, pointed tails. They live in open farm country, forests, woodlots, orchards, parks, suburban areas and inner city yards.

Mourning doves build flimsy stick nests (a design for a mourning dove nest cone can be found in *Woodworking for Wildlife*) and incubate two white eggs for two weeks. Their fledglings are fed a nutritious fluid called pigeon's milk, produced in the lining of the dove's crop.

Food: Sunflower, sorghum, ragweed, millet, barnyardgrass, browntop millet, California poppy, canarygrass, foxtail, bristlegrass, wild hemp and Japanese millet seeds.

Feeding habits: Mourning doves prefer searching for seeds where the ground cover is sparse and short, not in heavy or tall grass. They will eat a variety of small seeds that have fallen to the ground, but they also feed from perches on elevated feeders.

The best way to attract mourning doves is to provide an area of short grass, about three or

four feet in diameter, where sunflower seeds and millet can be scattered. This kind of feeding site develops naturally under hanging feeders during the summer. Patio blocks can also be set into the ground to create a bare area for feeding birds on the ground.

Mourning doves also adapt to large tray feeders near the ground or to self feeders where there is an ample perch for them, and they'll make use of adjacent bird baths or pools for obtaining water. Designs #1-3, 5 and 11-13 will all work for mourning doves.

References: Baskett et al. 1993, Culver 1991, Davison 1967, Longley (pers. comm.), Martin et. al. 1951 and Warton 1990.

The iridescence on the neck and the smooth transition area between the bill and head feathers help identify the morning dove on the left as an adult. The dove on the right has just fledged.

Mourning doves visit a feeder.

Some mourning doves attempt to winter in the north.

Red-headed woodpecker

Red-headed woodpeckers have bold black and white bodies with stunning red heads that almost glow in the sunlight. These were abundant birds in the early 1960s when Dutch elm disease killed thousands of American elm trees across the landscape. The dead trees created ideal nesting and foraging sites for red-headed woodpeckers, but now most of the American elm trees have rotted away or been removed to reduce the spread of the disease. As this happened, red-headed woodpecker numbers declined.

Now red-headed woodpeckers are uncommon, thriving only in woodlands, woodlots and farmsteads where people leave dead trees standing for the birds.

Red-headed woodpeckers have black and white bodies with red heads.

Red-headed woodpeckers can be found throughout most of the eastern United States and Great Plains east of the Rocky Mountains. They like orchards, urban backyards, hardwood and mixed hardwood forests, woodlots and farmsteads in agricultural regions. Although a few remain in northern regions during the winter, most red-headed woodpeckers migrate to the south central and southeastern states.

These woodpeckers excavate nest cavities in live or dead trees, cedar utility poles or fence posts. They are often seen along rural highways, nesting in power poles.

A woodpecker's clutch of five eggs requires 14 days of incubation, and the young fledge after about four weeks of parental care. These eggs, like most eggs laid in nest cavities, are pure white. Camouflage markings are not as beneficial for these birds' survival as they are for ring-billed gulls or pheasants that nest in the open.

Food: Apples, blackberries, dogwood, elderberries, grapes, huckleberries, mountain ash, mulberries, plums, raspberries, strawberries, poison ivy, corn and acorns; cornbread, peanuts, peanut butter and potato chips; ants, beetles, bugs, honeybees, caterpillars and grasshoppers.

In contrast to downy and hairy woodpeckers that eat 75 to 80 percent animal food, red-headed woodpeckers' diets consist of 60 percent animal food during the spring and summer and 20 percent animal food during the fall and winter.

Feeding habits: Red-headed woodpeckers cache small food items like acorns in the cracks and crevices of tree bark and in the grooves between shingles on roofs of buildings. At feeders, they may eat suet, corn, cracked walnuts, bread and peanuts, and in the summertime they can also be attracted to orange halves.

Partial albino woodpecker.
Photo by Thomas E. Keernan IV.

References: Davison 1967, Janssen 1987, Roberts 1932 and Warton 1990.

Northern flicker

Flickers are different from other Midwestern woodpeckers because they are "ant eaters" that spend most of their time foraging on the ground for ants. Flickers can extend their tongues three inches beyond their bills to capture their insect prey.

These birds have at least 132 common names around the country, including such oddities as yellowhammer, wick-up and yawker bird.

This male northern flicker is a hybrid. It has red mustache markings but yellow feather shafts.

Northern flickers are brown woodpeckers about 12 inches long. Their feather shafts are yellow, once earning them the name yellow-shafted flickers. Their brown backs are striped with black, their rumps have white patches, and their yellow bellies have small black dots. Their heads are gray and they have black collar marks.

A male flicker has black mustache markings that extend from the back of his bill, making it extremely easy to distinguish between the sexes. One western variety of northern flickers, rare in the Midwest, has red feather shafts and red mustache markings. Sometimes there are hybrids between these two color types.

Flickers have a broad breeding range that extends from Alaska across Canada and south into Mexico. Northern populations migrate south into the major portion of the United States and Mexico. Since a flicker's winter diet includes suet, seeds and fruits, it can winter from southern Minnesota west to Washington and east to Rhode Island, but most flickers winter farther south.

Flickers live in both coniferous and deciduous forests, farm groves, orchards, urban backyards and parklands. They return from the South in April or May and migrate from northern nesting areas in September and October.

Northern flickers were once common garden birds. In 1932, Dr. T. S. Roberts wrote that flickers, robins and grackles were the three most common native birds on city lawns in Minnesota. Flickers have declined significantly since that time as a backyard species, probably because of the overuse and misuse of lawn pesticides that are used to kill ants and other prey species that flickers eat.

Female flicker.

This species creates nest cavities from 2 to 60 feet above the ground. The six to eight shiny white eggs are laid at the bottom of a cavity that may be 10 to 36 inches deep. Incubation lasts 11 to 12 days. Both sexes incubate the eggs, with the male always incubating at night. The young fledge after 25 to 28 days.

Food: Beetles, bugs, caterpillars, cockroaches, crickets and grasshoppers; ampelopsis, blueberries, cherries, Virginia creeper, dogwood berries, poison ivy, blackberries, chokecherries, elderberries, grapes, honeysuckle, huckleberries, mulberries, red cedar, plums, raspberries, serviceberries, hawthorn, strawberries, bayberries and winterberries; suet, seeds from hackberries, corn, acorns, oats, ragweed, rye and wheat. Their primary food is ants. A researcher once counted 5,000 ants in the stomach of a single flicker.

Ninety percent of flickers' summertime diet is comprised of animal food, while 40 percent of their winter diet is animal food.

Feeding habits: Flickers can be attracted to suet feeders and to peanut butter. They also eat raisins and apples at feeders.

Male flicker.
Photo by Dick Peterson.

References: Culver 1991, Janssen 1987, Roberts 1932, Terres 1982 and Warton 1990.

Eastern bluebird

Although eastern bluebirds are inspiring and popular birds, few people in the Midwest saw them or heard their distinct sounds until a few years ago.

Eastern bluebirds have been a focal point of restoration efforts by the Bluebird Recovery Program of the Audubon Chapter of Minneapolis and the Minnesota DNR Nongame Wildlife Program since 1977.

These beautiful songbirds have made a dramatic recovery throughout much of the Midwest. Thousands of volunteers place and manage nest boxes for them in backyards, farms, and meadows. Bluebird numbers in Minnesota have increased at least tenfold in the past 15 years.

A male bluebird is rich blue with a rusty-red upper breast and a white belly. Females have similar but duller color patterns. Bluebirds are about two-thirds the size of robins.

Eastern bluebirds nest across most of the eastern half of the United States, the eastern Great Plains states from North Dakota to Texas, northern Mexico, and southern portions of the Canadian provinces from Saskatchewan eastward to the Atlantic Ocean.

Meadows, orchards, farms, cemeteries, golf courses, pastures, suburban and rural backyards and woodland edges will all make good habitats for bluebirds. In the fall bluebirds migrate to the southeastern states, Atlantic seaboard states and northern Mexico. A few bluebirds may winter in Minnesota and other northern regions where adequate food and shelter are available.

Bluebirds return from southern wintering areas between late March and mid-April. They nest in natural tree cavities, rotted wooden fence post tops, old woodpecker holes and nest boxes. Usually their clutches consist of four or five light blue eggs, which hatch after 12 to 14 days of incubation. The young fledge after 19 days of parental care.

Most bluebirds attempt to renest and raise a second brood during the same season. Their second clutch of eggs is usually smaller: three to four eggs. Sometimes a bluebird will raise three broods in one summer.

Food: Blackberries, blueberries, cherries, cotoneaster, Virginia creeper, dogwood, elderberries, honeysuckle, mountain ash, mulberries, eastern red cedar, viburnum, bittersweet, chokeberries, euonymus, poison ivy, raspberries, serviceberries and bayberries; dried currants, raisins, bread, cake, pitted

The female eastern bluebird's markings are more subdued than the male's markings.

dates, dried figs, peanuts, peanut butter and pecans; beetles, grubs, crickets, grasshoppers, weevils, ants, centipedes, cutworms, snails, sow bugs, spiders, caterpillars, earthworms and wasps. Bluebirds may feed pin cherries to their second brood.

A bluebird's diet consists of 90 percent animal food in the summer and 60 percent in the winter. Bluebirds can survive on bittersweet berries during cold weather prior to the emergence of insects in the spring.

Feeding habits: Eastern bluebirds are primarily insect eaters, so they usually don't come to feeders. And remember that if you use many chemicals to create a lawn with no insect life, you will have no food for bluebirds, either.

The new interest in using mealworm feeders and high protein mixes like the Janilla bluebird mix (see page 151) for insect-eating birds can now lure even the beautiful bluebirds to our backyards and patios.

If you wish to attract bluebirds during the summer, try feeding them mealworms in small containers or dishes with smooth, vertical sides (like tuna cans, soup bowls, the clear plastic trays used in meat markets, or clear plastic bases for flower pots like those sold in garden centers).

A male eastern bluebird has a rich blue back, a brick red upper breast area and a white belly.

Peterson T-post feeders (Design #22) and deck railing bluebird feeders (Designs #20 - 22) also work well.

Place your feeder on the ground within 15 or 20 feet of an occupied bluebird nest box near your house and place a few mealworms in the feeder. When the bluebirds see the movements of the mealworms, they will fly down and capture them. Then, if you wish, you can come by each day and move the feeder a few feet closer to a point that is visible from your home, deck, or picture window.

There are also special feeders on the market that look like self feeders with glass sides. They have holes on the sides and at each end so the bluebirds can get inside the feeder and eat. Larger birds cannot enter the feeder, and, since the front side is glass, you can watch the bluebirds when they're inside.

More information about attracting and feeding bluebirds can be found in *Bluebird Trails: A Guide to Success* by Dorene Scriven. It can be purchased from the Bluebird Recovery Committee, Audubon Chapter of Minneapolis, P.O. Box 3801, Minneapolis, MN 55403.

References: Culver 1991, Davison 1967, Martin et. al. 1951, Scriven 1989 and Warton 1990.

American robin

American robins, some of the first birds to return north after a harsh Midwestern winter, have become a welcome sign of spring. Their songs in the early morning and evening can evoke feelings of tranquility.

A robin's red-orange breast, brown-gray back and black head are well-known even to young children because they often nest in yards where children can witness the whole process of nest building, incubation and brood-rearing.

Robins are medium-sized birds, about ten inches long. A female robin's coloring isn't as bright as a male robin's coloring.

Robins are typically found in a variety of habitats ranging from suburban yards to farmsteads, woodlots and hardwood forests throughout most of the United States, Canada and Alaska. They winter in the southern United States, from Washington to California and into northern Mexico.

Nesting season for robins begins in late April or early May. They build cup-shaped nests of grass lined with mud in forks of trees or shrubs, on ledges of buildings or nesting shelves, or even in the nooks of farm equipment. Their four bright blue eggs will hatch after 12 to 14 days, and the young will fledge in two weeks.

Robins are usually regarded as worm eaters, but they do eat a wide variety of other foods. Fruits comprise about 25 percent of their summer diet, 75 percent of their fall diet, and 60 percent of their winter diet.

Food: Apples, barberries, blackberries, blueberries, cherries, cotoneaster, crabapples, cranberries, Virginia creeper, dogwood, elderberries, gooseberries, grapes, mountain ash, mulberries, plums, serviceberries, bittersweet, sumac, chokeberries, coralberries, hawthorn, bayberries and winterberries; beetles, bugs, caterpillars, centipedes, crickets, cutworms, flies, grasshoppers, millipedes, slugs, snails and spiders; bread, toast, cornbread, figs, prunes, raisins, nut meats, peanuts, peanut butter and grape jelly.

Feeding habits: American robins will eat apple slices stuck to nails on tray-type feeders. Bread, popcorn, raisins and especially mealworms will attract them during the summer.

References: Culver 1991, Davison 196, Martin et. al. 1951 and Warton 1990.

A robin pair selected a sheltered spot on a tractor tire for their nest. Spring planting may have to wait.

American robins are most well-known for their diet of earthworms, but they will also visit feeders to eat apples and mealworms. A newly-fledged robin is pictured here.

Varied thrush

Just when you think you have figured out what birds to expect at your feeder, something new and unexpected shows up: the varied thrush. About the size of a robin, it has orange wing-bars, an orange stripe above its eye and a gray-black band across the front of its breast.

This species symbolizes the delightful unpredictability of feeding birds. Varied thrushes do not fit the migration categories that typify regular migratory movements. They are regular winter visitors from the west.

This relative of the robin nests in moist coniferous forests of the Pacific northwest from northern California, Montana and Idaho north to Alaska. Thrushes normally winter from southern British Columbia to southern California. However, they frequently wander eastward to winter destinations including Minnesota, Wisconsin and even New York.

Food: Beetles, ants, wasps, caterpillars, earthworms, and other invertebrates; acorns, juniper berries, blackberries, raspberries and a variety of other wild berries.

Feeding habits: Varied thrushes usually come to tray feeders to eat sunflower seeds.

Reference: Proctor 1988.

Varied thrushes nest in Pacific coastal coniferous forests, but some migrate to the Midwest during the winter. Photo by Donald Waite/ Cornell Lab of Ornithology.

Northern mockingbird

Mockingbirds show up sporadically in Minnesota and have been recorded nesting in the state three times. The northern mockingbird has a remarkable distribution that covers all of the lower forty-eight states, Mexico and Cuba.

While mockingbirds may be less colorful than some other birds, their singing is unmatched. A male mockingbird's repertoire may contain more than 150 different songs. Where mockingbirds are abundant, they can confuse birdwatchers by mimicking the songs of other birds.

In recent decades there has been a steady increase in mockingbirds both in the northern states and in the Canadian provinces. They benefit from human-caused habitat changes in cities and suburbs, primarily the planting of berry-producing trees and shrubs.

A northern mockingbird is about ten inches long and more slender than a robin. Its upper parts are medium gray, with a pearly gray or white breast and belly. It has conspicuous white wing patches that become visible when it opens its wings.

Mockingbirds prefer residential and urban neighborhoods or hardwood forests, using twigs to make their nests in low shrubby cover. They will lay from two to six eggs in their nests, and may nest as many as three times per summer in southern states where the nesting season is longer. Incubation lasts 12 to 13 days, and the young fledge 12 to 13 days after that.

Food: Cottage cheese, apples, currants, nut meats, peanut butter, doughnuts, bread crumbs, suet and raisins, flies, beetles, bees, wasps, butterflies, ants, caterpillars and grasshoppers.

Mockingbirds are good examples of an omnivorous species: they eat just about anything. About half of their diet consists of arthropods and half is a variety of fruits and berries. During the nesting season they shift to eating about 85 percent insects and arthropods.

Feeding habits: If you have mockingbirds in your neighborhood during the summer, try placing slices of apple, raisins, peanut butter, suet or mealworms for them on a tray or fruit feeder.

References: Derrickson and Breitwisch 1992, Janssen 1987, Mahnken 1983 and Stokes 1987.

This northern mockingbird is eating raisins that were placed on a deck railing.

Northern mockingbirds are common in southeastern states but not in the upper Midwest. They readily adapt to backyard habitats.

Brown thrasher

A brown thrasher's bright rusty colors and speckled breast make it easily identifiable by even the most casual observer. A brown thrasher is slightly longer than a robin, but its body is more slender. The rusty color on its head, back and tail is unique, and the dark brown spots on its breast are very distinct.

Brown thrashers belong to the same family as mockingbirds and gray catbirds, and they can make a wide variety of calls and songs. Many of their calls are mimicked from other birds, and many of their song phrases are sung in pairs.

The bright, rusty markings of a brown thrasher make it an easy bird to identify.

Brown thrashers have a broad range, inhabiting the eastern half of the United States, the southern portions of the Canadian provinces from Alberta to the Atlantic, and the Great Plains states east of the Rocky Mountains. They are not common in large expanses of dense forest.

Habitats for brown thrashers include openings and edges of woodlands, farmsteads, shelterbelts, woodlots, orchards with brushy edges and urban lands with brushy cover for nesting.

Lyle Bradley of Anoka, Minnesota found that he could enhance the value of his hedges for brown thrashers and catbirds by throwing his shrub trimmings right back on top of the shrubs to make the cover thicker. Wild plum thickets provide excellent brown thrasher habitat.

Brown thrashers build bulky nests of twigs, weed stalks, grasses, bark from vines, and leaves. Nests are either on the ground or in low, shrubby cover. Between three and six eggs hatch after 12 or 13 days, and the young fledge after 14 days.

Food: Ampelopsis, beautyberries, blackberries, blueberries, cherries, Virginia creeper, currant, dogwood, eleagnus, elderberries, grapes, honeysuckle, mountain ash, mulberries, plums, poison ivy, pokeberries, serviceberries, strawberries, gooseberries, red cedar and bayberries; corn, acorns, peanuts and sumac; bread, peanut butter, raisins, sugar water and popped popcorn; beetles, ants, caterpillars, crickets, cutworms, dragonflies, earthworms, frogs, grasshoppers, lizards, mayflies, moths, salamanders, spiders and wireworms.

The diet of a brown thrasher includes 75 percent plant food in the fall and winter, 50 percent plant food in the summer, and 30 percent plant food in the spring.

Feeding habits: Brown thrashers are not common feeder visitors. It helps to have a shrubby grove or woodland nearby, one without all the understory removed for "neatness" purposes.

Brown thrashers will come to feeders for popped popcorn, bread, cheese, corn, broken walnuts, peanuts, sunflowers, peanut butter, raisins, suet and wheat. They are readily attracted to bird baths that have been placed near feeders.

Some brown thrashers will try to winter in northern regions by eating shelled corn or cracked corn, but they usually don't make it through the cold months.

References: Davison 1967, Janssen 1987, Roberts 1932 and Warton 1990

Rufous-sided towhee

One uncommon visitor to bird feeders is the rufous-sided towhee. These distinctive songbirds have unmistakable call-notes: either "towhee" or "chewink." Their song has been described as matching the phrase "drink your tea."

Towhees make their living by scratching for food among the ground litter of hardwood forests. They jump forward and then backward, their motion exposing food items hidden among the leaves. They are frequently seen feeding with fox sparrows, white-throated sparrows, white-crowned sparrows and dark-eyed juncos during migration.

Rufous-sided towhees were previously called red-eyed towhees because of their red eyes, and they were also called ground robins because of the rufous-red coloring on the sides of their breast. Slender compared to robins, towhees measure about 8 inches long.

Rufous-sided towhees are in the same family as sparrows and buntings, so you can think of them as rather large ground-feeding sparrows. Males have black backs, throats and upper chests, rufous sides, and white lower chests and bellies. Their white outer tail feathers are conspicuous when they flush. Females are similar to males, but their markings are brown where the males' markings are black.

As its name implies, the male rufous-sided towhee has rufous sides. He also has a black back and a white belly. Photo by Dave Maslowski/Maslowski Wildlife Productions.

Spotted towhees are a western race of rufous-sided towhees. Except for the white spots on their backs, spotted towhees are similar to the eastern race.

The range of the rufous-sided towhee covers most of the lower forty-eight United States into northern Mexico. They migrate from the northern Great Plains states, northern Midwest, Great Lakes states, and Northeastern states during the winter but are permanent residents farther south.

These are birds of eastern hardwood forests, not boreal forests or prairies. They like oak or mixed forests with lots of undergrowth and brushy cover. Minnesota's hardwood forest zone, from the southeastern to the northwestern corner of the state, has favorable towhee habitat.

Female towhees build bulky nests of leaves and twigs on the ground or in brush near the ground. They line their nests with hair and fine grasses. Three to five towhee eggs hatch after incubating for 12 or 13 days. Their young fledge in 10 to 12 days.

Food: Blackberries, blueberries, cherries, elderberries, grapes, raspberries, gooseberries, huckleberries, plums, mulberries, serviceberries, strawberries and bayberries; bristlegrass, canarygrass, corn, hickory nut meats, millet, acorns, oats, pine seeds, ragweed, sorghum, Sudan grass, sunflower, peanuts, walnut meats, watermelon seeds, wheat, barley, buckwheat and hemp; ants, bees, beetles, bugs, caterpillars, crickets, flies, grasshoppers, moths, spiders and wasps. Towhees eat 50 percent plant food in the summer and 80 percent plant food in the winter.

Feeding habits: Rufous-sided towhees are attracted to ground feeders with shelled corn, cracked corn, cracker crumbs, doughnuts, peanuts, nut meats, sorghum, sunflower seeds, watermelon seeds and wheat. They will also eat suet.

Lean-to feeders like the one shown on page 236 work well for towhees. The potential for towhee use increases if you have a large brush pile near your feeder.

References: Robbins, Bruun and Zim 1983, Roberts 1932 and Warton 1990.

This female rufous-sided towhee has a brown back but her general color pattern is similar to a male's. Photo by Dave Maslowski/ Maslowski Wildlife Productions.

Chipping sparrow

Usually seen scratching at the ground under a hanging bird feeder, a chipping sparrow is readily distinguished by its rusty-red cap markings and light gray unspotted breast. American tree sparrows also have rusty caps, but they have a dark breast spot and only visit feeders in the winter.

Chipping sparrows are only five inches long and the sexes look identical. They have brown backs and thin black stripes running through their eyes, and white bands on top of the black stripes. Immature chipping sparrows have streaked caps, breasts and bellies.

Chipping sparrows can also be distinguished by their high-pitched trills sung from the tops of trees.

These native sparrows have a broad range that covers almost all of North America from Mexico to Alaska and Canada's maritime provinces. They are migratory in the northern portion of their range and permanent residents in the southern portion of their range.

Their habitats vary from urban and inner city backyards to meadows, field edges, pastures, woodland openings and farms to northern tamarack and spruce bogs. If you're trying to attract them to your backyard, it helps to have some spruce trees nearby to provide nesting cover.

Chipping sparrows make tiny cup-shaped nests out of fine grasses and line them with any kind of hair, from horse to human. Their four

Adult chipping sparrow.

The slender brown streaks on this chipping sparrow's back and breast, as well as its pink bill, identify it as an immature bird.

This lark sparrow was feeding with indigo buntings on white proso millet scattered in a rock garden.

eggs require 11 to 14 days of incubation. The young leave the nest at about ten days of age.

Food: Amaranth, bristlegrass, canarygrass, cracked corn, crabgrass, dandelion seeds, millet, oats, panicum seeds, sunflower seeds, pine seeds, ragweed seeds, grain sorghum, bluegrass and chickweed; bread, cake crumbs, doughnuts, peanuts and peanut butter; ants, beetles, bugs, caterpillars, grasshoppers, leafhoppers, spiders, wasps and suet. They do not eat fruit.

Food items for chipping sparrows include 50 percent plant matter in the summer and 90 percent plant material in the winter.

Feeding habits: Chipping sparrows will eat red or white millet that has been scattered on the ground and they will sometimes take millet from cylindrical self-feeders or hopper feeders. They will also take mealworms at mealworm feeders. On rare occasions, chipping sparrows may attempt to winter in the north by staying near a feeding site.

References: Davison 1967, Janssen 1987, Roberts 1932 and Warton 1990.

Lark sparrow

A lark sparrow has unmistakable harlequin-like markings on its head and white feathers on the sides of its rounded tail. It has a chestnut patch behind its eyes, white stripes above its eyes and black stripes on each side of its chin. It also has a black spot in the center of its breast, similar to the marking on an American tree sparrow. Song sparrows also have this spot, but their breasts are striped.

Lark sparrows are summer residents in the Midwest. Their range includes most of the western states and western prairie provinces of Canada through the Ohio Valley. They are also found in Mexico.

Lark sparrows winter from southern California eastward to southern Florida and into Mexico. Northern populations are migratory and southern populations from Texas into Mexico are permanent residents.

Lark sparrows have fairly specific habitat needs. They are found in open, grassy habitats interspersed with hardwood forests or oak savanna. They usually construct grass-lined nests that are tucked into the sides of little bluestem clumps. Sometimes they nest in low shrubs. Near Detroit Lakes, Minnesota they nest in forest openings of alfalfa along roadsides and in cow pastures. Lark sparrows also live in abandoned fields and ditches.

These birds usually lay three to six eggs in their well-concealed nests, and the eggs require 12 days of incubation. The young leave the nest when they are nine or ten days old.

Food: Seeds of bristlegrass, cracked corn, knotgrass, oats, panicum, ragweed, sorghum, sunflower, wheat, amaranth and millet, plus grasshoppers, beetles and caterpillars.

Lark sparrows do not eat fruit. They eat 50 percent plant material in the summer and 100 percent plant material during the winter.

Feeding habits: Even though lark sparrows are uncommon at bird feeders, Bill and Mary Wyatt of Detroit Lakes, Minnesota have been able to attract some by scattering white proso millet in the rock garden by their home.

Song sparrow

Song sparrows are native birds with welcome summer songs. Their song patterns are distinctive: two or three clear notes followed by a musical trill. Dr. T. S. Roberts reported, however, that one person recorded 600 variations in this species' songs.

According to Roberts, "the sweet, cheery song of the Song Sparrow is one of the first to be heard at the breaking up of winter, just when the air is touched by the warmth of the first spring-like days but while the snow still lingers and the nights are cold and wintry."

A song sparrow is reddish-brown on top and streaked with black and gray. Its white breast is heavily streaked with black and rufous spots, including one large spot in the center. Due to the interesting variety of songs and plumage that song sparrows exhibit, as many as thirty subspecies are known.

Song sparrows are permanent residents through much of the central United States. This hardy species nests throughout most of North America from southern Alaska, across Canada and into most of the lower forty-eight states except for a region between New Mexico and Georgia.

Northern populations of song sparrows are migratory except for those in the southern regions of Alaska. Wintering areas for song sparrows include northern Mexico, New Mexico and the Gulf coast states.

Habitats of song sparrows are varied. They live in backyards, farms, woodlots, woodlands, forest openings, orchards, brushy fence rows and parklands.

Song sparrow nests are cup-shaped and made of coarse grasses, rootlets, and weed stems. They are usually one to four feet above the ground in a small shrub or conifer. Three to five eggs hatch after 12 to 13 days. The young fledge in about ten days.

Food: Amaranth, barnyardgrass, bristlegrass, canarygrass, cracked corn, crabgrass, dandelion seeds, hemp, millet, oats, panicum, pine, ragweed, smartweed, sorghum, Sudan grass, sunflower, walnut meats and wheat; dogwood, elderberries and mulberries; ants, beetles, bugs, caterpillars, crickets and grasshoppers.

Plant foods comprise 60 percent of a song sparrow's diet in the summer and 90 percent of its food in the winter.

Feeding habits: You can attract song sparrows to your feeders the same way you attract chipping sparrows. Throw some millet or cracked corn on the ground. Song sparrows may take peanut butter to feed to their young. It also helps to have some water or a brush pile nearby.

Song sparrows also feed on small seeds, like white proso millet, that have been scattered on the ground. They are common songbirds in woodland and meadow edges.

References: Davison 1967, Janssen 1987, Roberts 1932 and Warton 1990.

Red-winged blackbird

Along with the spring songs of chickadees and cardinals, the calls of returning red-winged blackbirds are memorable symbols of springtime in the Midwest. These birds are typically seen balancing on the old cattail stalks in our marshes, with males defending their territories. Bright red and yellow shoulder markings, or epaulets, on their wings provide a striking contrast to the drab brown of the dead cattails.

Red-winged blackbirds are smaller and more slender than robins, about nine inches long. Females have mottled brown and black patterning that provides them with ideal camouflage among the cattails.

Some female red-winged blackbirds are darker than others, and some may have lighter throats or a dark stripe through their eyes. If you see a bird at your feeder that resembles a female red-winged blackbird with an inconspicuous red wing-patch, it is probably a year-old male that has not yet molted into adult plumage.

Red-winged blackbirds are some of the most widely-distributed and abundant birds in North America. They have nested as far north as the cattail marshes of Alaska's Minto Flats and as far south as northwestern Costa Rica in Central America. They nest throughout all 48 states, Alaska, Canada, the Northwest Territories, Mexico and Central America.

Their habitats include freshwater cattail marshes, saltwater marshes, swamps, wet meadows, pastures, shrubby hedge rows, grasslands and field edges. Red-winged blackbirds nest among cattail stalks, grasses and shrubs.

A typical clutch contains three or four pale blue eggs that have irregular, scrawled stripes and blotches of brown and purple. The eggs hatch after 10 to 12 days, and the young fledge after ten days.

Food: Ants, beetles, cankerworms, caterpillars, grasshoppers, grubs, weevils, snails and spiders; barley, bristlegrass, canarygrass, corn, millet, oats, peanuts, ragweed, wheat, crabgrass and especially sunflowers. Red-winged blackbirds eat 50 percent plant matter in the summer and 95 percent plant matter in the winter.

Feeding habits: During fall migration, when thousands of red-

Red-winged blackbirds provide a welcome sign of spring when they return from their wintering grounds and stake out their territories in cattail marshes and shrubby wetland edges. They are a surprisingly regular visitor in backyards where they eat sunflower seeds.

The brown, heavily-striped female red-winged blackbirds are adept at balancing among the cattails that comprise their nesting habitat. They usually feed on the ground but will also use hanging feeders.

74

winged blackbirds congregate in the Great Plains, they can cause crop depredation problems. They can also become a nuisance at feeders when they congregate in large numbers.

Red-winged blackbirds will eat from the ground or perch on elevated or hanging feeders to get at sunflower seeds, shelled corn, cracked corn or millet.

References: Culver 1991, Davison 1967, Martin et. al. 1951 and Warton 1990.

Yellow-headed blackbird

A yellow-headed blackbird is marked just as its name implies: black, with a yellow head. A male is about nine inches long with white patches on the leading edges of his wings near the wrist joints.

The brown female has a white chin that blends down to an unstreaked yellow throat. They don't have streaks on their backs and sides like female red-winged blackbirds.

Female yellow-headed blackbirds are dark brown with a bright yellow upper breast area.

Perhaps the most distinctive feature of a yellow-headed blackbird is its incredible song. According to Dr. T. S. Roberts: "This fine fellow, perched aloft on a cluster of swaying reed stems, is straining every nerve in an attempt that results, after a few harsh preliminary, but fairly promising, notes, in a seemingly painful choking spell, which terminates in a long-drawn rasping squeal that is nothing short of harrowing...The rasping, scraping sounds are accompanied by a most intense bodily effort, as is evidenced by the widely spread tail, swollen throat, upturned head, and twisted neck."

Yellow-headed blackbirds live in Minnesota, Wisconsin and Iowa and the Pacific states, the Canadian prairie provinces and New Mexico and Arizona. They winter from southern California, Arizona, New Mexico and south Texas down into Mexico. Their habitats are usually deeper bulrush-dominated or wild cane marshes, although they can also nest in small cattail marshes.

The distinctive yellow-headed blackbird is a rare visitor at feeders.

Female yellow-headed blackbirds make their nests over standing water by weaving reeds and grasses among wild cane stalks or by weaving bulrush stems together. They will lay between three and six eggs, which will take 13 days to incubate and 12 days for the young to fledge. Yellow-headed blackbirds frequently nest in loose colonies.

There are some interesting differences between red-winged blackbirds and yellow-headed blackbirds. The red-winged variety arrive back from their wintering grounds in mid to late February, while yellow-headed blackbirds arrive about a month later. Red-winged blackbirds gather in enormous flocks of up to 250,000 or more during both spring and fall migrations. Fall concentrations of yellow-headed blackbirds usually do not exceed 200 birds.

Food: Bristlegrass, corn, oats, sorghum, wheat, barley, ragweed, sunflowers, beetles, caterpillars, grasshoppers and mayflies.

They eat 60 percent plant matter in the summer and 85 percent plant matter during the winter.

Feeding habits: While rare at bird feeders, yellow-headed blackbirds may appear among flocks of red-winged blackbirds where shelled corn, cracked corn or sunflower seeds are scattered on the ground. They may also use self or cylindrical feeders.

References: Culver 1991, Davison 1967, Janssen 1987 and Roberts 1932.

Common grackle

Minnesota has conservation groups that help bluebirds, wood ducks, bobwhites, pheasants, trumpeter swans, Canada geese, prairie chickens, sharp-tailed grouse, ruffed grouse and wild turkeys, but there are no conservation groups for grackles. A southern Minnesota town called Winthrop does, however, celebrate Grackle Days each spring to honor their return from winter migration!

Common grackles are often called blackbirds, but a close look at the male will show you an iridescent sheen of blue, purple, green, bronze and copper. In fact, these birds used to be known as bronzed grackles.

Male grackles are about 12 inches long. Females, black without the males' iridescent sheen, are slightly smaller. Their eyes are pale yellow or white.

The range of common grackles includes most of the lower 48 states and Canada east of the Rocky Mountains. Their habitats vary from inner cities to suburbs, farmlands, orchards, meadows, wetlands, fields and woodland edges. They usually migrate south in October and return from their migration in April.

Male common grackles have iridescent plumage when viewed in sunlight. This bird is blinking. The white membrane, called the nictitating membrane, passes over its eye when it blinks.

Grackles nest in places ranging from backyard spruce trees to bridge latticework. Sometimes they live in purple martin houses, and sometimes they live in the bottom of great blue heron stick nests.

Grackles often nest in loose colonies, with dozens of nests in the same vicinity. Females take 11 days to build their cup-shaped nests of grasses, mud and weed stalks. Their clutches of five eggs need 11 or 12 days for incubation, and their young fledge after 14 days.

Some people dislike grackles because they eat fruits in gardens and from trees. Others dislike them because they can damage agricultural crops and kill songbirds attempting to nest in backyards.

Grackles also have the unsavory habit of dropping the fecal sacs from their young into backyard swimming pools.

Food: Cherries, grapes, mountain ash, blackberries, chokeberries, dogwood, elderberries, mulberries, serviceberries, apples and bayberries; seeds, nuts and domestic grains like corn, acorns, oats, peas, pecans, pine seeds, sorghum, sunflowers, wheat, bristlegrass, canary-grass, hackberry seeds, hemp seeds, millet, ragweed and rye; bread, cornbread, peanut butter, potato chips, rice and figs; bees, crayfish, crickets, earthworms, grasshoppers, baby birds, bird eggs, suet, snails, sowbugs, spiders and minnows, and they have even been known to kill house sparrows.

The diet of common grackles includes 50 percent plant food in the summer and 80 percent plant food in the winter.

Feeding habits: Grackles are easily attracted to backyards that have spruce trees in which to nest. They come to ground feeders, tray feeders, deck railing feeders, screen feeders and self feeders looking for sunflower seeds, millet and cracked corn.

If grackles overwhelm a feeding area to the point that they are preventing other birds from feeding, it is possible to place a grackle log roller on some feeders to discourage them. See page 198 for details.

Grackles may also be discouraged from feeding at counter-weighted self feeders by adjusting the weight in the rear to close in response to a grackle's weight.

References: Culver 1991, Davison 1967, Roberts 1932, Stokes 1987 and Warton 1990.

This pure albino common grackle had recently left its nest. Pure albino birds have no pigment in their feathers and their eyes are pink. While such rare birds are often fascinating to humans, other birds of the same species tend to pick on albinos and they are conspicuous to predators.

Female common grackles are similar to males, but they have less iridescence in their feathers and their bills are more slender.

77

Two views of female brown-headed cowbirds.

Brown-headed cowbird

Male cowbirds are about seven inches long, with shiny dark brown heads and shiny black bodies. Females are gray-brown with white throats.

Cowbirds evolved with bison rather than cows, so they would probably be more appropriately named bison birds. They traditionally followed great herds of bison as they roamed over hundreds of miles of prairie and plains during the summer. Cowbirds caught grasshoppers and other insects that were flushed by the movement of the bison's feet.

Cowbirds couldn't have kept up with the bison herds if they had to stop, build nests, incubate eggs and rear their young, a process that takes many songbirds nearly a month to complete. Instead, cowbirds became infamous for removing eggs from other birds' nests and replacing them with eggs of their own. They are called nest parasites.

Birds that find themselves raising young cowbirds include yellow warblers, song sparrows, red-eyed vireos, chipping sparrows, eastern phoebes, rufous-sided towhees, ovenbirds, common yellowthroats, American redstarts, eastern bluebirds, lark sparrows, indigo buntings, red-winged blackbirds and field sparrows. At least 144 bird species have been reported to raise young cowbirds in their nests.

People have increased habitats for cowbirds by creating openings and meadows in forested regions, making more birds vulnerable to cowbird predation. As a result, cowbird numbers have increased dramatically while one rare bird, the Kirtland's warbler in Michigan, must be constantly monitored to reduce cowbird nest parasitism.

Cowbird eggs hatch after about 12 days of incubation, and the young fledge after ten days of care by their foster parents. A female cowbird may lay as many as 20 eggs per season in the nests of other birds. The aggressive cowbird chicks may push other chicks out of the nest or out-compete them for food brought by the parent birds.

There is only one bird that consistently prevents cowbird young from fledging in their nests: the American goldfinch. Goldfinches feed thistle seeds to their young, while most songbirds feed their young high-protein insects. Cowbird young that hatch in a goldfinch's nest invariably die of malnutrition.

In the winter, cowbirds migrate to Texas, northern Mexico and the eastern and southeastern United States. Some wintering roosts of blackbirds mixed with cowbirds can be enormous, constituting a local nuisance. One Kentucky blackbird roost contained five million birds, of which five percent were brown-headed cowbirds.

Feeding habits: Cowbirds frequently come to bird feeders stocked with cracked corn or millet. They are often in the company of grackles and red-winged blackbirds.

References: Culver 1991, Lowther 1993, Middleton 1993, Stokes 1987 and Warton 1990.

Male cowbirds have brown heads with iridescent black bodies. Cowbirds are a native species but they are a threat to the survival of declining populations of forest songbirds. Photo by Dave Maslowski/ Maslowski Wildlife Productions

CENTRAL AMERICAN MIGRANTS

Central American migrants are not very common at bird feeders because most of them are warblers and vireos that eat a high proportion of insects rather than fruits and seeds. These birds, called neotropical migrants by biologists, winter in the tropical habitats of Central and South America. Many neotropical migrant populations are declining due to the hazards of the long migration, loss of rain forest wintering areas and degradation of nesting habitats in North America. Nest parasitism by cowbirds may also be affecting the long term survival of these species.

Some birds, like yellow-bellied sapsuckers, winter from Illinois and Missouri south to Panama, so they can also be considered short-distance migrants.

Neotropical migrant birds routinely return to the Midwest in early May from wintering habitats that range from southern Mexico to northern Ecuador, Colombia and Venezuela in South America. Their woodland songs, fascinating habits and striking colors can enhance the beauty of the theater of seasons in your yard. Since these birds have so far to travel to their wintering grounds, most leave their summer habitats by September.

You will miss these birds if you only feed birds in the winter; give summer feeding a try. Nectar feeders will attract both hummingbirds and orioles. Apples will attract catbirds, and oranges and grape jelly attract orioles. Rose-breasted grosbeaks respond best to a feeder stocked with black oil sunflower seeds. The first time you have a northern oriole, rose-breasted grosbeak or ruby-throated hummingbird show up at your feeder, you will get hooked on summer feeding.

Ruby-throated hummingbird

Tiny ruby-throated hummingbirds can generate more interest and excitement than any other bird in the Midwest. There are 319 hummingbird species in North and South America, but only the ruby-throated is a regular breeding resident in the Midwest.

Hummingbirds possess many special qualities: they can hover and fly backwards, they never walk, their bills are adapted for sipping nectar at flowers, they can slow down their metabolic rate and become

boreal migrants

permanent residents

short-distance migrants

CENTRAL AMERICAN MIGRANTS

South American migrants

The darkened area is where the Central American migrants spend their winters.

A male ruby-throated hummingbird's bright red throat patch is called a gorget. Hummingbirds' feathers have structural colors, so they appear black when viewed from the side (photo on the left) and iridescent when the bird turns toward an observer or another hummingbird (below).

dormant during cold nights, and they can fly up to 60 miles per hour. Ruby-throated hummingbirds can beat their wings up to 75 times per second.

Only about three inches long, a hummingbird weighs between six and eight grams. Its back is iridescent green and its breast and belly are white.

A male's throat, or gorget, is a stunning ruby red when viewed in the sun. Without the refracted light, its throat appears black. Both the iridescent green and the iridescent red are not pigments in the feathers, but structural colors created when sunlight is refracted back from the feathers to your eyes. If these feathers are viewed with a light behind them, they appear gray.

Females are similar to males except that they have white throats rather than the red throat patches.

Ruby-throated hummingbirds nest throughout the eastern half of the United States and along the eastern edge of the Great Plains south to eastern Oklahoma and Texas. They also nest in the southern half of Alberta, Saskatchewan, Manitoba, Ontario, east central British Columbia and southeastern Canada.

The wintering range extends from southern Texas and Florida through Mexico to Costa Rica. By feeding heavily on flower nectar in southern states like Florida and Georgia, hummingbirds can add up to 50 percent of their body weight prior to flying 600 miles non-stop across the Gulf of Mexico to their wintering grounds in Mexico and Central America. The nectar is stored as fat reserves under the skin. Folklore explaining that hummingbirds migrate south on the backs of Canada geese is completely false; Canada geese never go to Central America in the winter!

Habitats of ruby-throated hummingbirds include hardwood forests and mixed hardwood forests, woodland edges and clearings, meadows, woodlots, forested urban and suburban parks, backyards and orchards. They are uncommon in open agricultural regions.

Hummingbird nests are about the size of walnut halves and are made of spider silk and plant down and lined on the outside with lichens. They are built on top of horizontal tree branches. Two tiny white eggs, only a half inch long, hatch after incubation periods of 14 to 16 days. The young fledge after three weeks.

Food: Hummingbirds have the highest rate of metabolism among all birds, so they must consume large amounts of high-energy food to sustain themselves. Most of this quick energy is derived from nectar in flowers. They use many flowers as nectar sources, including scarlet runner beans, bee balm (monarda), buckeye, cardinal flower, American columbine, coralberry, evening primrose, four-o'clock, fuchsia, gladiolus, hibiscus, honeysuckle, lilies, butterfly weed, morning glory, nasturtium, penstemon, petunia, phlox, scarlet sage, snapdragon, spotted touch-me-not, thistle, tithonia, trumpet creeper, bergena, weigela, zinnia, hosta and coral bells.

The nectar in these flowers helps supplement the sugar water at your hummingbird feeder. This subject is discussed in greater detail in the book *Landscaping for Wildlife.*

Feeding habits: These birds may eat up to 30 percent of their weight in nectar each day. When ruby-throated hummingbirds

This unusual view of a male ruby-throated hummingbird, at right, illustrates his incredible agility as he abruptly banks, turns and dives downward using his tail as a rudder.

first return in the spring there are few flowers blooming, so they lap the sap that flows from tree trunk wounds created by yellow-bellied sapsuckers. Their nectar diet is balanced by eating small insects and spiders.

At feeders, hummingbirds can be attracted by a nectar mixture of four parts water to one part cane sugar which is boiled, left to cool and then placed in a commercial feeder. The balance can be refrigerated until it's needed. Red coloring is not necessary in the water because most hummingbird feeders have red feeder ports. In warm weather the mixture may need to be changed every three to five days, and the feeder should be thoroughly cleaned. A small bag of over-ripe bananas or cantaloupe can be hung near the hummingbird feeder to attract fruit flies that are also eaten by the hummingbirds.

References: Culver 1991, Davison 1967, Roberts 1932 and Warton 1990.

A female ruby-throated hummingbird has an iridescent green back and a white throat, breast and belly.

Yellow-bellied sapsucker

Yellow-bellied sapsuckers have a unique diet: sap. These woodpeckers peck neat rows of quarter-inch diameter holes in tree trunks. Sap fills in the holes, and the birds lap up the sap. The wounds that they form provide a source of sap for hummingbirds, nuthatches, warblers, insects and even flying squirrels. They are known to use 275 species of hardwood and coniferous trees as a source of sap.

These woodpeckers are richly patterned. Males have barred backs, red foreheads, red throats and yellow speckled bellies. Females have white throats.

The yellow-bellied sapsucker's range includes both deciduous and coniferous forests in the Midwest, northeastern United States, eastern Canada and northwestward through the forests of the Canadian prairie provinces to northern British Columbia and the Northwest Territories. Suitable habitats include both natural forests and woodland groves and orchards. Wintering areas range from Missouri, Indiana and Illinois and south to Costa Rica and Panama.

Yellow-bellied sapsuckers nest in tree cavities that are from 3 to 30 feet above the ground. The cavities, made in either live or dead trees, are between 10 and 12 inches deep. Four eggs hatch after 11 to 12 days of incubation. Males incubate the eggs at night, and young fledge after a month of care.

Food: Apples, black cherries, Virginia creeper, dogwood, American elderberry, honeysuckle, poison ivy, strawberries, grapes, plums, ants, beetles, caterpillars, centipedes and spiders. They are best known for lapping the sap out of the tree wounds they create. They also eat the insects that get stuck in the sap flowing from their tree wounds.

Feeding habits: Yellow-bellied sapsuckers will also visit feeders for suet, peanut butter, cracked walnuts and fruits. They drink sugar water at hummingbird and oriole feeders.

References: Terres 1980 and Longley pers. comm.

Gray catbird

If a bird's beauty were judged by its song, the gray catbird would easily rank as one of our most beautiful songbirds. This gray bird of shrubby habitats is related to the mockingbird, and its bottomless repertoire of songs adds a special touch of nature to any backyard. Although the catbird is named for its cat-like "meowing" calls, it is one of our most accomplished songbirds. The catbird is also one of the few songbirds to sing at night, adding music to summer evenings.

Catbirds are slender birds, about nine inches long. Their bodies are uniform gray with black caps and rufous patches under their tails. The sexes look identical.

Gray catbirds nest across most of the United States except for the region from west Texas northwest to Oregon and west to California. They also nest in the southern portion of the Canadian provinces. This species winters from the Gulf Coast south to Costa Rica in Central America.

Catbirds live in thick, shrubby, brushy undergrowth in deciduous woodlands and gardens. They readily adapt to urban and backyard settings where there are thickets of fruiting shrubs that provide nesting sites and fruits to eat. Thickets of wild plums provide excellent habitats for both gray catbirds and brown thrashers.

Yellow-bellied sapsuckers visit feeders for suet, nectar or fruit.

A gray catbird is medium gray with a black cap and a rufous patch under the tail.

Nesting begins in mid-May. Catbird nests are bulky cup-shaped platforms of twigs, leaves and vines constructed near the ground in shrubby cover. Their inner linings are composed of rootlets. The four bright green-blue eggs hatch after 12 days, and the young fledge after 14 days.

Food: Apples, blackberries, blueberries, cherries, Virginia creeper, dogwood, elderberries, gooseberries, grapes, honeysuckle, mountain ash, mulberries, plums, raspberries, poison ivy, bittersweet, red cedar and bayberries; sumac, walnuts and alder; sliced apples, bread, cake, dried currant, peanuts, cheese and raisins; also ants, beetles, caterpillars, grasshoppers, bugs and spiders. Catbirds prefer fruits to seeds, and plant foods comprise 60 percent of their food intake in the summer and 80 percent in the winter.

Feeding habits: Catbirds are best attracted by having fruit-bearing shrubs, as explained in *Landscaping for Wildlife*. However, they are also attracted to feeders stocked with slices of apple, bread, cheese, grapes, peanuts, grape jelly, raisins, suet, mealworms and broken walnuts.

References: Davison 1967, Janssen 1987, Roberts 1932 and Warton 1990.

Yellow-rumped warbler

One of the most fascinating spectacles of spring bird migration is the passage of yellow-rumped warblers through Midwestern woodlands.

Many of these colorful warblers arrive in Minnesota in the second or third week of April along with eastern bluebirds, American robins, red-winged blackbirds, and eastern phoebes. They are among the first warbler species to arrive in the spring, and, in some years, their numbers totally overwhelm the numbers of other warblers in early May.

As they flit from one perch to another, they provide numerous opportunities for the quiet bird observer to see their delicate blue-gray and yellow markings. A male has a dapper blue-gray coloring on top with a yellow cap, yellow rump, and yellow spots on each side of his chest. His upper breast and sides are black. Females have similar but duller markings.

This species nests in pine forest and mixed woodlands throughout much of Canada, Alaska, and northern coniferous regions of the lower forty-eight states like Minnesota, Wisconsin and Maine, and also in pine forests of the Rocky Mountain states. Unlike some

Yellow-rumped warblers are among the first warblers to appear during the spring migration in late April and early May. The gray pattern with black highlights and the yellow patches on their heads, rump and upper breast make them easy to identify.

neotropical migrant warblers that have extremely limited wintering habitats, this one winters all the way from states in the lower Mississippi Valley and Gulf Coast to Panama. The status of its wintering habitat is therefore much less at risk than that of birds like bay-breasted warblers that only winter in the rain forests of Costa Rica, Panama and northern Colombia.

Yellow-rumped warbler's nests, built anywhere from 4 to 40 feet above the ground, are usually on horizontal branches of spruce or balsam fir trees. Warblers weave feathers into their nest lining so that the feathers arch over the top, like tree swallow nests. This provides camouflage from marauding jays or brown-headed cowbirds, both common nest parasites. Four or five warbler eggs will require 12 days for incubation. Fledging occurs after 10 to 12 days.

Food: Virginia creeper, dogwood, poison ivy, eastern red cedar, euonymus, butternut, hazel nut, hackberries, hickory, broken walnuts, sumac, almonds, bread, cake, cashew nuts, cornbread, cornmeal, peanuts, peanut butter and dried figs.

Feeding habits: Food habits of yellow-rumped warblers provide a fascinating deviation from that of most warblers: most are exclusive insect eaters, while yellow-rumped warblers eat 90 percent plant food during the winter. In fact, another common name for this warbler is the myrtle warbler, not after a woman named Myrtle, but because of the preference they show for eating waxmyrtle berries, or bayberries.

At wintering grounds, yellow-rumped warblers come to tray feeders stocked with orange slices, bread, cornmeal, nut meats, peanut butter, suet and bayberries.

References: Culver 1990, Davison 1967, Harrison 1984, Janssen 1987 and Roberts 1932.

Summer tanager

Stunning male summer tanagers are about six and a half inches long and red like cardinals. The females are an attractive yellow-orange. Young males molting into adult plumage are yellow-orange splotched with red. Their body profiles are similar to those of the scarlet tanager, but you can tell them apart by their wings: summer tanagers have red wings and scarlet tanagers do not.

Summer tanagers of the southeastern United States are found primarily in mixed oak and pine woodlands. Their range extends from the southeastern quarter of the United States westward into the southern Great Plains and California. In the winter, summer tanagers migrate to Central America where they are frequently seen visiting bird feeders stocked with bananas. Sometimes summer tanagers will try to winter in the north rather than migrate to Central America, but they're usually very rare in the northern regions of the Midwest, visiting only as spring migrants and occasionally at feeders in November.

Summer tanager nests are usually built in open oak-pine woodlands. These shallow cup nests, built from grasses and weed stems and lined with fine grass, are found on horizontal branches from 10 to 35 feet above the ground. They usually contain three to five eggs. Incubation requires 13 to 15 days, and the young fledge after about 15 days.

Female summer tanagers have yellow-orange plumage. This tanager was eating a banana at a bird feeder near Escazu, Costa Rica, while at its wintering grounds.

Male summer tanagers have stunning red plumage. This tanager was wintering in Panama

Food: Blackberries, cherries, dogwood, elderberries, grapes, mulberries, plums, ants, bees, beetles, bugs, caterpillars, wasps, bread, peanut butter, raisins, sugar water, cantaloupe seeds and suet.

Feeding habits: Summer tanagers seldom go to feeders in the summer, but in the fall and winter they visit feeders for sunflower seeds, suet, oranges and peanut butter. Walt Rohl, formerly of Forest Lake, Minnesota, once observed a summer tanager feeding on the fat of a deer rib cage that he hung up in his yard after deer hunting season.

References: Davison 1967, Harrison 1978, Proctor 1988, Robbins, Bruun and Zim 1983.

Rose-breasted grosbeak

One of the best ways to have other people envy your success in attracting birds is to have a procession of rose-breasted grosbeaks coming to your feeder.

Dr. T. S. Roberts compared the rose-breasted grosbeak's song to that of the American robin and the scarlet tanager. Grosbeaks' songs, he said, have a "loud, sweet, pure-toned warble" that is far superior to the other two birds. Males often sing while sitting on the eggs, and, like catbirds, they are one of the few songbirds that sings at night.

A male rose-breasted grosbeak has a black and white body and a beautiful rose-colored triangular marking on its breast. It is only eight inches long, with a stocky body profile compared to a cardinal. When seen in flight, there is little doubt about the identity of this species: bold black and white markings, a flash of the rose-colored bib, and perhaps a glimpse of the pink underwing linings will distinguish them.

Male rose-breasted grosbeak.

A female rose-breasted grosbeak is brown on top, with white wing stripes and well-marked white stripes above her eyes. She resembles a larger version of the female purple finch.

Rose-breasted grosbeaks are primarily found where mature hardwood forest is present. Their summer habitats are mature hardwood forests and adjacent woodlands, urban woodlands, parks, orchards and backyards. Grosbeaks live in the northern hardwood forests of the northeastern and east central United States, the Midwest, eastern Great Plains, and the Canadian provinces east of the Rocky Mountains. In the winter this species migrates to wintering grounds from southern Mexico through Central America, to Colombia and Ecuador.

Grosbeaks nest in northern white cedar, boxelder, elm, cherry, hawthorn and chokecherry trees. Their nests are from 4 to 15 feet above the ground and made out of small twigs, weed stems and plant rootlets. The four eggs require 12 to 14 days for incubation, and the chicks fledge at 10 to 15 days of age.

Food: Barberries, cherries, elderberries, mulberries, serviceberries, strawberries, blackberries, dogwood, corn, hemp, oats, sunflower, wheat, hickory nuts, ragweed and smartweed, suet, beetles, ants, bees, caterpillars, scale insects and wasps. They have voracious appetites for potato-bugs and have even been referred to as potato bug birds. Grosbeaks are also notorious among gardeners for eating their garden peas.

Rose-breasted grosbeaks eat 50 percent plant matter and 50 percent animal matter.

Feeding habits: The best way to attract rose-breasted grosbeaks is with a tray feeder, fly-through feeder, or self-feeder filled with black oil sunflower seeds. Look for them to arrive back from their wintering grounds in early May.

References: Davison 1967, Robbins, Bruun, and Zim 1983, Roberts 1932, Warton 1990.

Female rose-breasted grosbeaks, pictured above, look very different than their male counterparts, pictured on the right. Female grosbeaks look like large female purple finches with larger bills. Their heavy bills are adapted to cracking and eating larger seeds and fruits.

Indigo bunting

Among the most stunning of all native songbirds is the indigo bunting, a species of hardwood forests, brushy areas and woodland borders. The key to discovering indigo buntings is to learn their song: three paired whistled notes, two higher tones of the same pitch, two lower tones of the same pitch and two intermediate tones of the same pitch.

A male indigo bunting is about five inches long. He has rich blue to indigo structural coloring that is iridescent in bright sunlight. The lower portion of his bill, called the lower mandible, is bright white. A female indigo bunting is medium brown with a light tan breast and belly.

Indigo buntings are fairly common throughout the eastern half of the United States. They winter in southern Mexico, Central America, Colombia and the Caribbean.

Indigo buntings return from the south in mid-May. Females select nest sites and build their nests in shrubby cover within several feet of the ground. Three or four eggs hatch after 12 to 13 days. The young fledge after 9 to 12 days.

Food: Small spiders, caterpillars, grasshoppers, beetles, seeds of herbs and grasses, elderberries, blueberries, strawberries and blackberries.

Feeding habits: Although not typically birds that visit feeders, they will come to self feeders, tray feeders and ground feeding sites during the summer if they can get white proso millet. They will also feed at thistle feeders.

References: Culver 1991, Davison 1967, Janssen 1987, Payne 1992 and Warton 1990.

The brilliant colors of the male indigo bunting are structural colors like those of the blue jay and ruby-throated hummingbird.

This female indigo bunting has a subdued brown back with blue patches on her shoulders and tail. The clothesline provided a convenient perch for approaching the feeding area below.

Northern oriole

Brightly-marked northern orioles are instant favorites for anyone who has glimpsed their bright orange and black plumage and heard their mellow song.

Orioles are about eight and a half inches long, slightly smaller than catbirds. A male oriole has a black head, throat, back, tail and wings. He has white stripes on his wings while his chest, belly, vent, and parts of his tail are bright orange.

A female northern oriole is brown on top with white wing stripes and a pale orange breast and belly. She has a slender blackbird-style bill.

The eastern subspecies formerly known as the Baltimore oriole and the western subspecies formerly known as the Bullock's orioles are now considered northern orioles. They nest across almost all of the lower 48 states and the southern portions of the Canadian prairie provinces. They are absent as a nesting species only in the coastal plain region of the Gulf Coast states from Texas to North Carolina. Orioles winter from northern Mexico to northern Colombia in South America.

This species generally resides

Female and young orioles don't have the bright orange markings of the males.

in hardwood forests but it is also adapted to open woodlands, forest edges, urban backyards, parks, orchards and farm woodlots. When American elms were common, orioles frequently nested in them. Now they often use cottonwoods. Other nesting trees include birch, boxelder, maple, aspen and oak.

Orioles' hanging pouch-like nests are woven works of art created from milkweed down, dog hairs, weed fibers, wool and yarn or any other fibrous material that is available at nesting time. The pendulous nests are usually constructed at the tip of a long slender branch, making it difficult for predators to climb out to them. Four to five eggs hatch after 12 to 14 days of incubation. The young fledge in about 14 days.

Food: Blackberries, cherries, mountain ash, mulberries, apples, serviceberries, blueberries, elderberries, grapes, pears, peas, caterpillars, ants, beetles, bugs, grasshoppers, spiders and wasps. They are primarily fruit eaters.

Feeding habits: At feeders, orioles are attracted by orange halves, small trays of grape jelly, mealworms, broken walnuts, apple slices, suet and bread. They will visit nectar feeders containing a mixture of four parts water to one part sugar, the same colorless sugar water solution used for hummingbirds.

You can also attract orioles in the spring by hanging out clusters or string bags of long dog hair (like that of a Samoyed), yarn, string or milkweed silk saved from the previous fall. The orioles will take these fibers to build their nests.

References: Culver 1991, Davison 1967, Martin et. al. 1951, Roberts 1932, and Warton 1990.

Northern orioles can be attracted to feeders with orange halves, nectar or shallow trays of grape jelly. This male oriole is eating his jelly in an upside-down position.

SOUTH AMERICAN MIGRANTS

There are very few backyard bird species at feeders that migrate to South America in the winter. Only purple martins and scarlet tanagers are even incidental at bird feeding stations. Most migrants to this continent are insect eaters like swifts and swallows, shorebirds and some warblers and tanagers. Bobolinks and dickcissels are also notable as migrants to South America, but they don't visit feeders either.

boreal
migrants

permanent
residents

short-distance
migrants

Central American
migrants

SOUTH AMERICAN
MIGRANTS

This map indicates the approximate wintering area for South American migrant birds.

Purple martin

Their social behavior and insect-eating habits make purple martins popular birds in Midwestern backyards. As their name implies, male purple martins are purple or blue-black. Female purple martins are more drab-colored than the males, with dark backs, gray bellies and speckled throats.

These large swallows winter in Brazil and summer across the eastern United States, the Canadian prairie provinces and on the west coast. After returning from Brazilian wintering grounds in late April, purple martins lay four to five eggs in a martin house or hollow tree cavity. Incubation lasts 15 days, and the young fledge after four weeks.

Woodworking for Wildlife provides information on how to attract purple martins. They do not come to bird feeders because they catch insects on the wing. Purple martins have been included here because of a feeding technique that can be used to help them in the spring.

Purple martin experts recommend collecting egg shells, perhaps in quantity from a local restaurant. Break them into fragments smaller than a fingernail, lay them out in the air to dry, and serve them to the martins in a metal pie tin nailed to the top of a post near the martin house. The pie tin should have drain holes. The egg shells provide females with the calcium necessary to increase their nutrient reserves prior to laying eggs.

References: Culver 1991, Dennis 1994, Wade and Hill 1990 and Warton 1990.

The female purple martin is gray with few iridescent highlights.

Scarlet tanager

Scarlet tanagers are beautiful native songbirds. Males are bright red with black wings and black tails. Females and immature males have dull green backs, yellow bellies, and black wings and tails. In the winter males molt into nonbreeding plumage similar to that of the female.

Scarlet tanagers make a very long migration from summering habitats in the eastern hardwood forests of the northeastern United States to wintering grounds primarily in Colombia, Ecuador, eastern Peru and northwestern Bolivia. During the summer, their primary habitats are mature oak forests like those in the St. Croix River Valley in Minnesota and Wisconsin and the bottomland hardwood forests along the Mississippi River from Minnesota and Wisconsin southward.

Scarlet tanager nests are usually in hardwood trees, and they contain three to five eggs. Incubation takes 13 to 14 days, and the young fledge after two weeks in the nest.

Food: Beetles, caterpillars, wasps, moths, ants and other insects, blackberries, blueberries, cherries, grapes, mulberries and serviceberries.

Feeding habits: This species is not a typical visitor at bird feeders, but people who live in mature oak forest habitats might have scarlet tanagers visiting their bird baths or feeders stocked with orange slices or a mixture of cornmeal, peanut butter and suet.

The bold red and black markings on male scarlet tanagers make them beautiful and memorable songbirds.

References: Davison 1967, Ridgely and Tudor 1989 and Warton 1992.

93

4

population trends
and relative abundance
of birds that use feeders

population trends and relative abundance of birds that use feeders

Due to the continuing seasonal changes that occur in the species diversity and relative abundance of birds at a feeder, it is very difficult to draw conclusions about population trends of birds. There are many factors that can affect bird numbers at your feeders: types of feed offered, presence of other feeders in your neighborhood, population cycles, clearing of nearby woodlands for housing developments, roads and shopping centers, abundance of house sparrow populations and the presence of free-ranging cats.

Several sources of information are available to help you gain an understanding of what is happening to bird populations on a national scale, including an annual breeding bird survey.

The Office of Migratory Bird Management of the U. S. Fish and Wildlife Service conducts an annual Breeding Bird Survey across the nation to estimate the population trends of the nation's birds. The counts are done each June along hundreds of 25-mile routes in the United States. These routes have been run annually since 1966 and are an excellent source of trend information for the most common birds that can be detected along road routes. Table 1 contains a summary of bird population trends as determined by the Breeding Bird Survey:

Birds increasing at the national level and in Minnesota are such regular feeder visitors as black-capped chickadees, downy woodpeckers, hairy woodpeckers, red-bellied woodpeckers and white-breasted nuthatches. These birds have a broad tolerance for mixed meadow, woodland, residential and urban habitats and are broadly distributed across many habitat types.

That degree of adaptability, together with the security of a continuing food source at feeders, could make a difference in their survival. Winter feeding could bring more birds through the winter, and, where feeding stations are available, these birds might be in better physiological condition to produce larger broods of young.

The story for many other visitors at bird feeders is less clear. For example, how could blue jays, northern cardinals, dark-eyed juncos, European starlings, common grackles and house sparrows be decreasing over the past 25 years if they have access to so many millions of pounds of bird food?

How can so many species of birds be declining if they have access to so much bird food?

96

INCREASING SPECIES	National Trend*	Minnesota Trend**	DECREASING SPECIES	National Trend*	Minnesota Trend**
Downy woodpecker	+0.3	+2.5	Blue jay	-1.6	+2.8
Hairy woodpecker	+1.1	+3.1	Northern cardinal	-0.3	+3.4
Black-capped chickadee	+1.9	+5.9	Dark-eyed junco	-0.5	+0.4
White-breasted nuthatch	+2.2	+2.0	American goldfinch	-1.2	+1.7
Pileated woodpecker	+1.2	not counted	Gray jay	-0.9	-2.1
Red-breasted nuthatch	+2.2	+2.0	European starling	-1.0	+0.8
Common redpoll	+1.8	not counted	Song sparrow	-0.9	+0.8
Rock dove	+1.2	+0.5	White-throated sparrow	-1.4	+0.2
Red-bellied woodpecker	+0.6	+3.0	Red-winged blackbird	-1.0	+0.3
			Common grackle	-1.4	+0.2
			Pine grosbeak	-1.9	not counted
			Purple finch	-0.8	+0.9
STABLE SPECIES	National Trend*	Minnesota Trend**	Pine siskin	-0.1	-2.8
Mourning dove	0.0	-0.9	Evening grosbeak	-0.5	+1.6
			House sparrow	-1.4	+1.7

The answer probably lies in the habitat changes occurring across the nation: increasing urbanization, loss of large stands of forest, cowbird parasitism and the common tendency of landowners to clean out brushy, shrubby habitats needed by many songbirds.

The negative impacts of habitat destruction are severe, so bird lovers need to complement their feeding efforts with efforts to protect habitats and to landscape for wildlife. The Minnesota DNR publication *Landscaping for Wildlife* can show you how to make your yard a safe and healthy haven for birds. Supporting the work of state and federal conservation agencies to help wild birds that do not typically come to backyard feeders is also crucial.

References: Sauer and Droege 1989 and U.S. Fish and Wildlife Service 1991.

Table 1

A summary of population trends for birds that regularly use feeders.

*National Breeding Bird Survey population trends, 1966-1991, annual rate of change in percent. Source: USFWS 1991.

**Minnesota Breeding Bird Survey population trends for 41 routes, 1966-1990, annual median percent change.
Source: Minnesota DNR and Pfannmuller 1993.

Bird feeding and bird conservation: a funding dilemma

About 400 species of birds live in Minnesota, including migrants, accidental species and breeding species. About 234 species are nesting species, and only 44 of those are regular backyard species. The others are birds of wetlands, grasslands, forests and prairies.

More than half of the 234 bird species that breed in Minnesota are neotropical migrants, birds that winter primarily in Mexico, Central America and South America. This group includes warblers, vireos and tanagers. They receive no significant benefit either from the forces of urbanization or from backyard bird feeding. Twenty-eight of those neotropical species have been declining nationally at a rate of at least one percent per year from 1978 to 1988. Those species are listed in Table 2.

Blackpoll warblers are listed in Table 2 as declining neotropical migrant birds.

Other birds experiencing survival problems exist in such low numbers that they cannot be counted effectively by the federal breeding bird survey. They include the burrowing owl, Sprague's pipit, Baird's sparrow, chestnut-collared longspur, greater prairie chicken, upland sandpiper, marbled godwit, short-eared owl, trumpeter swan, piping plover, horned grebe, American bittern, yellow rail, king rail, common moorhen, Wilson's phalarope, common tern, Forster's tern and sharp-tailed sparrow.

Money needed by state conservation agencies to preserve all of our wild birds has traditionally come from voluntary donations made to the Nongame Wildlife Checkoff on the state's income tax and property tax forms. The amount being raised per year is less than half the amount needed to maintain our current wildlife populations at healthy levels.

And the amount raised per year has declined since 1988. At the same time, threats to our wildlife populations continue to increase.

Through excise taxes, special use stamps and fishing licenses, Minnesota anglers provide an average of $17.02 per person per year to the Minnesota DNR for fisheries conservation efforts. Hunters provide the Minnesota DNR with an average of $51.15 per person per year to help manage huntable game populations. People who watch, feed, photograph and enjoy wild birds (sometimes referred to as non-consumptive users) contribute only 50¢ per person per year for conservation, primarily through the Nongame Wildlife Checkoff on the state tax forms.

Franklin's gull	Chestnut-sided warbler
Black tern	Cape May warbler
Black-billed cuckoo	Black-throated green warbler
Yellow-billed cuckoo	Blackburnian warbler
Olive-sided flycatcher	Blackpoll warbler
Eastern wood pewee	American redstart
Northern rough-winged swallow	Ovenbird
Veery	Common yellowthroat
Wood thrush	Canada warbler
White-eyed vireo	Scarlet tanager
Blue-winged warbler	Rose-breasted grosbeak
Tennessee warbler	Bobolink
Northern parula	Northern oriole

Table 2
Neotropical migrant songbirds declining by one percent per year or more, 1978-1988.

Bird feeding has become a huge industry, growing as much as 20 percent per year due to the growing popularity of bird feeding. Expenditures for all wild bird related sales in Minnesota, including bird watching, feeding and photography, exceeded $360 million in 1991. Unfortunately for the wild birds struggling for survival, none of that revenue comes back to the state to help wildlife.

A new federal fee has been proposed on the sale of bird feed. This could increase the cost of bird feeding by no more than three or four dollars per year per person, yet it could generate millions of dollars each year for the conservation of the wild birds that really do need our help.

Bird lovers can do much to protect both backyard birds and birds that do not visit feeders. Report rare bird sightings to your state DNR, join conservation efforts, check off for wildlife on your state tax forms, and make a concerted effort to welcome birds onto your property by landscaping for wildlife.

And feed the birds. Even purely recreational bird feeding can instill a love and respect for wildlife that makes the rest fall into place.

Reference: Sauer and Droege 1989.

Relative abundance of birds at feeders

Each year between 1977 and 1986, Dr. Doug and Julie Keran of the Brainerd Technical College conducted a winter bird feeder study for Minnesota. The results give a good overview of the birds visiting midwestern feeders. The top 25 birds, in order of abundance, are listed in Table 3.

1. House sparrow	**8**	
2. Black-capped chickadee	**9**	
3. Evening grosbeak		
4. American goldfinch	**2**	
5. Redpoll	**27**	
6. Dark-eyed junco	**1**	
7. Blue jay	**3**	
8. White-breasted nuthatch	**11**	
9. Pine siskin	**15**	
10. Downy woodpecker	**6**	
11. European starling	**10**	
12. Hairy woodpecker	**17**	
13. American tree sparrow		

14. Purple finch	**22**
15. Northern cardinal	**7**
16. Red-breasted nuthatch	**18**
17. Pine grosbeak	
18. Common grackle	**14**
19. Gray jay	
20. Red-bellied woodpecker	**16**
21. Song sparrow	**20**
22. White-throated sparrow	**21**
23. Pileated woodpecker	
24. Red-winged blackbird	**19**
25. Mourning dove	**5**

Table 3
Relative abundance of winter birds as determined by Keran's study (ranking on the left) and Project Feeder Watch in 1993-94 (bold ranking on the right).

The count period for this survey was from October through March, so some of the results include fall migrants that did not stay through the winter. This list gives you an idea of which birds are most likely to show up at your feeders.

In addition to the Kerans' bird feeder study, a national winter bird feeder survey is currently underway by the Cornell Laboratory of Ornithology: Project Feeder Watch. In the 1993-1994 season, 8,700 volunteers submitted observations on winter birds throughout North America.

This survey is especially effective in tracking the southward movements of cyclical boreal birds when they invade feeders in the United States. The season of 1993-94, for example, was especially notable for southern movements of redpolls and red-breasted nuthatches.

The relative abundance of winter birds on a national scale as determined by Project Feeder Watch is shown by the rankings in bold type in Table 3. Keran's study included evening grosbeaks, pine grosbeaks, American tree sparrows and gray jays in the top 25 bird species, but these species did not show up in the top 25 of the Feeder Watch Study.

Conversely, the top 25 in the Project Feeder Watch study included house finches, American robins, tufted titmice, northern flickers, American crows, Carolina wrens and Carolina chickadees. This is a reflection of the recent increase in house finch numbers and of the many southern locations where species such as Carolina chickadees winter.

For further information on how to participate in Project Feeder Watch, write to P.O. Box 11, Ithaca, NY, 14851-0011. There is a fee to participate in this project.

Ovenbirds are listed in Table 2 as declining neotropical migrant birds.

99

NEW BIRDS ADAPTING TO FEEDERS

Through the process of natural selection, birds are continually adapting to the novel habitats and foods created by human activity—whether they were provided intentionally or not. The appearance of new species at bird feeders, and the subsequent appearance of urban raptors to prey on those feeder birds, is another fascinating example of adaptation and natural selection in our changing environments.

Indigo bunting

Many Minnesota bird feeders were visited by indigo buntings in the summer of 1993 when millet was offered either on tray feeders or self feeders. Some indigo buntings even showed up at thistle feeders. The cold wet spring and summer of that year could have changed the availability of preferred foods for the indigo buntings and caused them to forage at more unconventional sites like bird feeders.

Indigo buntings are primarily woodland birds that can be expected where a yard is in a larger woodland complex.

Eastern bluebird

Eastern bluebirds certainly aren't expected to visit typical bird feeders because they eat insects. The newest twist to bird feeding, however, is to provide shallow trays filled with mealworms.

The increasing success of the bluebird restoration effort and efforts to control house sparrows may allow bluebirds to nest in cities and suburbs where they previously could not compete. If they do appear in your yard, mealworm feeders can entice them to stay.

Eastern bluebird.

American crow

When crows were unprotected they were shot at with enough regularity to make them avoid yards and farms. Federal protection for crows since 1972 has allowed them to become more bold in their nesting and foraging near homes and at bird feeders.

Pileated woodpecker

Since suet has become a regular offering at many bird feeders, pileated woodpeckers have adapted to it as a food source and become regular feeder visitors.

RANGE EXPANSIONS

House finch

House finches were originally a western species that established themselves in New York, steadily spreading westward and northward. By 1990 they had become a nesting species in the Twin Cities area, and by 1994 they nested regularly in the Brainerd, Minnesota area. House finches' northward expansion continues.

Northern cardinal

Northern cardinals were first recorded in Minnesota in 1875. They were primarily residents southeast of Red Wing, Minnesota in the 1930s. By the 1960s, cardinals had expanded their range to include the southern half of Minnesota. The species continues this expansion with scattered reports in more northerly areas.

References: Janssen 1987 and Roberts 1932.

A female northern cardinal is pictured on the left and a male northern cardinal is pictured above.

Red-bellied woodpecker

Red-bellied woodpeckers have undergone a northern range expansion into Minnesota similar to that of northern cardinals. They were unknown in the state in 1892, and their first recorded sighting was at La Crescent in Houston County in 1893. By 1900 their range had extended to Red Wing, and by 1907 they were recorded in Rochester, Minnesota. A year later another one of these woodpeckers was recorded in Owatonna. Minneapolis was the northern limit of their range by 1930. Red-bellied woodpeckers now occupy the southern half of Minnesota and have dispersed to the South Dakota border and into central Minnesota.

References: Janssen 1987 and Roberts 1932.

Black-billed magpie

Black-billed magpies were formerly seen in western Minnesota only during the winter months. They became a regular nesting species in the late 1950s to early 1960s in western Polk, Kittson and Marshall counties. Since then their nesting range has spread to a larger portion of northwest Minnesota. Nesting has also been confirmed for several years near Palisade in Aitkin County.

5

unusual wildlife visitors at feeders

unusual wildlife visitors at feeders

Pine marten

Pine martens are mink-sized members of the weasel family found in a variety of habitats associated with the northern boreal forest in some extreme northern portions of the Midwest. They are 20 to 30 inches long, with long furry tails that measure about one third of their total length. Their tails are proportionally longer and fuller than mink tails. Mink are usually dark brown with small white throat patches, while martens are red-brown to yellow-brown with yellow throat patches.

Pine martens eat voles, eastern red squirrels, chipmunks, flying squirrels, birds, insects and some fruits and berries. They hunt in trees and on the ground. This species is occasionally attracted to suet feeders, sometimes for the suet and sometimes in search of voles, squirrels or backyard birds.

Reference: Hazard 1982.

This pine marten is visiting a suet feeder.
Photo by Janet C. Green

Fisher

Fishers are members of the weasel family, dark brown and about the size of a red fox. In Minnesota they are found in northern forests roughly from the Mille Lacs Lake area northwest to Detroit Lakes, north to Marshall County in the Thief River Falls area, and over to the northeastern tip of the state at Grand Marais.

Fishers may grow up to three feet long, including their tails, and they weigh up to ten pounds. Females are smaller than males and weigh approximately five pounds. Their fur is dark brown to black, while males sometimes have a grizzled appearance because of the white bands on their guard hairs.

104

Fishers live in both coniferous and hardwood forests, both younger secondary forests and in older forest stands. They are agile predators that hunt on the ground and in trees. Fishers are the only predators with specialized techniques for killing and eating porcupines. They also eat snowshoe hares, red squirrels, mice and birds. They are readily attracted to deer carcasses.

Because of many years of protection and a strictly controlled trapping season, fishers have increased in numbers and expanded their range to reoccupy forested areas where they had formerly been eliminated. Fishers will sometimes encounter suet feeders near woodland cabins and help themselves to a free meal. They do not pose a threat to people or pets and should be enjoyed as another important member of the northern forest ecosystem

Reference: Hazard 1982.

Like the pine marten, the fisher is a member of the weasel family. It is about the size of a red fox but its legs are shorter. Fishers are attracted to suet feeders in northern forests.

Flying squirrel

Flying squirrels are some of the most beautiful mammals to visit bird feeders and yet, because of their strict nocturnal habits, they are rarely seen. Two species are found in Minnesota: southern flying squirrels and northern flying squirrels. Southern flying squirrels are associated with mature oak forests. Larger northern flying squirrels are found primarily in the coniferous forests of the northeastern third of Minnesota.

Flying squirrels do not really fly. They glide. Their short gray fur is extremely soft, and their tail fur grows out on the sides so, during flight, their tails are flat and serve as rudders for maneuvering in the air.

Southern flying squirrels live in abandoned woodpecker holes or nest boxes. Females may raise two litters of three to five young per year. They primarily eat acorns, nuts and seeds. Northern flying squirrels usually nest in tree hole cavities, woodpecker holes or wood duck boxes, but sometimes they may make nests of cedar bark among tree branches. They typically raise one litter of three to six young.

Flying squirrels, like this southern squirrel, are rarely seen at bird feeders because they visit during the night. Their large eyes are adapted for night vision.

Flying squirrels may visit feeders at night to eat sunflower seeds or other food that has been left for the birds. Some people place a small red light near feeders where they suspect the squirrels are visiting. The red color is not visible to the squirrels, and it gives you a chance to watch one of our most beautiful native mammals.

Reference: Hazard 1982.

Virginia opossum

More than a few people have been shocked to look at their bird feeders and see a homely-looking opossum staring back at them. Opossums are grizzled, gray to black mammals the size of a house cat with long, bare tails. They are marsupials, meaning that the young are born after a very short gestation period and then live in a pouch on the female's belly until they are old enough to emerge. Their bare tails are prehensile, which means that they are adapted to wrap around or hold onto objects like tree branches.

Opossums may not look very bright, but they are an ancient species whose ancestors lived among the dinosaurs during the Cretaceous era. They are the only mammal to survive that tremendous time span in basically its original form.

Adult opossums are about 30 inches long, including the 10 or 12-inch tail. They weigh between four and eight pounds. Opossums are omnivorous, meaning that they eat a wide variety of plant and animal matter. They are easily attracted to foods placed at bird feeders, from suet to sunflower seeds, bakery goods and apples. And they will certainly create some excitement for the family dog.

Opossums have been expanding their range northward and westward in Minnesota. They now live as far north as Pine County and west to the South Dakota border. This species will not present any danger at feeders to people or pets, but if they become a nuisance they can be live trapped and relocated to another area.

Reference: Hazard 1982.

Virginia opossums are becoming increasingly common visitors at bird feeders.

Gray fox

Gray foxes are unexpected visitors at some bird feeders. They are most likely to visit feeders in backyards adjacent to large deciduous woodlands or river valley forests. Unlike most foxes, gray foxes can climb trees. This allows them to reach fruits and to pursue live prey in trees.

Omnivorous animals, gray foxes may come in search of dog food, seeds or fruits, or they may be hunting for cottontail rabbits or voles that can be common in yards. Insects sometimes comprise a significant portion of their diet.

A gray fox weighs 8 to 12 pounds. Its body is grizzled gray with a prominent black stripe down its back and tail. The tip of its tail is black and its legs, feet and belly are buff yellow.

Brushy hardwood forests are gray foxes' preferred habitats. They live in forests from Latin America northward to Ontario and Quebec. In Minnesota they are associated primarily with the southeastern hardwood forest along the Mississippi River and its tributaries. They are also found in lower densities through the forest transition zone of central Minnesota and occasionally in the western counties.

Gray foxes are omnivorous so they will visit bird feeders for sunflower seeds as well as suet.

Gray foxes raise one litter of about four young each year. The litter would normally be born in May after a gestation period of about 50 to 60 days. They are shy visitors at feeders and do not pose a threat to people or their pets.

Reference: Hazard 1982.

Red fox

The common and elusive red fox will sometimes pay a cautious visit to bird feeding stations. For several years, Mary McGee of Minneapolis, Minnesota, had a family of red foxes come into her back yard on a regular basis. Originally they were visiting to eat bird food, but she eventually set out dog food on the edge of her yard for the foxes and their pups.

This is an excellent example of how another wildlife species is adapting to urban environments. Red foxes are being reported in urban and metropolitan areas with ever-increasing frequency. This is already a common phenomenon in England where foxes may even live in burrows in the crawl spaces under houses.

Red foxes, as their name implies, have rusty-red coats, black legs and feet, black ears and white-tipped tails. Colors vary, and some color phases can be black, silver or a grizzled gray-red with a dark cross over the back and shoulders. Foxes with this type of coloration are called cross foxes. Red foxes usually weigh between 9 and 13 pounds.

The red fox's range includes both Eurasia and North America. They are found throughout the Midwest in open agricultural areas, woodlands, and urbanized areas.

Red foxes breed in January and February, and their young are usually born in April. A litter may contain from 4 to 11 young, who begin dispersing from their den area in the fall.

As with gray foxes, red foxes are omnivorous. They eat small mammals like ground squirrels, chipmunks, cottontail rabbits, field mice, voles, insects, fruits, dog food, suet, birds and bird food. They

On rare occasions, red foxes will visit bird feeders to eat sunflower seeds, dog food or suet. They usually visit at dusk or during the night. Photo by Mary McGee.

are also quite shy and do not pose a threat to children or pets. While it is theoretically possible for foxes to carry rabies, most rabies in the Midwest are carried not by foxes but by skunks.

Reference: Hazard 1982.

Cottontail rabbit

Cottontail rabbits are not generally considered regular visitors at bird feeders, unless you use shelled corn. Then they will appear regularly to share the corn with the blue jays.

Cottontails are the most abundant and widespread rabbits in the Midwest, living in a variety of farmland, meadow, woodlot and urban habitats. People often assume that rabbits are large rodents, but they are actually grouped with a different order of wildlife species called Lagomorphs. This group includes rabbits like the cottontail and hares like the snowshoe and the white-tailed jackrabbit.

Cottontail rabbits will eventually learn to visit bird feeders for a free meal.

A cottontail rabbit is distinguished by grizzled gray fur, long ears, a fluffy white tail and a white belly. Their fur does not change to white during the winter like that of snowshoe hares or jackrabbits. They are primary prey for many larger predators like red foxes, coyotes, great horned owls and red-tailed hawks.

These rabbits have adapted extremely well to backyard environments. They frequently live out their life cycles among the trees, shrubs, flowers and vegetables in residential areas. Most active at dawn and dusk, cottontails feed on a variety of succulent leaves, twigs, sapling bark, grain, vegetables and flowers. The territory of cottontail rabbits may range from about two to ten acres, and the females defend home ranges against other females.

The cottontail's range stretches from southern Saskatchewan to Quebec and southward to Central America. Cottontails begin breeding in late February and have litters of four to six young a month later. One female may have up to four litters per summer in northern regions or up to seven litters per summer in southern regions!

Cottontail young are born in a nest on the ground lined with fur that the female has pulled from her own body. Young cottontails are naked and blind at birth, but they can open their eyes after about a week. They are weaned at a month of age and disperse after that. Females can begin breeding at three months of age.

This species is frequently considered a nuisance in gardens. If you provide them with a feeder of shelled corn, perhaps they won't do as much damage to your flowers and vegetables. Or maybe you will just end up with more rabbits!

Reference: Hazard 1982.

Another unusual visitor at a feeder, this hen common goldeneye apparently mistook the feeder for a nest box but couldn't find the entrance hole.
Photo by G.N. Rysgaard.

6

hawks, owls, falcons and shrikes at feeders

hawks, owls, falcons and shrikes at feeders

If you feed the birds, sooner or later you will see a bird of prey, like a hawk, owl, falcon or shrike, visiting your backyard in search of smaller birds. Such visits can generate a flurry of wings as sparrows, juncos, siskins, redpolls, chickadees and goldfinches fly into nearby escape cover.

Birds are more vulnerable if the feeder is close to bushes or trees where birds of prey, also called raptors, can approach closely before attacking. Feeders that are placed close to trees or bushes should be encircled with two-inch by four-inch wire mesh, three feet high, to disrupt the approach of both cats and raptors. Otherwise, birds prefer feeders that are out in the open where they can watch for approaching predators.

Adult sharp-shinned hawks capture and eat small birds like sparrows and juncos.

There is an increasing frequency of people reporting that raptors are nesting in urban parks and backyards and making a living by eating the birds that use feeders. This is a classic example of natural selection and adaptation occurring before our eyes. We have created an artificial situation in which small birds are concentrated at bird feeders. The feeders become attractive hunting sites for birds of prey. Over the next 10 to 20 years we will probably see more birds of prey adapt to urban environments to exploit this relatively new food resource.

Predation by raptors is a natural phenomenon that we may not enjoy but should tolerate. The songbirds in your yard will usually become more elusive after a few days of consecutive raptor visits. The raptor will move on and things will return to normal.

The exception, of course, is when the raptor decides to nest in your yard. While this provides a unique opportunity for you to see the life history of a raptor, you may have fewer songbirds around that year. If a raptor does take one of a pair of songbirds, the remaining mate will usually take a new mate immediately, keeping the songbird territory occupied.

Sometimes raptors or crows learn that if they fly towards a group of birds at a feeder near a picture window, the birds scatter and some knock themselves out on the window. This gives the crow or raptor time to grab the stunned bird and fly off with it. If this becomes a problem, you should stretch some cherry tree netting outside the window. Fasten the netting three or four inches out from the glass. It will prevent the birds from being injured and is nearly invisible from inside the house.

There are a variety of hawks and falcons that may show up in your backyard either on a casual basis during migration or to begin nesting.

Sharp-shinned hawk

Sharp-shinned hawks are woodland accipiters, which are short-winged hawks with long, slender tails that primarily eat smaller birds.

An adult sharp-shinned hawk has a blue-gray back, dark gray to black cap, red eyes, white breast with fine horizontal barring and a tail that has three grayish bars and a white tip. Males weigh about 3.6 ounces and females weigh about 6.3 ounces. Their body length is about ten and a half inches, comparable to a blue jay. These hawks are named for their bare yellow lower leg, or shin, area.

Sharp-shinned hawks hunt in a manner similar to the Cooper's hawk. They usually pursue small birds through thick woodland cover after watching from a perch. The prey of the sharp-shinned hawk is primarily small birds like sparrows, juncos, and siskins. Chickadees are very elusive and are seldom taken by sharp-shinned hawks.

Immature sharp-shinned hawks have slender yellow legs and vertical brown stripes on the breast.

Cooper's hawk

The Cooper's hawk is a larger member of the accipiter group, measuring about 15 inches long. An adult Cooper's hawk has a blue-gray back, a black cap, red eyes and finely-barred horizontal rusty striping on its white breast. Its tail has three black bands and a white rounded tip, contrasting the smaller sharp-shinned hawk's tail that is straight across the tip.

An immature Cooper's hawk is brown with vertical brown stripes on its breast. Immature female Cooper's hawks can easily be confused with immature male northern goshawks.

A female Cooper's hawk weighs just over a pound, while a male averages just under a pound. Males can be confused with female sharp-shinned hawks. In general, a Cooper's hawk is about the size of a crow and a sharp-shinned hawk is the size of a blue jay.

Cooper's hawks prefer prey the size of starlings, robins, grackles, meadowlarks and flickers, but the larger females can even take ruffed grouse. They also eat chipmunks and eastern red squirrels. This hawk hunts by watching from protective cover, then flying suddenly from its perch to seize its prey. Cooper's hawks pluck their prey before eating.

Immature Cooper's hawks have brown backs and vertical stripes on their breasts.

Northern goshawk

Northern goshawks are 19-inch northern woodland raptors that feed primarily on large forest birds like ruffed grouse. Sometimes they will also take larger songbirds like crows and blue jays, but they are seldom found in backyard situations except during migratory periods.

Goshawks are frequently so aggressive that they will follow their prey right into a window, crashing into the glass along with the smaller bird. This usually results in a broken neck and a dead goshawk. Each year several dead goshawks are turned in to the Minnesota DNR by people who have found them below their picture windows.

An adult goshawk has a blue-gray back, red eyes, a slate-brown tail tipped with white, a light stripe above its eyes and a light-colored breast finely barred with gray stripes. Its wings are relatively short and rounded, and its tail is long

114

in proportion to its body size to give it exceptional maneuverability when chasing prey through woodland cover. An immature goshawk is mottled brown above with vertical brown barring on its breast. Its eyes are green-gray, and it has dark bars on its brown tail feathers.

Goshawks have become relatively uncommon in recent years and, although they can create some dramatic chase scenes with their prey, they are not frequent backyard visitors.

The northern goshawk is the "tiger of the air" among the accipiter hawks. It can capture birds up to the size of a ruffed grouse. And adult is pictured above and an immature goshawk is pictured on the left. Immature goshawk photo by Chip Clark.

American kestrel

American kestrels, members of the falcon family, are generally more well-known than most raptors. A male kestrel is about ten inches long with a rusty back and tail, slate blue wings and two black whisker marks on each side of his face. The top of his head is slate blue. Females are larger than males and rufous over their entire backs with fine dark barring. Male kestrels average 3.8 ounces and females average 4.2 ounces.

Kestrels inhabit open farm country interspersed with farm groves, woodlots, meadows, haylands and roadside ditches. They also nest in cities and parks where woodlands are interspersed with urban openings, backyards, cemeteries and golf courses. This falcon will hover over likely grassland sites or wait quietly on perches until spotting a field mouse, vole or grasshopper. Then it drops onto its prey.

Extremely adaptable, kestrels may nest in hollow trees, nest boxes intended for wood ducks or crevices in the roofs of buildings. They will nest in backyards and exploit the local house sparrow population. In the winter they migrate to Mexico and Latin America.

Kestrels can be expected to continue increasing in numbers in urban and backyard habitats, but they are not primarily bird-eating falcons like merlins. They are more adapted to eating grasshoppers, field mice, voles, small reptiles and amphibians. While kestrels may occasionally take a small songbird up to the size of a bluebird, the impact of this predation on songbirds is inconsequential compared to the effects of house sparrows, starlings, house cats and habitat loss.

Adult male American kestral.

115

Merlin

In the early 1960s, Dr. Lynn Oliphant of the University of Saskatchewan in Saskatoon documented the adaptation of merlins to larger cities in southern Saskatchewan prairie cities like Saskatoon and Regina. Often considered a wilderness or forest species, merlins adapted to new and unexploited prey resources in urban habitats: house sparrows in the summer and Bohemian waxwings in the winter. Merlins began nesting in abandoned crow nests in urban backyard spruce trees.

Merlins were formerly known as pigeon hawks, implying that they eat pigeons. Pigeons, however, are bigger than merlins. Members of the falcon family, male merlins weigh about 6.3 ounces and females weigh about 7.8 ounces.

Adult male merlins have dark slate gray backs and heads. Unlike prairie falcons and peregrine falcons, they have no conspicuous sideburn markings. Their tails are gray with black bands and their wings are narrow and pointed. The crowns and backs of both female and immature merlins are dark brown rather than slate gray, and their tails are light brown with dark brown bars. Their breasts and bellies are heavily streaked with brown.

There is a healthy population of merlins in northeastern Minnesota's Boundary Waters Canoe Area Wilderness. Merlins often nest on islands there. However, the urban adaptation that occurred in Saskatchewan thirty years ago now seems to be happening in Minnesota. Northeastern cities like Hibbing, Grand Rapids, International Falls, Virginia and Duluth are attracting nesting merlins that feed on the variety of small birds, like house sparrows, that are attracted to backyard feeders.

Merlins also migrate through western Minnesota from breeding areas in the Canadian prairie provinces. They winter from Texas to Louisiana, on Caribbean islands and southward into Venezuela and Ecuador. Their hunting behavior involves flying low over the ground to capture their prey. They do not stoop from great heights like peregrine falcons.

Merlins continue to expand their breeding range southward into east central Minnesota. Perhaps the Richardson's subspecies of merlin in Canada will expand to western cities like Fargo and Moorhead. While this may be unsettling to people who feed birds, it is a natural phenomenon. With the unnaturally high concentration of small birds now living in cities, there is obviously a habitat niche waiting to be filled by this small urban falcon.

Please report any new urban merlin nests in northeast Minnesota to the Regional Nongame Wildlife Specialist, Minnesota DNR, 1201 E. Highway 2, Grand Rapids, MN 55744.

Merlins are members of the falcon family and eat birds the size of house sparrows. This merlin is an immature female. Photo by Dr. Lynn Oliphant.

References: Brown and Amadon 1989, Sodhi, Oliphant, James and Warkentin 1993.

Peregrine falcon

Peregrine falcons are not expected in most backyards. They are stunning and beautiful birds of prey that usually feed in larger, open areas either over water, high above city streets, or over fields and meadows. The forested, shrubby, enclosed cover present in most backyards does not lend itself to the hunting style of peregrines. They stoop or dive from great heights to capture blue jay to pigeon-sized flying birds.

Peregrine falcons are about 15 inches long, the size of a crow. An adult is slate gray over its back and tail with black helmet markings on top of its head and down through its eyes. Its breast is white with light barring. An immature peregrine has a brown back, vertical brown stripes through its eyes and a light tan to white breast that also has vertical brown stripes. Males average 1.4 pounds and females average 2.2 pounds.

Peregrine falcons were absent from Minnesota as a breeding species from the 1950s to the mid-1980s because of illegal killing and DDT contamination in the environment. As a result of a restoration program that began in 1982, peregrines are now a Minnesota breeding species. The first pair of Minnesota peregrine falcons nested in downtown Minneapolis in 1987. This restoration project is a cooperative effort by The Raptor Center at the University of Minnesota, the Minnesota DNR's Nongame Wildlife Program, the Bell Museum of Natural History, the Minnesota Falconers' Association, The Nature Conservancy, the U.S. Fish and Wildlife Service, the U.S. Forest Service and a number of other conservation organizations.

These falcons now nest in the Twin Cities, Rochester, Stillwater, Becker, Duluth and on several cliffs in northeastern Minnesota. They also nest at several other metropolitan sites in the Midwest. In addition to the nesting birds, there are also migrant falcons that pass through Minnesota from the arctic en route to Central and South American wintering areas.

Peregrine falcons are included here because they are frequently blamed for the predation done by other birds of prey in backyards,

Peregrine falcons are not adapted to attacking birds at feeders. They strike their prey on the wing at speeds exceeding 180 miles per hour. Most backyards are not big enough to accommodate aerial chases at those speeds. This adult female peregrine falcon is standing over a black-billed cuckoo.

117

probably sharp-shinned hawks, Cooper's hawks or goshawks.

It is possible for peregrines to make a rare backyard appearance. The immature peregrine shown here was photographed eating a sharp-shinned hawk in a Bemidji yard by Minnesota DNR wildlife biologist Steve Maxson. Since the peregrine could be approached within several feet, it was believed to be an arctic migrant that had never before encountered people.

References: Brown and Amadon 1989 and Maxson, pers. comm.

This immature peregrine just killed a sharp-shinned hawk and was eating it in a Bemidji, Minnesota backyard. Photo by Stephen Maxson.

This is a red-phase screech-owl. Gray owls may be a part of the same brood as red screech-owls.

Eastern screech-owl

Screech-owls are about nine inches tall, and they are either rust or gray. They are the only small owls with ear tufts. They nest in tree cavities or in screech-owl or wood duck nest boxes. While they do not represent a threat to songbird populations, they could reduce bird numbers in a yard where they are nesting. The opportunity to see screech owls raise their young in your yard is a very special treat that few people ever get to see.

Screech-owls are opportunists that eat what is available. Their foods range from birds to small mammals, fish, crayfish, salamanders, spiders, snails, beetles, moths and reptiles. They may eat robins, downy woodpeckers, northern orioles, house sparrows, goldfinches, chipping sparrows, white-throated sparrows, song sparrows, indigo buntings, barn swallows, cedar waxwings, yellow warblers, catbirds and redstarts.

If a screech-owl takes one songbird of a pair, the other songbird will immediately take a new mate, so the owl's predation does not usually result in a noticeable decline in birds. If an owl takes a mated pair of songbirds in the same night, however, that territory may remain unoccupied for the remainder of the nesting season.

Barred owl

Barred owls are probably not interested in eating songbirds at your feeder; they're looking for squirrels, mice and voles that are also visiting the feeder. Although the barred owl shown on the next page lurked around a bird feeder, it had no interest in the birds, who continued to feed in the owl's presence. The owl was seen taking a gray squirrel that was feeding on fallen sunflower seeds, and it stayed in the vicinity for several days.

Barred owls may even eat other owls. Naturalist Edward Howe Forbush reported that the stomach of a barred owl contained a long-eared owl, and the stomach of the long-eared owl contained a screech-owl!

Barred owls are not the only owls that approach bird feeders. Minnesota DNR Nongame Wildlife Specialist Katie Haws reported that boreal owls, hawk owls and great horned owls have also been seen near feeders in northern Minnesota.

References: Roberts 1932.

Barred owls may visit feeders because they provide opportunities to capture squirrels and voles --not birds.
Photo by Dr. Walter Breckenridge.

Northern shrike

Northern shrikes migrate to the Midwest from Canadian breeding grounds in October and return north by April of the following spring. Although they look like songbirds, they function as birds of prey.

About ten inches long, a northern shrike is pearly gray with black wings and a black mask and tail with white feathers on the sides. Northern shrikes are slightly larger than summer resident loggerhead shrikes.

The time of year that you see a shrike is usually the key to its identification. Shrikes you see between May and September are probably loggerhead shrikes. In the winter you're more likely to see a northern shrike, and in the spring and fall you might see either species. There are subtle differences in their markings: a northern shrike has a faintly barred breast, a black mask that does not extend in front of its eyes, a large bill, light-colored lower mandible, and a thin white line of feathers above its upper bill. A loggerhead shrike has a dark lower mandible with no faint barring on its breast and no thin white line above its upper bill.

Shrikes sit quietly in bushes or trees watching for field mice, voles or small birds. They will quickly fly down and pounce on their victims. They use their powerful bills to kill the prey, but since they do not have strong talons to hold their prey down, they sometimes impale it on a thorn or on a barbed-wire fence. They may do this to hold the animal while eating it or to store it for later consumption. Shrikes periodically regurgitate pellets of undigested bones, fur and feathers like other birds of prey. Their primary foods include grasshoppers, beetles, caterpillars, mice, voles and sparrow-sized birds.

Shrikes frequently visit bird feeders in the winter because of the abundance of small birds and small rodents. Shrikes may stay around for several days until the birds become so shy that the hunting is more difficult. Then they will move on to another area.

References: Robbins, Bruun and Zim 1983 and Roberts 1932.

Although northern shrikes are not hawks or owls, they act as birds of prey by killing and eating large insects, field mice, voles and small birds.

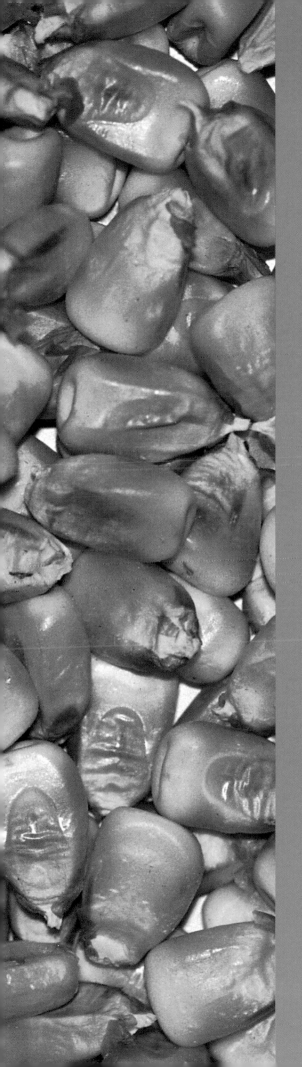

problem animals at feeders

7

problem animals at feeders

Black bear

Black bears live throughout much of the northeastern third of Minnesota, roughly from Chisago County northwest to Kittson County. Many people who feed birds in northern Minnesota simply stop during the summer to avoid having their feeders trashed by the bears. But there are other strategies:

1.) Bring all of your feeders into the house or garage at night, when most feeders are visited and destroyed.

2.) Wait until a bear visits a feeder. Then remove all your feeders for at least a week so the bear will forage elsewhere and not look to the feeders for regular meals.

3.) Suspend your feeders on a pulley system so the feeder is at least 12 feet above the ground and at least 8 feet from poles or tree trunks. A rope on the pulley system allows easy refilling of the feeders.

4.) Provide alternative attractions for birds instead of the traditional seeds: bird baths, fountains, dusting sites and nest structures.

Thank goodness for hibernation! When the bears begin to hibernate in October and November they typically cease to be a problem for the remainder of the winter.

Black bears can be a major nuisance at bird feeders during the summer in northern forested regions.

This photo could provide a new chapter in the Goldilocks story: "Someone has been visiting *my* bird feeder, and they ate it all up!" If a bear raids a feeder, try taking it down for a week or bringing it inside at night.

122

Raccoon

Raccoons are some of the most widely distributed nuisance animals at bird feeders. They are so intelligent and agile that they will figure out how to raid most types of feeders. By late summer they will be bringing their whole family to eat the seeds and suet that were placed for the birds.

Raccoons are a lot like Canada geese in this regard. At first it is fun and interesting to see them coming to eat. Soon the numbers multiply, you have to step around their droppings in the yard and deck, and they become so bold that they hardly get out of your way when you are present.

Feeding raccoons should be discouraged. They regularly carry distemper in the Midwest, and this can be transmitted to dogs or cats. Rabies can also be transmitted by raccoons, although that problem is more prevalent in the eastern and southeastern United States than in the Midwest. Raccoon droppings can also contain parasitic roundworms that can be fatal to humans.

Raccoons may be attracted either to suet feeders, nectar in hummingbird feeders, or seeds like sunflower seeds. To avoid raccoons, you can hang suet in mesh bags from small branches that are too slender to support a raccoon's weight. You may need to temporarily remove your nectar feeders to break the pattern of visiting raccoons. You might also want to place your feeders on top of posts smeared with lithium grease. Raccoons don't like getting grease in their fur!

The last alternative is to get clearance from your local conservation officer to live trap the raccoons and turn them over to the local animal control officer for disposition. Live traps can sometimes be borrowed from an animal shelter or they can be rented from rental stores that provide lawn and garden equipment.

But don't place the trap on the ground, because the kind of bait that attracts raccoons (like sardines, fried chicken or dog food) will also attract skunks. Surely you do not want to try the fine art of removing a skunk from a live trap without getting sprayed. Set your raccoon live trap on a picnic table or other elevated surface so you don't accidentally catch a skunk!

References: Janilla, pers. comm.

A raccoon can be a major pest at a bird feeder by eating large amounts of seeds and damaging the feeder itself.

123

Striped skunk

Striped skunks are found throughout the Midwest, and sooner or later they will show up in your yard searching for grubs, beetles, mice, fruits or other foods. They may check out the area under your feeders for some tasty morsels. If you discover skunks regularly visiting your feeders, clean up the area on the ground to remove the type of food that is attracting them. This should cause them to move to other areas where they won't be a problem.

Skunks are normally nocturnal, so if you see one out in the daytime it could be sick with rabies. Skunks are primary carriers of rabies in the Midwest. In the city, you should contact the local police department for skunk disposal. In rural areas where skunks are suspected of having rabies they should be shot to prevent spreading the disease to kids, pets or livestock.

Yearling fawns.

White-tailed deer

White-tailed deer are found throughout most of North America and as far south as Venezuela. They are found throughout a variety of habitats in the Midwest, including agricultural regions, hardwood forests, coniferous forests and urban areas.

By late November or early December deer gather in herds to winter in areas that provide adequate food and cover. When these areas are in urban sites, the deer become opportunists that may

124

explore yards in search of food, anything from dog food to bird food.

When only small numbers of deer are involved, they can be a beautiful and entertaining addition to your list of backyard wildlife visitors. They will quickly learn to visit bird feeders stocked with shelled corn or sunflower seeds. LeRoy and Donna Sellman of Blaine, Minnesota, have a herd of deer that regularly visits their yard in the winter for the shelled corn that they scatter on the ground.

While this can be entertaining, the deer also browse on trees and shrubs and, unless deer repellent or other protection is used, they can cause significant damage to plants. "Hinder" and "Deer-Away" are examples of effective deer repellents. Cylinders of fencing at least four feet tall can be placed around individual trees to reduce deer damage. Consult with your local DNR wildlife manager for the latest recommendations on effective use of deer repellents and other deer damage control techniques.

A doe watches attentively while her triplet yearling fawns eat shelled corn in a driveway.

House cats

House cats, whether they are your own, a neighbor's or feral cats without owners, can be some of the most persistent and devastating causes of songbird mortality at otherwise successful bird feeding sites. Most people do not realize the extent of the problem caused by house cats because they either love cats as pets or they only see cats with one dead bird at a time.

Nationwide, however, cats are a huge problem. Estimates vary as to how many cats live in the United States; some estimates are as high as 60 million. Even with conservative estimates, the toll on songbirds quickly becomes astronomical. It was estimated that if the national cat population was 55 million, and if 80 percent of those cats were either feral or allowed outside where they could hunt, and if only one cat in ten caught one bird per day, that would still be a conservative total of 4.4 million birds killed per day!

Predator scent post surveys by the Minnesota DNR have shown that feral house cats in rural areas are some of the most abundant wild predators in the state, and that their numbers have been steadily increasing since the surveys began in 1976. Cats were recorded on 72 percent of all survey routes, exceeded only by red foxes and striped skunks.

In a University of Wisconsin study, Department of Wildlife Ecology research assistant John Coleman estimated that 1.2 million cats lived in rural areas of Wisconsin, and that they killed about 19 million songbirds per year. This study found a density of 57 cats per square mile in rural areas and 1,295 cats per square mile in urban areas.

What is wrong with this feeder? A pile of downy woodpecker feathers at the base of this feeder showed how effective this cat was at capturing birds.

So how can you protect your birds from cats? If the cat in question belongs to your neighbors, you can ask them to please refrain from allowing it to roam into your yard. You can also fasten several (not one) bells to the cat's collar, but this is usually ineffective. The only really effective way to keep cats from killing birds is to keep them indoors. Feral, free-ranging cats should be caught in live traps, using sardines or pieces of fried chicken for bait, and turned over to the local animal control officer for disposition.

Make sure your feeders and bird baths are at least six feet from nearby trees, bushes or other hiding places where cats can wait to ambush the visiting birds. If you have a feeder or bird bath close to a bush or tree, encircle the feeder or bath with two by four-inch mesh wire fencing that is at least three feet high. Escaping birds can hop through the mesh or fly upward to escape the cat's approach.

Commercially-made live traps can usually be borrowed from humane shelters to capture nuisance house cats in urban settings. They can also be rented from lawn and garden rental stores. Albert Weikert has developed a stray cat live trap that is reported to be quite effective. Contact him at 303 E. 5th St., Villisca, IA 50864 or by phone at (712) 826-2420.

If you prefer more natural control, tolerating a local population of coyotes will help keep the house cats in check. They eat house cats.

References: Minnesota DNR 1993, Stallcup 1992 and Washington Dept. of Wildlife 1993.

Some cats should be confined to keep them from killing neighborhood songbirds.

Cats are excellent hunters and very skilled at stalking and killing birds. These two hen pheasants escaped.

House cats quickly learn that bird feeders are excellent places to get some fast food.

House sparrow

House sparrows are a major nuisance at many bird feeders. Although they look harmless, they can be a significant source of songbird mortality. House sparrows enter the nesting cavities of tree swallows, bluebirds and chickadees, and they kill both the incubating females and chicks by cracking their skulls open with their bills.

House sparrows should be selectively removed from any nest boxes or humanely trapped and euthanized by using a repeating-style live trap like the Cedar Valley Live Trap. This is mentioned in the house sparrow species account on page 53.

House sparrows can overwhelm a feeding area, turning it into a sparrow slum.

One way to discourage house sparrows at bird feeders is to use house sparrow brackets fitted with monofilament fish line. A grid of monofilament fish line, with lines spaced about 12 inches apart and extending over the roof and sides of the feeder all the way to the ground, disrupts the approach of house sparrows. Other birds do not seem to be affected.

House sparrow brackets are made from one eighth by one half-inch or one eighth by three quarters-inch aluminum strapping that can be purchased in six-foot lengths at most hardware stores.

Cut the strapping into six 8-inch pieces with a hacksaw. Also cut one five-inch piece that will be placed at the top center of the feeder. Drill a one sixteenth-inch diameter hole on one end of all the pieces, about one half inch from the end. File the area around each hole to keep rough edges from cutting the line.

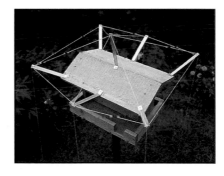

House sparrow brackets with monofilament fish line to deter sparrows at feeders.

On the other end of each bracket, drill a larger hole that will accommodate a deck screw or wood screw, to be screwed into the edges of the feeder roof. This hole should also be about one half inch from the end of the bracket.

Place the end of each bracket with the larger hole in a vise and bend it about 30 degrees, as shown in the accompanying photograph. The bracket for the top center of the roof should be bent so the bracket is vertical after being attached.

Screw all the brackets in place as shown in the photograph. Then string 20-pound monofilament line through the holes. A yellow cord is shown on the accompanying photo instead of monofilament line to make it more visible in the photograph, but is not suggested for actual sparrow control. The line should be tied snugly and each hanging line should extend to the ground where it is either pinned down or tied to large fishing sinkers.

Cedar Valley live trap.

This idea was first developed by graduate students at the University of Nebraska at Lincoln and further refined by Steve Mortenson, a fish and wildlife biologist at the Leech Lake Indian Reservation in Cass Lake, Minnesota.

European starling

European starlings are also an unwelcome nuisance species at Midwestern bird feeders. This is not just because of the food they eat, but because they also compete with native songbirds for available nesting cavities. They will drive away bluebirds, tree swallows, chickadees and other native species from natural cavities. They may even preempt nest boxes from wood ducks.

European starlings are an exotic species from Europe first released in New York City in 1890. Since then, they have spread throughout North America and are not protected by state or federal laws. Many people who feed birds try to control or eliminate excessive starling visits.

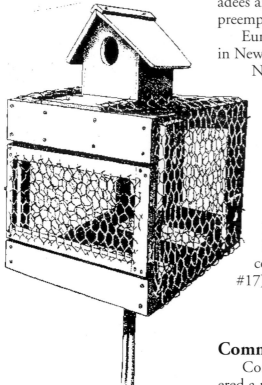

Starlings can be shot in rural areas where firearms ordinances permit. They can also be live-trapped and humanely killed, but they cannot be transported somewhere else and released, because they will probably return.

Tom Webb of Turner Valley in Alberta, Canada, has developed an effective starling trap. Plans can be obtained from him at Box 472, Turner Valley, Alberta, Canada T0L 2A0. Please enclose two dollars (US) to cover postage and handling costs. Starling-proof suet feeders as shown on page 210 (Design #17) also help reduce starling use at feeders.

Webb starling trap.
Drawing by Gary Ross.

Common grackle

Common grackles are native birds that are not usually considered a nuisance species. However, in some situations they can be so abundant that they overwhelm a feeder site and prevent smaller birds from using it. In these cases, a grackle log roller device can be placed on the wooden self feeders to discourage grackle use. See page 198 for details.

Eastern gray squirrel

Gray squirrels are the most common tree squirrels throughout much of the Midwest. About 19 inches long, including their eight-inch tails, these squirrels quickly make their presence known. Dozens of gray squirrels can become regular visitors at a well-stocked feeder.

Attitudes about these squirrels vary. Some people enjoy having them at their feeders and watching their antics. Others find that they eventually get overwhelmed with too many squirrels and need to reduce their numbers to an acceptable level. Squirrels can also become destructive and can chew up expensive wooden or plastic feeders in minutes. They can eat large quantities of seeds and can prevent songbirds from using feeders.

Gray squirrels are usually gray, but they can also be black or white. They live in eastern hardwood forests and mixed hardwood-coniferous forests, and are particularly well adapted to oak forests where they eat acorns. By storing and burying acorns, they help plant oak trees for the future. Gray squirrels often make their dens

128

in the cavities of large trees, but they sometimes cause problems by nesting in peoples' attics.

The more you watch squirrels plundering feeders that are supposed to be squirrel-proof, the more you learn to appreciate how incredibly intelligent, determined and agile they can be. You will also learn how quickly their populations can increase. Each March female gray squirrels give birth to between two and four young, and then they have another litter in July or August. There is usually a significant dispersal of young squirrels in the fall. Squirrel problems may be particularly acute as the young squirrels roam through the countryside looking for available territories and feeding areas.

The solution to your squirrel problem is up to you. Here are six suggestions:

1.) You can catch squirrels in live traps and move them at least five miles away, although this solution just transfers the problem to someone else. The ability of squirrels to survive once relocated is questionable at best.

2.) You can live trap the squirrels and humanely euthanize them. In Minnesota, a homeowner may kill either cottontail rabbits or squirrels on their own property at any time of the year if the rabbits or squirrels are doing damage and need to be controlled. This is permitted outside of the normal hunting seasons and without a special permit.

3.) You can live trap squirrels during the legal hunting season and humanely kill and eat them, or give them to someone else to eat.

4.) You can use squirrel-proof feeders or put protective shields on your feeder posts to prevent squirrels from visiting your feeders.

5.) Some people take five-gallon plastic buckets, fill them a quarter full with shelled corn and set them off to the side of their squirrel-proof feeders. The squirrels will learn to sit in the bottom of the bucket, eating their fill without spilling any grain and without being forced to go elsewhere.

6.) In areas where firearm ordinances allow shooting, problem squirrels can be shot and properly disposed of, or eaten if taken during the hunting season.

Reference: Hazard 1982.

Gray squirrels are the most common woodland squirrels in Midwestern forests. They can become abundant pests at feeders unless precautions are taken to limit their use.

Fox squirrel

Fox squirrels are relatively large tree squirrels found in agricultural regions of the Midwest. They are common in open areas like farm groves, woodlots, and riparian (river valley) forests in agricultural areas, and usually don't come to backyard habitats in high numbers like gray squirrels. They are 22 inches long, including fluffy ten-inch tails. Their name comes from their rufous-red coloring, which is similar to the coloring on red foxes.

Fox squirrels live in leaf nests more than gray squirrels do, but they will also use cavities in trees for their dens. They do very well where they have access to corn: in fields, corn cribs or at feeders. Fox squirrels will eat acorns, tree buds and fruits, and are one of the only mammals that can eat and digest the poisonous seeds of cockleburs without any ill effects.

Fox squirrels will also eat walnuts and ears of corn that have been left for them. Walnuts can be drilled with small holes and strung on wires to provide hours of viewing enjoyment. Ears of corn can either be placed on large spikes or strung end to end on wires to keep the squirrels busy—and away from the birds' feeding sites.

When control is necessary, the techniques recommended for gray squirrels will also work for fox squirrels.

References: Hazard 1982, Orr (pers. comm.)

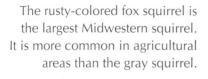

The rusty-colored fox squirrel is the largest Midwestern squirrel. It is more common in agricultural areas than the gray squirrel.

Eastern red squirrel

Eastern red squirrels are small attractively-marked squirrels living in northern coniferous forests and mixed hardwood-coniferous forests. They are also found in many urban areas, woodlots and rural farm areas where conifer plantings are present, but they're not as abundant as gray squirrels in oak woodlands. Red squirrels are frequent prey of pine martens and northern raptors.

Eastern red squirrels measure about 12 inches long, including a five-inch tail. Their winter fur is orange-red on the back and sides and their ears are tufted. During summer, eastern red squirrels have no ear tufts and their white bellies and gray backs are separated by a long black line. Usually one litter of two to five young is born each year.

Red squirrels eat seeds of spruce, fir, pine, elm, maple, basswood and cedar. They cache cones containing the seeds as a winter food supply, and they defend the territories where their food caches are stored against other red squirrels. Red squirrels also eat mushrooms, berries, maple and elm buds, acorns, insect larvae, small birds, birds' eggs, and even young gray squirrels and cottontail rabbits.

Red squirrels readily come to bird feeders to eat whatever seeds are available. They will sometimes kill songbirds at feeder sites. The biggest problem with tolerating red squirrels is that they will often nest in nearby houses, garages or other buildings. If they chew through the wiring of those buildings, they can cause a fire. Whenever red squirrels are found nesting in a building, they need to be immediately trapped and removed. Control methods for red squirrels are the same as those listed for the gray squirrel.

The eastern red squirrel can be very aggressive at bird feeders.

Eastern chipmunk and least chipmunk

Eastern chipmunks are distinctive woodland mammals with one dark stripe and two white stripes down their backs. The white stripes are edged with thin dark brown or black stripes. They are sandy brown with white bellies and reddish rumps. They have stripes on their faces and stripes on their backs that extend only as far as the rump area. They are about ten inches long, including a four-inch tail.

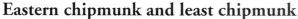

Eastern chipmunks are a woodland variety of ground squirrel common around cabins, houses, and outbuildings as well as in natural forest habitats.

Least chipmunks are another species of chipmunk living in boreal forests. They are also found in openings and disturbed areas within boreal forests. These chipmunks are smaller than eastern chipmunks and do not have reddish rumps. The stripes on their backs extend all the way to the base of their tails. They raise two litters per summer: one in April and another in August. They hibernate during the winter and do not create problems at feeders during that season.

Chipmunks have an unusually diversified diet: tree buds and seeds, fruits, hazel nuts, acorns, pine seeds, black cherries, mushrooms, frogs, small snakes, nestling birds and occasional songbirds including juncos, house sparrows and starlings. They may also visit bird feeders.

A few chipmunks can be fun to watch at a feeding area because they add action and variety. They tend to move into your house or garage, locate your stored bird food and nest among stored boards, garage supplies and in the walls. At that point they change from being cute to being pests.

Excessive numbers of chipmunks can be trapped and killed humanely using snap-type rat traps baited with peanut butter. They can also be removed with small live traps and transplanted to natural woodlands several miles away, but the chances of transplanted animals surviving is poor.

Reference: Hazard 1982.

Many people enjoy the presence of eastern chipmunks until they move into the garage and begin nesting in the storage shelves.

131

Here are two ways to prevent squirrels from using your feeders: purchase feeders with a wire cage (immediate right) or place feeders on support posts that have a hanging covered section of stove pipe as a squirrel guard (far right).

Squirrel-proof feeders and feeder support posts

You can use several strategies to reduce or eliminate the number of squirrels using your feeders. Metal self-feeders with a counterweight on the back will close when a squirrel stands on the front. These cost about $35 to $50. While they may seem expensive, they'll save a lot of money on feed that would otherwise be eaten by the squirrels.

Gilbertson PVC cylindrical feeders are largely squirrel-proof. The perches on this feeder flip down whenever a heavy animal tries to use them. Place them at least six feet out on the limb of a tree and hanging from three feet of wire. Squirrels must jump to reach the feeder, but they have so much momentum when they hit the feeder that they fall off.

When all else fails, squirrels can be trapped and removed with a live trap.

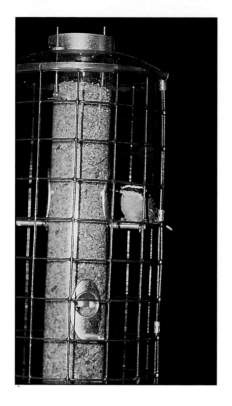

A red-breasted nuthatch visits a cylindrical feeder in a wire cage in the photo on the far left. This feeder is squirrel-proof.

If you want to keep the squirrels busy and away from your bird feeders, try putting up a special feeder for them. The wires pictured on the immediate left were strung with ears of corn and walnuts and kept the squirrels busy for a long time. Photo by Janice Orr.

It's important to hang these feeders at least five feet away from tree trunks. If squirrels can hop to the feeders from a short distance they can hang from the feeder ports by their front paws as they eat the seeds inside.

A multiple feeder support on a single post is easy to make squirrel-proof by placing either a long section of stove pipe over the support post or by placing a cone-shaped baffle (or even several baffles) around the post. Baffles should have a radius of at least 16 inches to keep squirrels and raccoons from going over them.

Pipes that are either three quarters or one inch in diameter can be used for feeder support posts and smeared with lithium grease to prevent squirrels and raccoons from climbing them. The grease will need to be replaced frequently in order for this technique to be effective.

This feeder has a counterweight on the back. The front will close when an animal as heavy as a squirrel sits on it.

Ducks and geese

Mallard ducks and Canada geese are increasingly adapting to urban settings, and many mallards nest in yards under shrubs. A few mallards, attracted to shelled corn, may come to backyard feeders during the summer and provide an interesting variety to the regular assemblage of birds.

However, the gatherings of waterfowl in lakeshore yards and along rivers can grow from dozens to hundreds and create a public nuisance. In some municipalities it is illegal to feed ducks and geese. City waterfowl feeding that results in the concentration of dozens or hundreds of birds should be discouraged. It makes the surrounding area unsanitary from all their droppings, and it exposes the waterfowl to the transmission of avian diseases.

133

8

types of bird food

types of bird food

There are so many choices of bird food available that a novice bird lover can easily become confused and overwhelmed. Some types of food may be cheap but they may not be the ones that will attract lots of birds to your feeder. If you use the right kinds of "good" bird foods, you can probably double the number of species you attract.

In the past, many people fed the birds by trial and error. Twenty-five years ago people fed birds their table scraps and stale bread. Now there is a multi-million dollar wild bird food industry that has developed around this popular pastime.

The big breakthrough in knowledge about bird food preferences came with the publication of a report called "Relative Attractiveness of Different Foods at Wild Bird Feeders" by Aelred D. Geis (1980) of the U.S. Fish and Wildlife Service.

The Geis study revealed that many commonly used feed grains were not preferred by birds, or that they attracted the "wrong" kinds of birds. For example, bread, cracked corn and millet seeds are highly preferred by house sparrows, an undesirable exotic species that competes with native birds for nesting cavities. House sparrows need to be discouraged from using bird feeders by not placing the foods that they prefer and/or live-trapping and removing them.

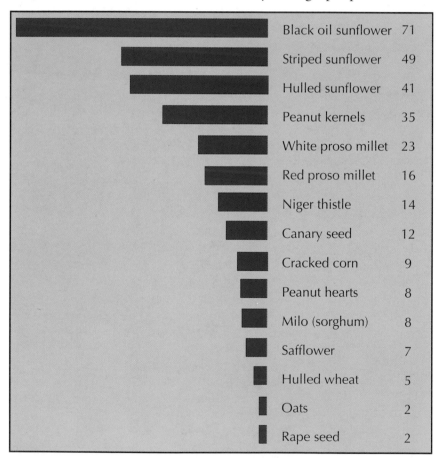

Black oil sunflower	71
Striped sunflower	49
Hulled sunflower	41
Peanut kernels	35
White proso millet	23
Red proso millet	16
Niger thistle	14
Canary seed	12
Cracked corn	9
Peanut hearts	8
Milo (sorghum)	8
Safflower	7
Hulled wheat	5
Oats	2
Rape seed	2

Table 4
Relative preference of seeds to desirable native birds; scored from 1 to 100, with 100 points being most preferred by birds.

Before beginning a bird feeding program, you should become familiar with the choices of bird food available. Then you can make the best use of your budget and attract the birds that you want to have at your feeder. You will also discover that by offering different kinds of food in different seasons, you can attract the greatest variety of native songbirds.

SEEDS AND NUTS

This blue jay has selected a black oil sunflower seed.

There are at least 21 different kinds of seeds available for feeding birds. You should include at least five or six of them in your feeders to attract a variety of birds.

It is confusing to consider the seed preferences of individual bird species, because most people try to attract a variety of birds to their feeders, and the best feed choices will vary from one season to the next.

Ten bird species were chosen to make the chart shown in Table 4: northern cardinals, black-capped chickadees, evening grosbeaks, purple finches, American goldfinches, house finches, blue jays, tufted titmice, white-throated sparrows and mourning doves. The bird food listed was scored for its relative attractiveness to these birds, according to the Geis study results.

It is apparent from this comparison and from the recommendations of people who feed birds that the most important seeds are black oil sunflowers, peanut kernels, white proso millet and Niger thistle. There are also special situations in which hulled sunflower hearts, sunflower chips, peanut hearts and safflower are important. Canary seed, cracked corn, milo, wheat, hulled oats, and rape seed are generally not needed or preferred by birds. However, new varieties of milo are now on the market that may be more popular with birds than older varieties.

These recommendations are only general preferences. Seed preferences will vary depending on the types of birds present, outdoor temperatures, moisture and rainfall, location of feeders with respect to nearby water, hardwoods and conifers, availability of seeds in nearby fields and croplands, and the time of year. You may wish to try your own feeder preference tests to see what works best for you.

Reference: Brooks Pennington (pers. comm.)

Black oil sunflower seeds and striped sunflower seeds

The undisputed champion of the wild bird food contest is black oil sunflower. It should be the primary component of any bird feeding project, comprising at least 75 percent of the seeds you offer the birds.

It is important to distinguish between the black oil sunflowers and the traditional striped sunflowers. The striped seeds have a longer, thicker shell that is more difficult for many birds to crack. Even smaller birds like chickadees, purple finches, pine siskins and house finches have no problem cracking the thin seed coat of the black oil sunflower.

Black oil sunflower seeds.

Other birds that readily feed on black oil sunflower seeds are blue jays, northern cardinals, evening grosbeaks, tufted titmice, mourning doves, dark-eyed juncos, white-throated sparrows and song sparrows. Over 40 different bird species are known to eat black oil sunflower seeds. It makes a good food because the oil content exceeds 40 percent. Research is currently underway to continue improving the nutritional value of sunflowers.

One note of caution is appropriate for sunflower seeds. Normally birds will crack open the seeds, eat the hearts and drop the hulls. An active bird feeding station will eventually have an accumulation of sunflower hulls on the deck or on the ground under the feeder. These should be regularly cleaned up and not placed in flower beds, gardens or compost piles. The hulls contain a plant growth inhibitor that could disrupt or prevent the growth of your garden plants.

Striped sunflower seeds.

Hulled sunflower hearts

Smaller birds like white-throated sparrows, American goldfinches and house finches like hulled sunflower hearts because they don't have to crack the seed coat. Also, there aren't any hulls to clean out from under your feeders.

Sunflower chips and finch mix

Sunflower chips are small, broken pieces of sunflower hearts. They do not create a mess under your bird feeder, and they are readily eaten by goldfinches, redpolls and pine siskins. The pieces are small enough to be used in thistle feeders, hanging cylindrical self feeders or two-liter hanging pop bottle feeders with small feeder ports that are under a quarter inch in diameter.

Hulled sunflower hearts.

If you are being visited by so many goldfinches that you can't afford to keep up with the cost of Niger thistle, try using sunflower chips instead. However, they absorb moisture more readily than Niger thistle seeds and can mold in the feeder, so you'll need to check your feeder regularly and keep it clean.

A half and half mixture of sunflower chips and Niger thistle seeds in a hanging pop bottle feeder is an excellent food combination for redpolls, pine siskins and goldfinches. You can also use this mixture in cylindrical self feeders designed for sunflower seeds.

Reference: Jones, pers. comm.

Sunflower chips.

Finch mix.

Male redpoll with finch mix.

Peanut kernels and peanuts in the shell

Peanuts are an up-and-coming popular bird food, especially if you like to feed blue jays, downy woodpeckers, hairy woodpeckers and tufted titmice. Other birds that eat peanuts are red-winged blackbirds, indigo buntings, northern cardinals, gray catbirds, black-capped chickadees, American crows, purple finches, goldfinches, evening grosbeaks, dark-eyed juncos, ruby-crowned kinglets, red-breasted nuthatches and white-breasted nuthatches

Chipping sparrows, fox sparrows, house sparrows, song sparrows, white-crowned sparrows, white-throated sparrows, brown thrashers, rufous-sided towhees, wild turkeys, yellow-rumped warblers, red-bellied woodpeckers, red-headed woodpeckers, eastern bluebirds, northern mockingbirds and American robins will eat peanut kernels, too.

Provide peanuts in the hanging hardware cloth feeder shown in Design #23. Blue jays, woodpeckers and black-capped chickadees will work the peanuts out of the quarter-inch wire mesh. Peanuts in the shell can also be offered as bird food.

Reference: Davison 1967 and Martin et. al. 1951.

Peanuts.

Peanut hearts

Peanut hearts are the tiny chips left when peanut halves are broken apart. They are as nutritious as regular peanut kernels and their small size makes them perfect for smaller birds. They are primarily

Peanut hearts.

Peanut pickouts.

eaten by white-throated sparrows, common grackles, blue jays, starlings and northern cardinals. Peanut hearts could be mixed in with white proso millet and sunflower chips in a hanging pop bottle feeder with ports no more than a quarter inch in diameter.

Peanut pickouts and cardinal mix

Peanut pickouts are a mixture of peanuts, pistachio nuts, pecans, cashews and other nuts. This is an excellent food to add to black oil sunflower seeds to increase its attraction to northern cardinals. Try mixing 90 percent black oil sunflower seeds with five percent peanut pickouts and five percent safflower seeds for a great cardinal mix.

Cardinal mix

White, golden, and red proso millet and millet mix

White proso millet is one of the most controversial components of wild bird food. It is cheaper than many other seeds, and highly desired by wild birds like northern bobwhites, northern cardinals, mourning doves, purple finches, dark-eyed juncos, chipping sparrows, fox sparrows, song sparrows, American tree sparrows, white-throated sparrows, rufous-sided towhees, wild turkeys, common grackles, blue jays and ring-necked pheasants.

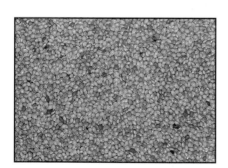

White proso millet.

A dark-eyed junco eats at a bird feeder stocked with millet mix.

White proso millet is also attractive, however, to house sparrows and brown-headed cowbirds. House sparrows compete with local songbirds for nesting areas, and cowbirds reduce the numbers of native birds by laying their eggs in the songbirds' nests. Many of the other birds that eat millet will do just as well with black oil sunflower seeds, which attract fewer sparrows.

During the summer white proso millet can be scattered on the ground or in cylindrical or tray feeders near the ground for indigo buntings or mourning doves.

In the spring and fall it can be scattered on the ground for white-throated sparrows, dark-eyed juncos, white-crowned sparrows and fox sparrows. During the winter it can also be scattered on the ground for American tree sparrows and dark-eyed juncos. Golden millet and red millet are less used and less popular than white proso millet.

Some bird feed mixes contain 90 to 95 percent white proso millet. These are useful mixes to scatter on the ground during the spring and fall for native sparrows and juncos.

These mixes should not be confused with those that are primarily comprised of black oil sunflower seeds and a smaller portion of white proso millet, safflower, and other assorted seeds.

If you want to attract more birds to your feeders, at least 75 percent of the seed offered should be black oil sunflowers. If you try to save money by feeding millet mixes instead of sunflower seeds, you will get fewer species of birds and more house sparrows.

Red millet.

Niger thistle

Niger thistle is one of the most popular wild bird foods because it is so attractive to American goldfinches. It is also eaten by purple finches, redpolls, mourning doves, song sparrows, dark-eyed juncos, white-throated sparrows, red crossbills and house finches. Indigo buntings may also visit finch feeders to eat thistle seeds. If you use pop bottle feeders with slightly larger holes, a mixture of thistle seeds, sunflower chips and peanut hearts will attract goldfinches, pine siskins and redpolls in the winter.

The word "thistle" may cause confusion. Niger thistle is grown in Ethiopia and India and imported to the United States. It is treated at the U. S. port of entry to prevent it from maturing and to kill foreign noxious weeds like parasitic dodder that could devastate crops in the United States. Niger thistle is not a noxious weed like Canada thistle and it does not pose a threat to domestic crops.

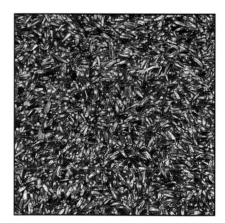

Niger thistle.

Niger thistle is one of the more expensive wild bird foods, frequently costing more than a dollar per pound in small quantities. You may want to buy it in 40 or 50-pound sacks. If the seed is purchased in bulk, you can split the bag and its cost with your friends or family.

Canary seed

Canary seed is not a very common or necessary component of wild bird food. It is primarily eaten by house sparrows, mourning doves, cowbirds and white-throated sparrows.

Black oil sunflower seeds will serve the mourning doves and white-throated sparrows just as well as canary seed and not be as attractive to the house sparrows or cowbirds.

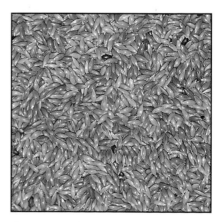

Canary seed.

141

Cracked corn

Cracked corn is eaten by many birds: red-winged blackbirds, yellow-headed blackbirds, bobwhites, indigo buntings, northern cardinals, crows, mourning doves, rock doves, wood ducks, purple finches, goldfinches, common grackles, rose-breasted grosbeaks, blue jays, dark-eyed juncos, mallards, ring-necked pheasants, common ravens, chipping sparrows, fox sparrows, lark sparrows and song sparrows.

Other species that eat cracked corn include American tree sparrows, white-crowned sparrows, white-throated sparrows, brown thrashers, rufous-sided towhees, wild turkeys, hairy woodpeckers, downy woodpeckers, pileated woodpeckers, red-bellied woodpeckers, red-headed woodpeckers, brown creepers, northern flickers, evening grosbeaks, white-breasted nuthatches and American robins. The main problem with cracked corn is that it may attract "problem birds" like house sparrows, brown-headed cowbirds and starlings. If house sparrows and starlings are a problem they may need to be trapped and removed.

Cracked corn can be mixed with white proso millet and scattered on the ground during spring and fall for feeding migrant sparrows, juncos and other ground-feeding birds.

Reference: Davison 1967 and Martin et. al. 1951.

Cracked corn.

Shelled corn

Shelled corn is an excellent food choice for blue jays, red-bellied woodpeckers, mallards, ring-necked pheasants, wild turkeys, red-headed woodpeckers, bobwhites, northern cardinals, common crows, mourning doves, common grackles, common ravens and rufous-sided towhees. They will need to compete, however, with the many squirrels that are also attracted to corn.

You can make an excellent shelled corn feeder for pheasants by making a three-foot high half-inch mesh hardware cloth cylinder to create a double layer of wire. This way the kernels won't fall out too easily. Wire the feeder to a small sheet of plywood, fill the feeder with shelled corn and wire the top shut so squirrels cannot eat all the corn from above. See the photo on page 207.

Reference: Davison 1967.

Shelled corn.

Ear corn

Ear corn can be fed to ring-necked pheasants, red-bellied woodpeckers, wild turkeys, mallards, Canada geese, deer, cottontails, squirrels and crows. The wire fence feeder on page 205 is an excellent ear corn feeder for pheasants and wild turkeys.

Ear corn can also be stuck onto a headless spike that is driven into a tree branch to feed red-bellied woodpeckers and squirrels. Several ears can be strung onto long wires by pushing the wire through the pith in the center of the cob. This can create a challenging chain of corn for squirrels that distracts them from your other feeders.

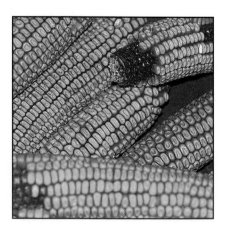

Ear corn.

Milo (sorghum)

Milo, or sorghum, is mainly eaten by red-winged blackbirds, yellow-headed blackbirds, bobwhites, indigo buntings, northern cardinals, brown-headed cowbirds, crows, mourning doves, wood ducks, Canada geese, common grackles and blue jays.

Other species that eat milo include dark-eyed juncos, mallards, ring-necked pheasants, chipping sparrows, fox sparrows, lark sparrows, American tree sparrows, white-crowned sparrows, white-throated sparrows, rufous-sided towhees, wild turkeys and American goldfinches.

Sorghum should be scattered on the ground where it can be used by ground-feeding birds. Probably the best thing about sorghum is that house sparrows don't like it very much.

Reference: Davison 1967 and Martin et. al. 1951.

Milo.

Safflower.

Safflower

Safflower has become an increasingly popular bird food because it is excellent for cardinals, rose-breasted grosbeaks, chickadees, nuthatches, mourning doves, house finches and white-throated sparrows. House sparrows and starlings don't seem to like it, though! Even squirrels don't eat safflower seeds.

This cardinal is eating safflower.

143

Try it as an alternative to black oil sunflower seeds or millet mixes if you are being plagued by house sparrows, starlings and squirrels. Dave and Jan Ahlgren of Stillwater, Minnesota, reported that when a black bear visited the bird feeders on their deck it ignored the safflower seeds. Perhaps safflower seeds should be tried in the northern bear range as a way of discouraging bear damage at bird feeders.

 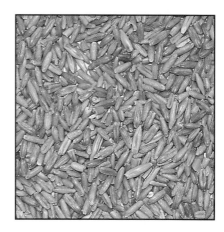

Wheat.
Far right: Hulled oats.

Wheat, hulled oats and rape seed

Wheat, hulled oats and rape seed are not popular as wild bird food. Wheat and oats are eaten by a variety of birds, but they can be too attractive to birds like house sparrows, starlings and brown-headed cowbirds.

Wheat and oats are eaten by red-winged blackbirds, yellow-headed blackbirds, bobwhites, indigo buntings, northern cardinals, crows, mourning doves, rock doves, Canada geese, common grackles, rose-breasted grosbeaks, blue jays, dark-eyed juncos, mallards, ring-necked pheasants, chipping sparrows and purple finches. Additional species include American goldfinches, fox sparrows, lark sparrows, song sparrows, American tree sparrows, white-throated sparrows, rufous-sided towhees, wild turkeys and northern flickers.

Rape seeds are only eaten by bobwhites, mourning doves, American goldfinches, common redpolls, purple finches and dark-eyed juncos.

Reference: Davison 1967.

Rape seed.

Popped popcorn

Not many people would think of popped popcorn as a likely bird food, but Pat and Rose Deutz of Marshall, Minnesota discovered that brown thrashers will eat it. They have an old wooden wheelbarrow that serves as an adaptable and movable feeder for many different birds, including red-headed woodpeckers and brown thrashers. The brown thrashers, however, didn't come to the feeder until popcorn was scattered in the wheelbarrow.

There is also a habitat lesson here: brown thrashers need shrubby, brushy cover for nesting. The Deutz's old-fashioned farm grove has been intentionally left brushy for the birds. They also left the dead trees standing for red-headed woodpeckers. A clean, neatly-mowed farm grove will not support many species or numbers of wild birds.

Broken walnuts and nut meats

Les and Jean Orr of Waukon, Iowa, have found that broken walnuts are an excellent bird food. Although walnut meats are very nutritious, they are not available to most songbirds until the husk is removed and the hard shell is broken. Walnut meats are eaten by at least 24 species of wildlife. Among the birds that eat black walnut meats are northern cardinals, gray catbirds, crows, blue jays, dark-eyed juncos, ruby-crowned kinglets, song sparrows, white-crowned sparrows, tufted titmice, yellow-rumped warblers, downy woodpeckers, hairy woodpeckers, red-bellied woodpeckers and pileated woodpeckers.

There are many places in the Midwest where black walnut trees grow in farm groves, woodlots and orchards. Where the walnuts are not picked up for human use, they can be collected for bird feeding. After the husks have been removed and the shells have been allowed to dry, break open the nuts with a hammer and place the pieces of broken nuts into a self feeder where the slot is wide enough at the bottom (about two or three inches) to allow the birds to pull them out. The birds then search among the shell fragments for the nut meats. Be sure to wear safety goggles while pounding on the nuts with a hammer.

Popped popcorn and peanuts.

Cracked walnuts in a self feeder.
Photo by Janice Orr.

Rose-breasted grosbeak at a feeder.

145

FRUIT AND KITCHEN FOODS

Apples

Slices of apple, impaled on a nail, will attract gray catbirds, blue jays and American robins. If you get the birds started in spring, they will visit your apple feeding station all summer, and they may bring their young to the feeder after they fledge. The best part of this technique is that you can use apples that are below human eating standards. The birds don't care. And wormy apples are just fine.

Oranges

Orange halves are attractive to northern orioles, red-headed woodpeckers and red-bellied woodpeckers. Cut the orange in half and impale each piece on a nail so the birds can feed on the orange juice. The feeder nails can be placed on the top side of sloping tree branches, tree stump feeders or deck railing feeders (Design # 23).

Orioles eat orange halves primarily in the first two weeks after they return in May. After that they strongly prefer grape jelly.

This red-headed woodpecker is eating juice from an orange half.

Bananas

You might want to use bananas in your feeders during the spring warbler migration. Slice the bananas down the middle and lay them on a spring warbler and tanager feeding tray with some apple slices, orange halves, day-old bread, broken cookies, biscuits, cornbread, crushed egg shells and a mealworm dish. That should be an irresistible combination during the last two weeks of April and the first

146

two weeks of May as many neotropical migrants pass through.

Tennessee warblers, summer tanagers and northern orioles frequently feed on bananas at tray feeders in Costa Rica during January and February. It is fascinating to see them on the wintering grounds sharing feeders with such exotic birds as blue-crowned motmots, blue-gray tanagers, scarlet-rumped tanagers, golden-hooded tanagers, spotted-crowned euphonias and clay-colored robins.

An American robin eats an apple.

A blue-winged mountain tanager eats watermelon at a feeder in Venezuela. While you shouldn't expect to see this species at your bird feeder, you'll be surprised which birds will show up if you're creative in the fruits you offer.

Watermelons

Small slices of watermelon can be added to a spring warbler and tanager tray as described in the banana section. In the Venezuelan cloud forests people provide watermelon slices for the local birds and migrants. These watermelon slices attract such incredibly beautiful birds as blue-winged mountain tanagers, golden tanagers and ridge-billed toucanets. But don't hold your breath waiting for a toucanet to show up in the Midwest. In Minnesota we could expect, perhaps, a passing scarlet tanager.

Be creative with the food you offer the birds. Try something new once in a while, like bananas or watermelon slices. Perhaps the birds will surprise you. See page 240.

A blue-crowned motmot (above) and a Tennesee warbler (below) visit a Costa Rican feeder for bananas.

Raisins and dried currants

Raisins and currants, whole or chopped, are eaten by eastern bluebirds, gray catbirds, northern mockingbirds, American robins, summer tanagers, brown thrashers, northern cardinals and white-crowned sparrows. They're more palatable if you soak them before placing them out for the birds. Raisins or dried currants can be placed in enclosed feeders for bluebirds, set out on Linda feeders as shown in Design #21, or scattered in deck railing feeders like the one shown in Design #23.

Reference: Davison 1967.

Grape jelly

Grape jelly is an excellent food to offer in small trays during the summer for northern orioles and gray catbirds. The jelly can be offered in the Linda tray feeder (Design #21), Peterson T-Post feeder (Design #22) and the deck railing feeder (Design #23).

A northern oriole eats grape jelly.

Peanut butter

Peanut butter is a nutritious, high-energy food that can be smeared into the holes in hanging log feeders for woodpeckers (see page 212). It can be smeared on tree bark or mixed with cornmeal and placed in trays for the birds. Peanut butter is also used in the Janilla bluebird mix.

Smear trees with peanut butter to attract woodpeckers, nuthatches, chickadees and brown creepers. Photo by Janice Orr.

Bakery goods

Bakery goods that are surprisingly attractive to birds include white bread, corn bread, doughnuts, cake, cornmeal and cookies. White bread, biscuits and crackers are eaten by red-winged blackbirds, northern cardinals, gray catbirds, black-capped chickadees, brown creepers, rock doves, common grackles, blue jays, dark-eyed juncos, northern mockingbirds, white-breasted nuthatches, common ravens, American robins, chipping sparrows, fox sparrows, song sparrows, American tree sparrows, white-crowned sparrows, white-throated sparrows and European starlings.

White bread is also eaten by summer tanagers, brown thrashers, tufted titmice, rufous-sided towhees, black-throated blue warblers, yellow-rumped warblers, orange-crowned warblers, pine warblers, cedar waxwings, downy woodpeckers, red-bellied woodpeckers, red-headed woodpeckers, eastern bluebirds, northern orioles and even ring-necked pheasants.

Cake and cookie crumbs are eaten by eastern bluebirds, gray catbirds, northern mockingbirds, chipping sparrows, tufted titmice, yellow-rumped warblers and pine warblers.

Cornbread is eagerly eaten by red-winged blackbirds, northern cardinals, purple finches, white-throated sparrows, tufted titmice, yellow-rumped warblers, orange-crowned warblers, pine warblers, yellow-throated warblers and red-headed woodpeckers.

Doughnuts are eaten by black-capped chickadees, blue jays, dark-eyed juncos, red-breasted nuthatches, white-breasted nuthatches, chipping sparrows, white-throated sparrows and many other species. Doughnuts can be set out on a dowel for the birds to eat.

There are many bakeries and restaurants that must discard old bakery goods that are no longer suitable for human consumption. These old baked goods are excellent for bird food because of their starchy nutritional content.

The only caution about using bakery goods is that, like white proso millet, they can attract lots of house sparrows and starlings. If you provide bakery goods for the birds, be prepared to do some trapping and removal of house sparrows and European starlings so that

148

you are not inadvertently helping increase the local sparrow and starling population to the detriment of the other birds.

Be sure to set out a variety of bakery goods along with several fruits and some crushed egg shells on the tanager and warbler tray during the last two weeks of April and the first two weeks of May. As you can see from the list of warblers attracted to white bread, crackers, cornbread and doughnuts, you may get some great spring migrants stopping at your feeder. See page 240.

Egg shells

Egg shells can be collected from restaurants, dried out and crushed for a nutritional supplement in the spring. Place the crushed egg shells on elevated trays near purple martin houses, or else place them on warbler and tanager trays in the early spring. Many birds benefit from the calcium in the egg shells.

Nectar or sugar water

Sugar water solutions, either commercial mixes or homemade mixes, simulate the nectar that birds obtain from flowers. Sugar water can be used in nectar feeders to attract ruby-throated hummingbirds, northern orioles, white-breasted nuthatches and downy woodpeckers.

Commercial nectar mixes are available, but hummingbird nectar is easy to make. Boil four parts water with one part cane sugar. Let the mixture cool. Then fill your nectar feeder and place the rest of the solution in the refrigerator.

In extremely hot weather, the nectar can spoil in two or three days. The water will become cloudy and a black fungus will develop. In spring and early fall it will last longer. Each time you change nectar or refill your feeder, you should soak the feeder for an hour in a diluted solution of chlorine bleach (two ounces of bleach mixed with 1 gallon of water). Then allow the feeder to dry out before refilling it.

Do not use honey to make hummingbird nectar because it spoils too quickly. Red food coloring is also unnecessary and may not be good for the birds. Most hummingbird feeders have little red plastic flowers to attract the hummingbirds.

Bees and wasps can create a problem at feeder ports. Some feeders come with bee guards, but you can also discourage bees and wasps by rubbing Avon Skin-So-Soft®, Off Skintastic® or similar insect repellents around the feeder ports. They repel bees without causing problems for the birds.

Dog food

Dry dog food that is formed as small pellets or nuggets can be a popular and nutritious food for birds like blue jays.

Doughnuts, cornbread and other bakery goods are eaten by a variety of birds.

Sugar water can be used to attract hummingbirds, white-breasted nuthatches, downy woodpeckers and orioles.

149

ANIMAL FAT, MEALWORMS, INSECTS AND OTHER BIRD FOOD

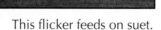

This flicker feeds on suet.

Suet cakes can be purchased commercially or mixed at home.

Suet

Suet is a high quality animal fat found in the kidney area of cattle. The name can also be used to refer to any fat trimmings from livestock that can be placed in suet feeders for the birds. Suet is sold at most grocery stores in the meat section.

Suet is an extremely popular food for many birds: gray catbirds, black-capped chickadees, brown creepers, American crows, purple finches, northern flickers, common grackles, rose-breasted grosbeaks, blue jays, gray jays, dark-eyed juncos, golden-crowned kinglets, ruby-crowned kinglets, northern mockingbirds, red-breasted nuthatches, white-breasted nuthatches, northern orioles, chipping sparrows, fox sparrows, American tree sparrows and white-throated sparrows.

Other birds that eat suet are European starlings, house sparrows, summer tanagers, brown thrashers, tufted titmice, yellow-rumped warblers, downy woodpeckers, hairy woodpeckers, red-bellied woodpeckers, red-headed woodpeckers, pileated woodpeckers and even eastern bluebirds, northern cardinals and American robins.

Reference: Davison 1967.

Suet cakes

One problem with suet is that, in warm weather, it can turn rancid. Many people feed suet only from September through May to avoid spoilage in the summer. If you stop, however, you will miss the delight of seeing woodpeckers and orioles bringing their young to the feeder and feeding them suet.

Suet cakes are made by melting suet down twice in a double boiler and mixing nutritious little tidbits of food like cornmeal, raisins, chopped peanuts and rice into the suet before it congeals into a hardened cake. Suet cakes don't turn rancid as quickly in warm weather and are eaten by many kinds of birds. Suet cakes can be purchased commercially, or you can make them at home, a fun activity to do with children. Here are the instructions for making suet cakes:

150

Grind up beef suet in a food grinder. This breaks the suet into small parts so it will melt down evenly. Then place the ground-up suet into the inner pan of a double boiler so it melts. Allow the suet to cool until it congeals. Then melt the congealed suet in the double boiler a second time.

Make suet cakes by pouring the liquid suet into aluminum foil cake forms or aluminum foil dishes that are left over from frozen foods. The liquid suet can also be poured into holes drilled into hanging log suet feeders like the one shown on page 213 or into a coconut feeder as shown on page 215.

This downy woodpecker is eating suet.

Other nutritious ingredients for suet cakes are finely crushed egg shells, oatmeal, cracked corn, millet, dried currants and cooked noodles or spaghetti. If you have access to natural berries in the summer or fall, like red osier, gray dogwood or mountain ash berries, you can air dry them and put them in the suet cakes.

Put your additional ingredients in the aluminum foil form. Let the melted suet cool slightly so that it begins to set. Pour the semi-liquid suet into the form, the log or the coconut and over the seeds or dried fruits. Stir up the mixture so the seeds and fruits are distributed throughout the suet cake. Then let the mixture cool.

You could also dip pine cones into the melted suet or suet mixture. Depending on the space between the pine cone scales, you may need to use a spatula to force the mixture inside.

Dave Maslowski of Maslowski Wildlife Productions in Cincinnati, Ohio, mentioned that a brown creeper was attracted by a suet mixture of two parts ground suet (not melted), two parts cornmeal, and one part peanut butter. This was mixed well and placed in a suet feeder. You could also smear it onto the bark of a tree with an upward stroke, since brown creepers climb up rather than down trees and probe into the crevices of the bark from below.

A nutritious bluebird food mix that contains suet was developed by Linda Janilla of Stillwater, Minnesota. The recipe is as follows:

1 cup peanut butter	4 cups yellow cornmeal
1 cup rendered (melted) suet	1 cup flour
1 cup peanut hearts	1 cup sunflower chips
1 cup Zante currants (small raisins)	

Mix well. The mixture should be granular, but it should still stick together. If it is too sticky, add more corn meal.

This mix can also be pushed into the cavities of a Peterson T-Post Feeder, shown in Design # 22, or a hanging log feeder for woodpeckers and nuthatches shown on page 213. It can also be offered to bluebirds on an open tray or platform or in an enclosed bluebird feeder. Enclosed bluebird feeders with glass sides manufactured by Dave Ahlgren are available at many wild bird stores.

Venison fat and deer rib cages

Minnesota's deer harvest was approximately 200,000 in 1993. That's a lot of deer.

Each deer provides a considerable amount of venison for human consumption. However, each deer probably has between 10 and 15 pounds of fat that are meticulously cut away from the meat and thrown away. Since the fat congeals at room temperature, it is avoided when cooking venison.

This means that perhaps as many as two million pounds of venison fat are available each year in Minnesota as a perfectly suitable suet alternative for the birds. And it is probably free for the asking; just find a successful deer hunter. Or perhaps you prefer to pay $1.19 per pound for beef fat in the local meat market. Bear fat can also be used to feed the birds.

The fat trimmings from the deer can be placed in a suet dispenser like Designs #17 through 19. It can also be hung in mesh bags like onion or potato sacks.

Another part of the deer that usually goes to waste is the rib cage. There is very little meat, and quite a bit of fat. Black-capped chickadees, common ravens, downy woodpeckers, hairy woodpeckers, summer tanagers and even pileated woodpeckers and black-billed magpies will dine on the deer ribs throughout the winter. The rib cage may be sawed down the center of the vertebral column and each set of ribs can be hung on the side of a tree. The whole rib cage could also be suspended from a tree or hung on a post to provide a nutritious source of fat for the birds.

The sight of a rib cage hanging in a backyard might be rather unsettling to your neighbors, so if you try using ribs, place them where they won't offend your neighbor's view.

This downy woodpecker is a regular visitor at a deer rib cage.

A red-bellied woodpecker stops at a suet feeder.

152

Bacon fat drippings (melted fat from the frying pan)

Some people save their bacon fat, or get it from restaurants, so they can use it to feed the birds. Most birds that feed on suet will also eat bacon fat. You can use melted fat from beef, pork, veal, lamb or poultry. Heat the fat until excess moisture has evaporated, and then strain the fat into a container that can be either refrigerated or frozen. This can be mixed into suet recipes.

Grit

Grit consists of sand or fine particles of gravel that are eaten by birds to aid in grinding up seeds and other food in their gizzards. Some people place trays of sand near their bird feeders to provide a source of grit. It can also be mixed with bird food.

Mealworms

Mealworms have become a great new item for bird feeding enthusiasts. They're the larvae of small black beetles that are typically found in stored grain. They have been used in the pet trade for many years as food for chameleons. Give them a try.

Feeding mealworms to wild birds can provide hours of viewing enjoyment. Place them where eastern bluebirds, northern cardinals and gray catbirds can see their movement and capture them as they would natural prey items.

Mealworms can be raised at home to feed songbirds.

This is an excellent way to encourage feeding activity if you have bluebirds nesting near your yard. They will even come onto your deck to get mealworms.

If you don't have bluebirds, try this anyway. You might be surprised at how many birds show up at the feeder.

The list of birds that can be attracted to mealworms is quite impressive. They actually attract more species than black oil sunflower seeds! The list includes woodpeckers, jays, chickadees, titmice, nuthatches, wrens, bluebirds, robins, catbirds, mockingbirds, brown thrashers, vireos, warblers, cardinals, rose-breasted grosbeaks, indigo buntings, rufous-sided towhees, chipping sparrows, field sparrows, song sparrows, juncos, cowbirds, blackbirds, grackles, orioles, scarlet tanagers, purple finches and evening grosbeaks.

Mealworms can be purchased from your local pet store or bait shop. Larger quantities can be ordered from several places: Rainbow Mealworms, Box 4907, Compton, CA 90224 (1-800-777-WORM); Grubco, Inc., Box 15001, Hamilton, OH 45015 (1-800-222-3563); and Georgia Mealies, Route 7, Box 508, Tifton, GA 31794. They cost about $5 per thousand, plus shipping and handling.

You may wish to raise your own mealworms. A good container is a plastic shoe box or a plastic container that is four to six inches deep, 12 to 14 inches wide, and 18 to 24 inches long. Place several inches of bran in the bottom of the container. It can be mixed with poultry laying mash or other ground-up feed grains. This will be the main food supply for the mealworms.

This chipping sparrow is eating mealworms.

A bluebird eats mealworms from a Linda Tray.

Cut out a piece of cardboard from the side of an empty breakfast food box and lay it on top of the bran. Then place several pieces of carrots, sliced the long way, on the cardboard. This introduces just enough moisture to sustain the mealworm colony. These slices will need to be replaced weekly as they dry out. Too much moisture from other sources, or moisture in the bran itself, will cause a fungus to develop and the mealworms will die.

Lay several sheets of newspaper, cut to the shape of the container, on top of the carrots. The top of the container should be sealed to prevent the escape of adult beetles, and there should be small air holes for ventilation.

You can buy several hundred mealworms to start your colony. Place them in the bran, and they will do the rest. Allow several weeks for the first mealworms to transform into adult beetles. They will mate, lay eggs and die. That life cycle will sustain itself throughout the summer.

The optimum temperature for your mealworm colony is 80 degrees or above. To make the mealworms contain a higher protein

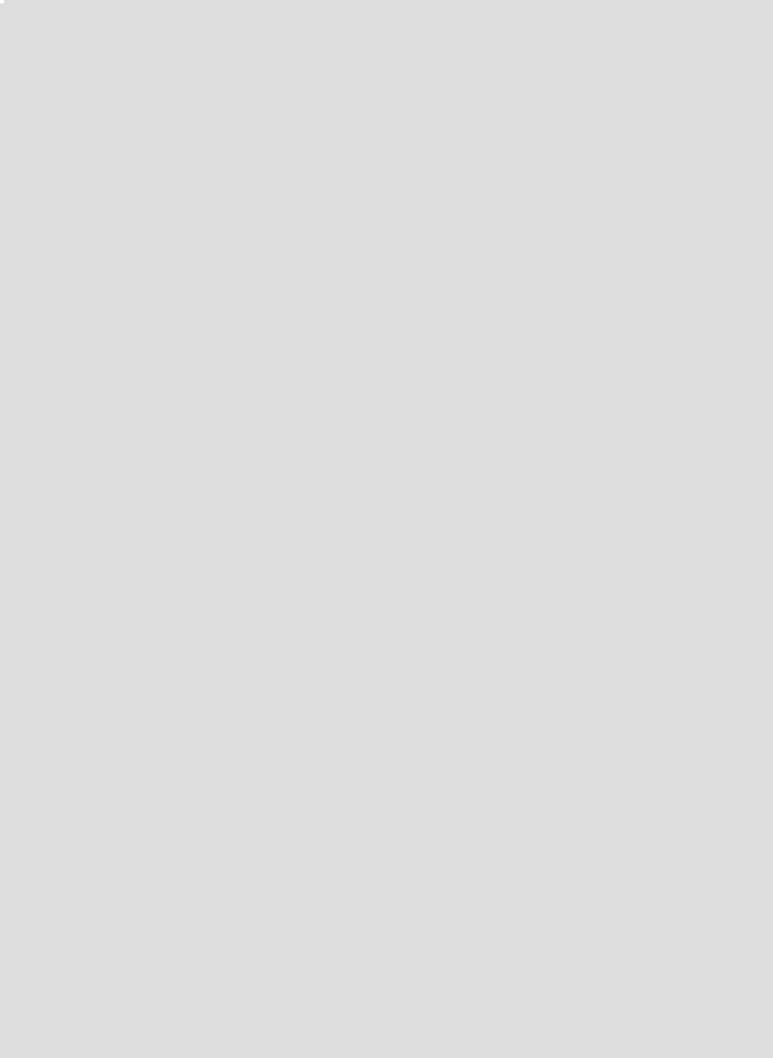

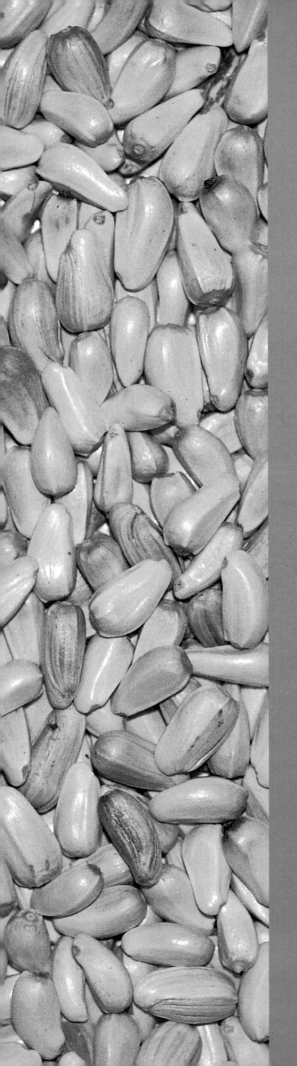

9

*woodshop basics for
feeder construction*

woodshop basics for feeder construction

The past several chapters have dealt with the creatures that visit bird feeders and the types of food that can be used to attract birds. The next chapter covers the feeders that can be placed on your property to attract wildlife. Some of these feeders can be purchased commercially, but many can be made at home. You can make feeders from natural objects like tree branches and hollow logs or household waste items like empty two-liter pop bottles.

More than two dozen feeders can be made from new or scrap wood. Since many of the feeders in this book require construction with wood, this chapter is an introduction to woodworking tools, tips and safety precautions. This information will help you build the wooden feeders described in the following chapter safely and efficiently.

If you buy bird feeders you're missing out on one of the more enjoyable hobbies associated with wildlife conservation: woodworking. Whether you are building bird houses, nest platforms, or bird feeders, there is a tremendous amount of satisfaction in creating simple structures that will attract wildlife to your yard. The plans in this book involve basic tools and simple techniques.

Woodworking can be a fun activity for people of all ages.

Building nest boxes and wildlife feeders does not require the high levels of sophistication and woodworking skill required for making more advanced projects like cabinets and furniture. Woodworking can be simple, easy and fun for your family and friends. But whether you are working with a hammer and nails or a power saw, you need to be continually aware that woodworking safety is the primary concern. It is important to complete each project with the same number of fingers that you had when you started. Most safety considerations involve the use of common sense.

Plan ahead for your time in the woodshop. Make sure you assemble in advance the right tools for the job, and that they are sharp and properly fitted with the right attachments, bits, blades or guards. Carbide-tipped blades provide an excellent cutting edge on saw blades for circular saws, jigsaws, table saws and radial arm saws.

Most of the designs in this book can be cut out with hand tools, but you would undoubtedly find it easier to use power tools. Many of the cuts can be made with a jigsaw or portable circular saw, and a reversible cordless drill is great for drilling holes and screwing deck screws into the feeder parts.

The great thing about woodshop techniques for bird feeders is that they're very basic. And birds are forgiving. If you make a mistake, they won't care.

It's a good idea to locate a family member or friend who has a table saw or radial arm saw. You will be able to make more precise cuts, including kerf cuts, with these saws. If you can get a small group of people together to cut out and assemble some bird feeders, hopefully one of them will have a simple woodshop where you can work efficiently.

The first rule of using the power equipment is to wear safety goggles or glasses to protect your eyes. Use them every time you cut or drill.

The second safety rule is to work with a partner whenever possible. Your partner can help in laying out and measuring boards, double-checking measurements and holding boards as they are being cut or drilled. And partners can help remind each other about special safety concerns that need to be considered during the construction process.

Reference: Williams 1981.

Woodworking is much easier and safer with a partner.

It is important to use safety goggles while working with power tools.

TOOLS AND TECHNIQUES FOR FEEDER CONSTRUCTION

Claw hammer

Claw hammers are essential for pounding and pulling nails. If you don't want to pound nails, you could use a cordless reversible drill and deck screws.

Cordless reversible drill and screwdriver

A cordless, reversible, rechargeable drill is a wonderful tool for assembling bird feeders. If you make a mistake, you can simply back the screw out and start it over. This tool is also safer than a hammer, especially when children are involved.

The tools and equipment pictured above are all useful when making bird feeders.

Electric drill

You can use an electric drill to pre-drill the holes for deck screws. You could also use a cordless drill for this purpose, but if you have a drill bit in this drill and a Phillips screw bit in a cordless drill, you don't have to keep switching the bits back and forth. An electric drill is also helpful for drilling holes in hanging log feeders, hanging screen feeders, starling-proof suet feeders and dowel suet feeders.

Rip saw and crosscut saw

Hand saws provide the simple straight cuts required for making bird feeders. Rip saws are used for making lengthwise cuts on boards, and crosscut saws are used for cutting across the grain. Rip saws have five and a half teeth per inch and crosscut saws have seven teeth per inch.

Jigsaw

Jigsaws are available in one sixth to one half horsepower. They can be used for crosscuts, rip cuts, bevel or angle cuts and scrolling or curving cuts. This is the best saw to use for curving cuts like the front of the Rustad chalet feeder unless you have access to a band saw, which can also be used to make curved cuts. It is, however, more difficult to cut a perfectly straight line with a jigsaw than with a circular saw, radial arm saw or table saw.

The best blade to use in cutting wood up to one inch thick is a medium wood blade that has about nine teeth per inch. Be careful not to cut your electric cord while using this saw!

Jigsaw.

Circular saw

A portable, electric circular saw provides the straight cuts associated with bird feeders, especially when cutting plywood sheets or two by four-inch boards. This saw can also be used for rip cuts, crosscuts and bevel cuts. More powerful than a saber saw, a circular saw has one and a quarter to two and a half horsepower motors.

The circular blade for this saw is typically seven and a quarter inches in diameter. The best blade to use for general bird feeder construction is a combination blade designed for both crosscut and ripsaw purposes. A plywood blade, which has more teeth per inch, should be used for cutting plywood.

The teeth of a circular saw tear upward, so you should place the good, or outer side of your board face down when you cut. This will give you a cleaner cut on the side of the plywood that shows. A straight-edge guide is useful for making straight, accurate cuts with this saw.

Circular saw.

Table saw

A table saw provides the best alternative for making most of the cuts essential for constructing bird feeders. Most table saws use a nine or ten-inch diameter blade. The rip fence on a table saw allows you to make long, straight cuts to rip a board or to cut up a piece of plywood.

This is the best saw to use if you need to rip boards into a narrower width. For example, a table saw is ideal for ripping a one by six-inch board into two halves to make side pieces for a bird feeder. This is also the best saw for making the bevel cuts that serve as the peaks of roof sections. The saw's tilt gauge allows you to tilt the saw blade to the angle you need.

Table saws are also helpful for making the kerfs (grooves) on screen feeders that serve as insertion points for screens or panes of glass.

When working with a table saw, you must use the safety guard that fits over the top of the saw blade. You should also make a pusher stick

Table saw.

that looks like a walleye with its mouth open. Use it to push the boards as they are cut so you can keep your fingers away from the saw blade.

Radial arm saw

A radial arm saw is an efficient saw to use for cross cuts, and it can also be rotated to make rip cuts and bevel cuts. The length of a radial arm saw cut is limited to a stroke of about two feet, so it is not quite as versatile as a table saw, especially if you're cutting up a piece of plywood.

A radial arm saw usually has a ten-inch diameter blade and can easily cut two by four-inch boards. Radial arm saws are recommended for crosscuts on one or two-inch thick boards, but table saws are better for ripping boards and cutting beveled edges on long roof sections more than two feet long.

Spring clamps and C-clamps

Spring clamps are useful for holding wood to a workbench, especially if you're using saber saws or circular saws. Spring clamps are especially important if you don't have a partner to help hold the boards. C-clamps are also useful for fastening boards to workbenches.

Screws and nails

Soft wood like cedar, fastened with smooth galvanized nails, may loosen up over time due to freezing and thawing moisture. You can avoid this problem by using deck screws, size 4D ring-shank nails or size 4D concrete-coated sinker nails. If you are fastening a three quarters or seven eighths-inch piece of wood into a two by four-inch gable, or into the end of a piece of thicker wood, you may want to use size 6D ring shank or concrete-coated sinker nails.

The main fasteners for nearly all of the following bird feeder designs are one and five-eighths-inch deck screws, ideal for fastening two pieces of wood that are each between three quarters and one inch thick. You can pre-drill the holes with a 7/64-inch drill bit and insert the screws with a rechargeable cordless drill and a Phillips bit. It is quick, easy and safe.

If you want a more finished look to your feeder, try using 4D or 6D headless finishing nails on the roof and edges and a router to give a rounded edge to feeder sides.

You can use 6D or 8D finishing nails to hold fruit halves in place when you build fruit feeders. Since the nails have no heads, it is easy to press the fruits onto the nails.

Lag screws (a quarter inch by two or two and a half inches) have hexagonal bolt heads that can be tightened with a wrench. They work well for attaching feeders to the sides of trees. Be sure to place a washer under the head of the screw. Each year, these screws must be loosened by a couple of turns to allow for the growth of the tree.

Screw eyes have holes on the top. If you screw them into the top of hanging log suet feeders, you can twist a hook or wire through the hole and attach it to a deck support or tree limb. You can also use screw eyes in the ends of feeders so you can hang them up in the garage when you're not using them.

Pusher stick.

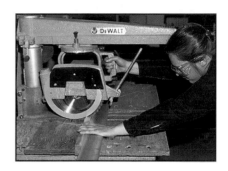

Radial arm saw.

Spring clamps.

Deck screws.

161

WOODWORKING TIPS

Bevel (angle) cuts

Bevel cuts are cuts made at an angle. They are necessary on roof sections along the peaks of fly-through feeders or self-feeders. Depending on the feeder, the angles are either 19 or 23 degrees. The backs of Rustad chalet feeders require 33-degree bevel cuts.

The easiest way to make bevel cuts is with a table saw. Roof sections may be cut out with a radial arm saw or a circular saw. You could use a saber saw, but they don't make straight cuts as easily.

Although table saws and radial arm saws have scales marking the angle of bevel cuts for adjusting the blade, they are not necessarily correct. If you want a perfect angle that matches the angle of the gable sections, use one of your gable scraps as indicated on the appropriate design. Set the scrap on its short end adjacent to the saw blade as you tilt the angle of the saw blade. Change the angle of the blade until it lies flush on the sloping surface of the gable scrap as shown in the accompanying photo.

When you want to make an angle cut on a feeder section, save the scrap from your gable cut and use it to set the angle on the table saw.

Set the gable scrap so the angling surface is adjacent to the table saw blade. Adjust the angle of the saw blade until it lies flush on the sloping surface of the wood scraps.

Above: Cut the roof sections so the angle fits at the peak of the feeder.

Right: Place the gable sections the proper distance apart. Then attach the roof sections to the gables with deck screws and glue.

Kerfs (dadoes or grooves)

A kerf is a cut made by a table saw or radial arm saw that penetrates only partway through a board. There are two kinds of kerfs. "Dadoes" are kerfs that run across the grain of the wood. "Grooves" run with the grain. The designs in this book involve the use of grooves.

Self feeder side pieces (Designs #15 and 16) have grooves that

are three eighths of an inch deep in boards that are either three quarters or seven eighths of an inch thick. The saw blade creates a groove one eighth of an inch wide that allows glass or Plexiglas panes to be slipped into the boards on the completed feeder. Similarly, grooves allow screens to be fitted into boards used for screen feeders (Designs #10 and 11).

The designs in this book have avoided the use of kerfs as much as possible because they can become a problem if you don't have a table saw or radial arm saw. Grooves can be made with other saws, but it's more difficult.

One alternative for screen feeders with kerfs is to staple the screen to the bottom of the feeder and omit the kerf. You could also rip three eighths of an inch of wood off the bottom of the feeder sides, staple the screen onto the bottom of the altered feeder, and then screw the three eighths-inch piece of wood back onto the bottom of the feeder to secure the screen. See the photos of the Perry extra large screen feeder for this technique.

Ripping

Ripping means cutting a board lengthwise. It can be done with a hand rip saw, a saber saw, circular saw, radial arm saw or a table saw. A table saw is the best choice.

Many of the feeder designs in this book have edges made from one by three-inch boards (actually two and a half inches wide). If you are unable to obtain a board this size from your local lumber yard, you can buy one by six-inch boards and rip them into feeder sides that are two and three quarters inches thick. Either width is acceptable for feeder use, and this will not affect the other measurements on the designs. Some lumber yards will rip boards for you for an extra fee.

A safety note on ripping: be sure that the safety guard on the table saw is in place while ripping. If not, the saw can bind on the wood and throw the board completely across the workshop—or into you—like a spear! Do not stand directly behind the saw path.

Marking wood and using a square

When marking boards prior to cutting them, use a carpenter's square to ensure that you are making accurate right angles. Lay the long edge of the square along the edge of the board and mark the wood along the short edge at the proper intervals.

Remember that saw blades may take out one eighth of an inch of wood each time they cut a board. You must allow for the width of the saw blade when making your marks. Add that width to the length of each piece to be cut.

When making two or four identical pieces, like the four corner supports of a fly-through feeder, mark and cut out one support. Then use it as your model for marking and cutting out each successive piece. Compare them afterwards to be sure they are all the same length. If not, a radial arm saw works well for trimming any excess wood on the ends of the longer pieces.

Also, remember the carpenter's first rule: "Measure twice, cut once!"

You will be amazed how easy it is to mark a board wrong and not discover your error until after cutting the wood. Always review your marks, or have your partner check them, before you proceed. It also helps to buy a couple of extra boards before cutting out several bird feeders. They can be used to replace wood that splits or pieces that are cut wrong.

Once you have cut out all the pieces of a feeder, it's a good idea to assemble them by holding the pieces together and checking their fit. This is called a dry fit. You may need to do some minor trimming to get a tighter fit.

Making a kerf.

Ripping.

Pre-drill nail or screw holes to keep the wood from splitting.

Two examples of using a square.

Table 5. Traditional and actual dimensions of boards referred to in bird feeder designs.

Gluing seams.

Gluing seams, joints and screen feeders

You can add extra strength to bird feeders by laying a bead of exterior, water-resistant wood glue or adhesive along the edges of wood being nailed or screwed together. This is especially important when fastening roof sections to gable sections and gluing roof sections together along the peak. Glue should also be used in the kerf groove of screen feeders to hold the screen in place.

There are a variety of acceptable woodworking glues on the market. Among excellent new waterproof glues are Titebond II®, Weather-Tite® slow set epoxy and Resorcinol®. They come in squeezable plastic containers or in tubes that are inserted into caulking guns. If you need to fill in cracks, grooves or nail holes, try mixing glue with the sawdust from the feeder. The sawdust and glue mixture will match the color of the wood and fill the holes and grooves quite nicely.

Dimensions of boards

Except for plywood, the traditional, advertised dimensions of boards are not the same as the real dimensions. A two by four-inch board is actually one and a half by three and a half inches. One-inch thick lumber ranging from 2 to 12 inches wide is usually three quarters of an inch thick, but it may also be five eighths of an inch or seven eighths of an inch thick.

Number one grade rough cedar, a good choice for making bird feeders, is usually seven eighths of an inch thick, but may be one inch thick. Table 5 gives the traditional and actual dimensions of boards referred to in this book.

Traditional dimensions (inches)	Actual dimensions (inches)
1 x 2	3/4 x 1 1/2
1 x 3	3/4 x 2 1/2
1 x 4	3/4 x 3 1/2
1 x 6	3/4 x 5 1/2
1 x 8	3/4 x 7 1/4
1 x 10	3/4 x 9 1/4
1 x 12	3/4 x 11 1/4
2 x 2	1 1/2 x 1 1/2
2 x 4	1 1/2 x 3 1/2

Boards are sold in two-foot increments, usually starting with lengths of six feet. You can buy boards in lengths of six, eight, ten and 12 feet or longer.

The designs in this book provide materials lists that show the traditional dimensions and the actual length of board needed for a feeder. If you need 54 inches of one by six-inch wood for a feeder, you would probably buy a one by six-inch board in the smallest commercially-available length over 54 inches. In this case, you would need a six-foot board and you will have 18 inches of extra wood to use on another feeder.

The actual size of the wood is listed in the feeder diagrams, and a wood thickness of three quarters of an inch is assumed. Be sure to measure the thickness of the wood you are using. If it is thicker or thinner than three quarters of an inch, the lengths of some pieces of the feeder will need to be changed. Each piece that changes is marked with an asterisk, and a new length (for a seven eighths of an inch thickness) is indicated at the bottom of the diagram.

If the wood is one inch thick, add another quarter inch to the dimensions shown for a seven eighths of an inch thick board. If the wood is only five eighths of an inch thick, subtract a quarter inch from the original dimension shown for the three quarters of an inch thick wood.

One benefit of making bird feeders is that it gives you the opportunity to use wood scraps that accumulate in your woodshop. Leftover boards from construction sites can also be used, as long as you have the project manager's permission. Even if you don't have a supply of scrap lumber available, most of these feeders don't cost more than ten dollars using new boards. For example, the Linda tray feeder (Design #21) costs less than $3.50 using number one cedar for prices quoted in August of 1994. A medium deck railing feeder costs under ten dollars using new number one cedar. The bottom line is that bird feeders are not expensive to build, and they make excellent gifts for friends.

Several of the feeder designs in this book use three quarters of an inch thick exterior plywood as floors and roof sections, and the Rustad chalet feeder is made entirely from plywood. A-C or B-C grade exterior plywood is acceptable. Plywood is sold in four by four-foot or four by eight-foot sheets, so where plywood is shown in designs you will need to buy a half or whole sheet and use it to make components for several feeders. Plywood will need to be painted or stained and treated with wood preservative.

Number one cedar boards are the best choice for most bird feeder designs. This wood weathers well, needs no painting, is easy to drill and cut, and is relatively straight-grained and knot-free. Feeders made from cedar look very rustic and make especially nice gifts. They don't cost much more than pine boards, which don't weather as well.

Other woods, in addition to cedar, that weather well include redwood, cypress, Douglas fir and lodgepole pine. Pine bird feeders should be painted with outdoor paint or treated with wood preservative. Be selective when choosing boards. Look for boards that are flat, straight, relatively free of knots and free of large cracks on the ends.

Reference: Williams 1981.

Using the techniques and designs in this book, you can learn how to build all these feeders.

10

bird feeders
and feeder designs

bird feeders and feeder designs

TRAY FEEDERS

Tray feeders are among the most popular and adaptable of all bird feeders. They are very easy to make and should last a long time.

Almost any type of lumber or wood scraps can be used to create tray feeders. Some people even use a sheet of plywood on a stump or the top of a picnic table as a winter tray feeder. The feeder designs shown here provide several options, depending on what size of boards are available. In general, the larger the tray, the more birds the feeder can accommodate.

This medium tray feeder appears to be the site of a board meeting for the local association of evening grosbeaks. This feeder's size makes it easy to accommodate on decks.

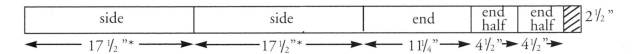

| side | side | end | end half | end half | 2½" |

← 17½"* → ← 17½"* → ← 11¼" → 4½"→ 4½"→

* This dimension assumes a ¾" thick board.
  Sides should be 17¾" if board is ⅞" thick.

Design #1

Small Tray Feeder

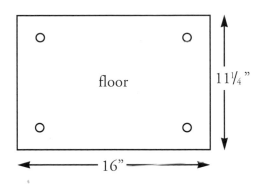

floor

11¼"

← 16" →

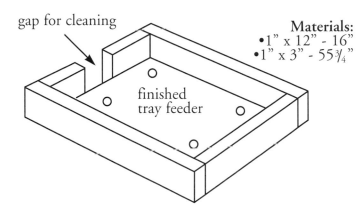

gap for cleaning

finished
tray feeder

Materials:
•1" x 12" - 16"
•1" x 3" - 55¾"

One benefit of tray feeders is that they give birds a wide scope of vision, allowing them to feel relatively secure from predators. If tray feeders are close to trees, bushes or other obstacles, there is a danger of ambush by cats or raptors.

Tray feeders should have some drain holes in the bottom and a cleaning gap on the side to make it easier to scrape out old or moldy seeds. It is better to regularly place smaller amounts of seeds in a tray feeder (no more than 1/4 inch deep) than to fill it all the way to the top, which promotes the growth of mold or the germination of wet seeds. It also helps to stir up the seeds after a rain to help them dry out. Waste seeds under and around the feeder will need to be periodically cleaned up to avoid attracting mice, voles or rats.

Small tray feeders may be fastened to a post or stump.

Small tray feeder

Small tray feeders are easy to build and easy to accommodate in small yards, decks or garden areas. These feeders can be attached to the tops of stumps, posts or pipes from 1 to 5 feet above the ground. The simplicity of this design makes it an excellent choice for small children to assemble.

These all-purpose feeders are used by a wide variety of common feeder birds like chickadees, cardinals, blue jays, house finches, purple finches and grackles. Since these are small feeders, they can easily be dominated by a single aggressive blue jay or gray squirrel. They can be stocked with sunflower, safflower, corn or millet mixes.

Due to territorial spacing, only a few birds will feed in a small space at the same time. For this reason you may want to have several of these feeders scattered around your garden, deck or yard.

This feeder also serves as the base for the small fly-through feeder (Design #6).

Medium tray feeder

When it comes to bird feeders, bigger is better. A larger feeding surface means more birds. The design for medium tray feeders expands on the small tray feeder to give it a larger feeding area. It also serves as the base for medium fly-through feeders (Design #7). The main difference with this feeder is that the ends also serve as the legs, so the feeder is self-supporting. Yet the design is still fairly simple and can be assembled within an hour.

Large tray feeder

Keeping with the "bigger is better" theory, this large tray feeder can accommodate many birds at once: everything from cardinals, chickadees, juncos, doves, evening grosbeaks, redpolls and blue jays to ring-necked pheasants.

The only difference between this feeder and the previous design is the size of the tray. The large tray feeder design calls for a feeding surface of 18 by 20 inches. This surface can also serve as the base for the large fly-through feeder with dimensions shown in Design #8.

This medium tray feeder has leg sections so it can stand by itself.

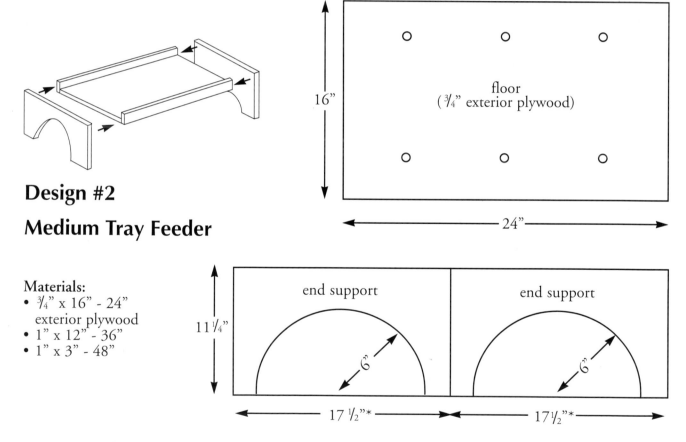

Design #2

Medium Tray Feeder

Materials:
- ¾" x 16" - 24" exterior plywood
- 1" x 12" - 36"
- 1" x 3" - 48"

floor
(¾" exterior plywood)

16"

24"

end support   end support

11¼"

6"   6"

17½"*   17½"*

* This dimension assumes a ¾" thick board for sides. Change to 17¾" if sides are ⅞" thick.

2½" high

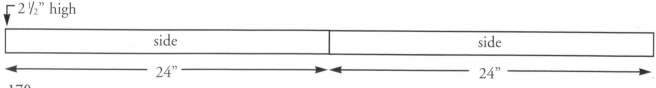

side   side

24"   24"

170

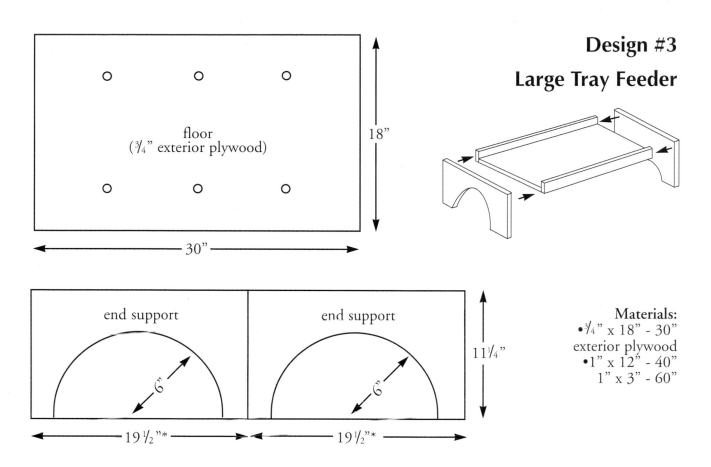

floor
(¾" exterior plywood)

18"

30"

Design #3

Large Tray Feeder

end support

end support

11¼"

6"

6"

19½"*

19½"*

Materials:
• ¾" x 18" - 30"
exterior plywood
• 1" x 12" - 40"
1" x 3" - 60"

* This dimension assumes ¾" thick side boards.
Change to 19¾" if sides are ⅞" thick.

2½" high

side

side

30"

30"

Leg sections added
to the ends of your feeder
allow it to stand alone.
This feeder is popular
with ground feeding birds.

171

Birds frequently assert their dominance over other birds at feeders. This is called the "pecking order." Here two juncos, identified by their white outer tail feathers, compete through displays to see who is dominant.

Design #4

Medium Deck Railing Feeder

Materials:
•1" x 8" - 48"
• 2 - 1" x 2" - 48"
• 2 - 1" x 3" - 57"
See additional diagrams on the next page.

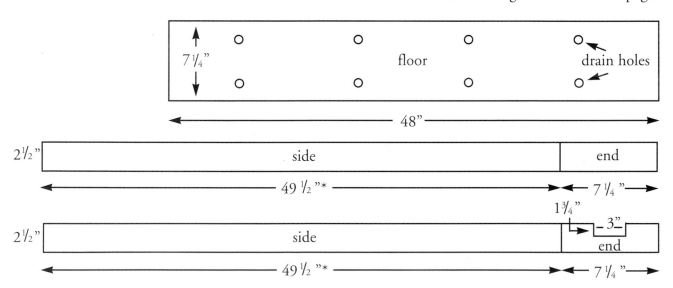

$7\frac{1}{4}$"   floor   drain holes

48"

$2\frac{1}{2}$"   side   end

$49\frac{1}{2}$"* $7\frac{1}{4}$"

$1\frac{3}{4}$"

$2\frac{1}{2}$"   side   3"   end

$49\frac{1}{2}$"* $7\frac{1}{4}$"

* This dimension assumes this board is $\frac{3}{4}$" thick. If it is $\frac{7}{8}$" thick, change the dimension to $49\frac{3}{4}$."

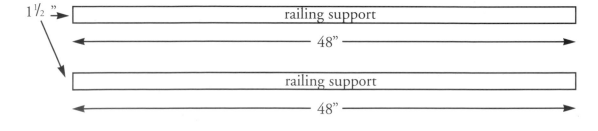

$1\frac{1}{2}$"   railing support

48"

railing support

48"

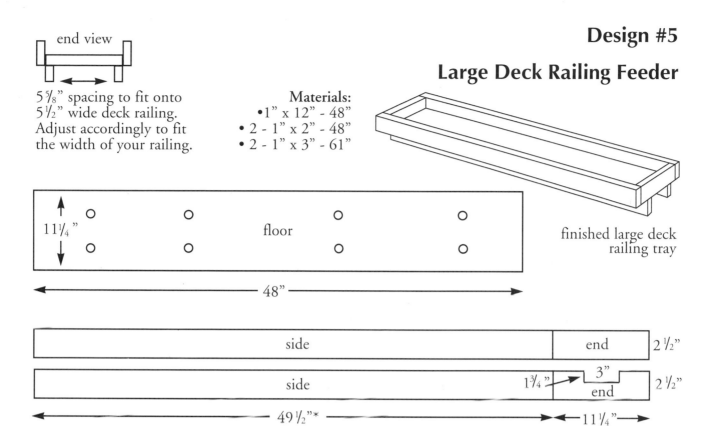

end view

5⅝" spacing to fit onto
5½" wide deck railing.
Adjust accordingly to fit
the width of your railing.

Materials:
• 1" x 12" - 48"
• 2 - 1" x 2" - 48"
• 2 - 1" x 3" - 61"

Design #5

Large Deck Railing Feeder

finished large deck
railing tray

11¼"   floor   ○ ○ ○ ○ / ○ ○ ○ ○

← 48" →

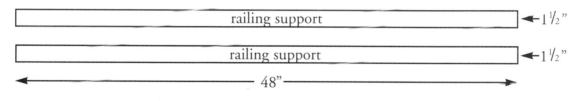

| side | end | 2½" |
| side   1¾" → 3" end | | 2½" |

← 49½"* → ← 11¼" →

This dimension assumes this board is ¾" thick. If it is ⅞," dimension should be 49¾."

| railing support | ← 1½" |
| railing support | ← 1½" |

← 48" →

This large deck railing feeder
is 4 feet long and the base is a
piece of 1-inch by 12-inch wood.
The twenty-four redpolls and
one house finch demonstrate
how successful this feeder is
in providing space for many
birds at one time.
The railing supports should
be screwed or fastened into
the deck to keep the feeder
from tipping.

173

Medium deck railing feeder

This design combines the simple structure and effectiveness of the tray feeder with the popularity of decks with railings in many American backyards. Many people have a deck with either a 3 1/2 or 5 1/2-inch wide railing that makes an excellent support for a long, slender deck railing feeder.

Medium deck railing feeders use a 4-foot long, 1-inch by 8-inch board on the bottom. You can adapt this to a 2-foot or 3-foot length if you wish, but remember that the more space you allow, the more birds that can feed at one time.

The 1-by-2s that serve to bracket the deck railing may also need to be fastened onto the railing with some deck screws or wooden dowels to prevent the feeder from accidentally tipping off.

With medium deck railing feeders you can attract cardinals, blue jays, purple finches, house finches, pine siskins, redpolls, goldfinches, chickadees and dark-eyed juncos.

You may want to take the feeder down in the spring to avoid messy sunflower seed hulls and bird droppings on your deck. And, since the seeds are subject to getting wet, don't put too much in the feeder at once.

Large deck railing feeder

Large deck railing feeders use large feeding surfaces that can accommodate many songbirds at one time.

These feeders should also be screwed or clamped onto the deck to prevent tipping. You may wish to use them in the fall and winter when you are not using your deck because the feeder generates problems with waste seed and bird droppings.

Seeds in large deck railing feeders are also subject to getting wet, so don't put too much seed into the feeder at one time.

The Deutz wheelbarrow feeder is essentially a tray feeder on a wheelbarrow base. This red-headed woodpecker visited the feeder to get peanuts in the shell. Brown thrashers also eat popcorn at this feeder.

174

Deutz wheelbarrow feeder

Pat and Rose Deutz of Marshall, Minnesota, turned an old wheelbarrow into a bird feeder. It had a large, shallow cargo area that essentially served as a tray feeder.

The beauty of the feeder is that it is very easy to move when you mow your lawn. Among the interesting visitors at this feeder are brown thrashers that came for popcorn and red-headed woodpeckers that came for peanuts in the shell.

Bullwinkle moose antler feeder

Art Hawkins of Hugo, Minnesota, started using this novel feeder on his deck several years ago. Nuthatches, chickadees and other birds would land on the tines of a medium-sized moose antler, and then hop down to the palm of the antler to feed on the sunflower seeds scattered there. Squirrels also enjoy nibbling on the antler tips for a calcium supplement. Drill a screw through the center of the antler's palm onto the deck railing.

Obviously, there is a very limited supply of moose antlers to provide this type of feeder. If you want a feeder like this, find some friends in the moose' northern range and ask them to keep their eyes open for a naturally shed antler that could be added to your bird feeding station.

You could also place an antlered deer skull in a ground feeding site. The birds land on the antlers before hopping down to feed.

Blue jays, chickadees, nuthatches and juncos are regular visitors at this Bullwinkle antler feeder.

175

FLY-THROUGH FEEDERS

This medium fly-through feeder has the same base as the medium tray feeder, but its roof keeps out rain and snow. The male common grackle on the right is "sky pointing," a display of dominance that happens during courtship or as grackles compete for space at feeders.

Fly-through feeders get their name because the feeders have a roof and corner posts but no sides. The birds can fly into the feeder and still have a full field of view around them. This helps them see approaching predators.

The roof also keeps the seeds drier than the open tray feeders. Fly-through feeders are used by a wide variety of birds from chickadees and juncos to cardinals and blue jays.

Generally, the larger the feeder, the more birds the feeder will accommodate. The variety of feeder designs provided here allows you to build a feeder that will fit your available space and to use a

variety of small and medium wood scraps left over from other projects. These feeders use the same bases as previously explained for Designs #1, 2 and 3.

Small fly-through feeder

The small tray feeder serves as a base for the small fly-through feeder. A roof section and four corner posts have been added to keep the seeds dry.

This is a simple feeder to construct, but you will need to make an angled cut of 19 degrees along one longitudinal side of each roof half. This is done most easily with a table saw. The four corner posts are set into the corners of the tray feeder, and they fit inside the gables to provide a firm support for the roof. The

Small fly-through feeders can be placed on stumps, posts, poles or deck railings. Three house finches are visiting this one.

gables must be set 16 inches apart to accommodate the corner posts. A cleaning gap is provided on the end of this feeder so you can periodically scrape out old sunflower seed hulls.

Medium fly-through feeder

Medium fly-through feeders use the same base unit as medium tray feeders. The floor is 16 by 24 inches, so it will accommodate quite a few birds and still keep the seeds dry. The gables on the small fly-through feeder are cut from the same board as the sides and roof supports and are either 3/4 or 7/8 inch thick. The gables on the medium fly-through feeder, on the other hand, are cut from a piece of 2 by 4 that is 24 5/16 inches long. This provides a stronger support for the larger roof halves.

Notice that the angle cut along the side of the roof halves is slightly different than the cut on the previous feeder: it is a 23 degree angle. To set a perfect roof angle on a table saw for these cuts, take one of your gable scraps and set it upright on the short end against the blade as you adjust the saw. See the photo on page 162. The angle cut will exactly match the angle of the gables.

The gables need to be spaced 24 inches apart to accommodate the corner posts. This feeder can be set on a stump, post or pole, or else you can make end sections with legs as shown for the large and Perry extra large screen feeders (Designs #12 and 13).

Large fly-through feeder

Large fly-through feeders use the same 18- by 30-inch base unit as large tray feeders. Be sure to use exterior plywood for the base, not interior plywood. If plywood is not available, you could use several 30-inch long boards aligned side-by-side to achieve the 18-inch

Design #6

Small Fly-through Feeder

Materials:
• 1 x 12 - 16"
• 1 x 8 - 36"
• 1 x 6 - 58," ripped

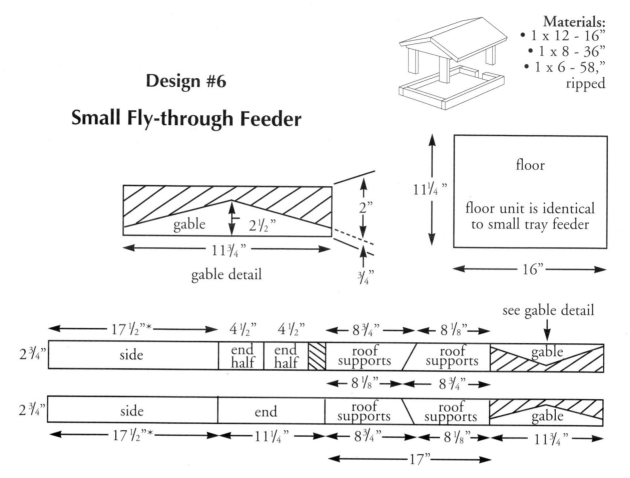

gable 2½"

gable detail

11¾"

2"

¾"

11¼"

floor

floor unit is identical to small tray feeder

16"

see gable detail

17½"* 4½" 4½" 8¾" 8⅛"

2¾" side | end half | end half | roof supports | roof supports | gable

8⅛" 8¾"

2¾" side | end | roof supports | roof supports | gable

17½"* 11¼" 8¾" 8⅛" 11¾"

17"

* These dimensions assume a board thickness of ¾." If it is ⅞" thick, sides should be 17¾."

cut this edge at a 19° angle

7¼" roof half | roof half

18" 18"

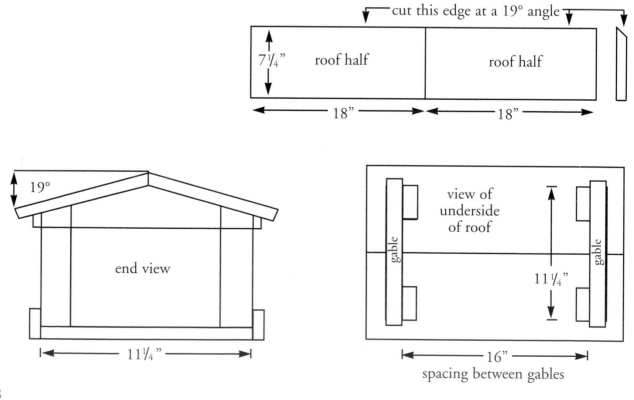

19°

end view

11¼"

view of underside of roof

gable gable

11¼"

16"

spacing between gables

178

The feeder being assembled in these photos is a medium fly-through feeder with dimensions listed on the following page. The procedure for assembling small, medium and large fly-through feeders is similar.

1. The completed roof unit for the medium fly-through feeder.

2. The four corner posts are fastened on the inside of the gable sections.

3. The roof section with attached legs is set into the medium tray feeder and the legs are fastened to the end pieces.

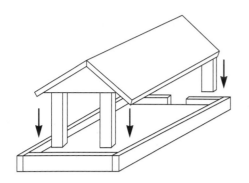

Materials:
- 16" x 24" exterior plywood (¾" thick)
- 1" x 12" - 60"
- 2" x 4" - 25"
- 1" x 6" - 72" (ripped)

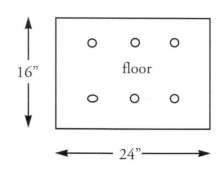

16"

floor

24"

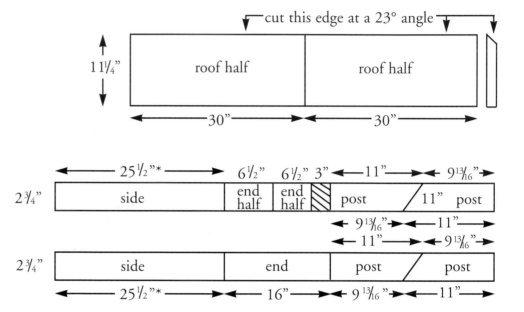

cut this edge at a 23° angle

11¼"

roof half | roof half

30" | 30"

25½"* | 6½" | 6½" | 3" | 11" | 9¹³⁄₁₆"

2¾" side | end half | end half | post | 11" post

9¹³⁄₁₆" | 11"

11" | 9¹³⁄₁₆"

2¾" side | end | post | post

25½"* | 16" | 9¹³⁄₁₆" | 11"

* These dimensions assume a board thickness of ¾."
If it is ⅞" thick, sides should be 25¾."

Design #7

Medium
Fly-through Feeder

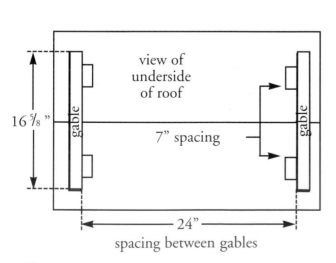

view of underside of roof

16⅝"

gable

gable

7" spacing

24"

spacing between gables

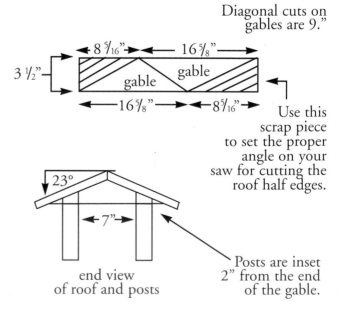

Diagonal cuts on gables are 9."

8⁵⁄₁₆" | 16⅝"

3½"

gable | gable

16⅝" | 8⁵⁄₁₆"

Use this scrap piece to set the proper angle on your saw for cutting the roof half edges.

23°

7"

end view of roof and posts

Posts are inset 2" from the end of the gable.

180

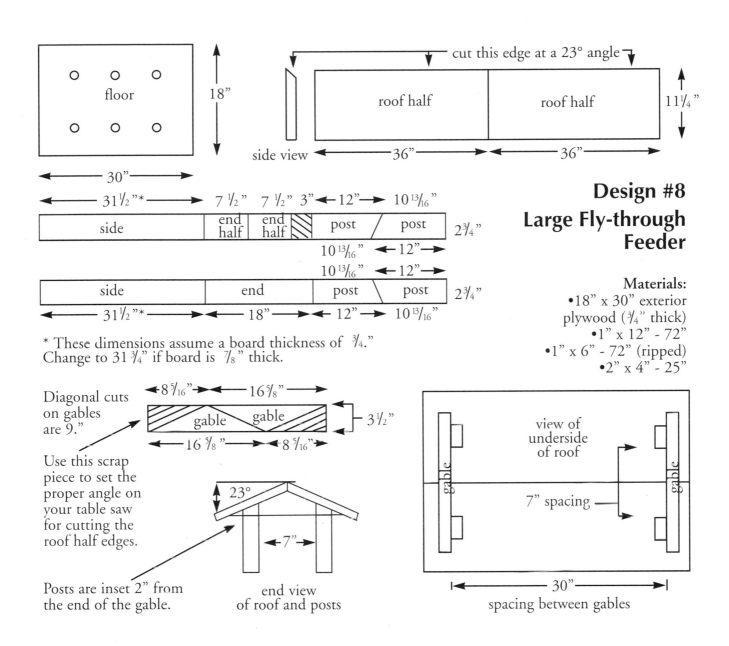

floor

18"

cut this edge at a 23° angle

roof half   roof half

11¼"

side view   ◄— 36" —► ◄— 36" —►

◄— 30" —►

◄—— 31½"* ——► 7½" 7½" 3" ◄—12"—► 10 13/16"

| side | end half | end half | | post | post | 2¾" |

10 13/16" ◄—12"—►

10 13/16" ◄—12"—►

| side | end | post | post | 2¾" |

◄——— 31½"* ———► ◄— 18" —► ◄— 12" —► 10 13/16"

**Design #8
Large Fly-through
Feeder**

Materials:
•18" x 30" exterior
plywood (¾" thick)
•1" x 12" - 72"
•1" x 6" - 72" (ripped)
•2" x 4" - 25"

* These dimensions assume a board thickness of ¾."
Change to 31¾" if board is ⅞" thick.

Diagonal cuts
on gables
are 9."

◄8 5/16"► ◄—16 5/8"—►

gable   gable

3½"

◄—16 5/8"—► ◄8 5/16"►

Use this scrap
piece to set the
proper angle on
your table saw
for cutting the
roof half edges.

23°

◄—7"—►

Posts are inset 2" from
the end of the gable.

end view
of roof and posts

view of
underside
of roof

gable   gable

7" spacing

◄——— 30" ———►

spacing between gables

This free-standing fly-through
feeder has end pieces with legs.

181

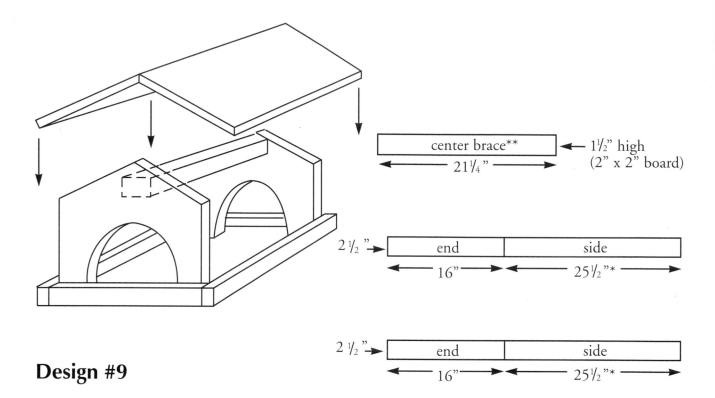

center brace**
21¼"

← 1½" high
(2" x 2" board)

2½" → | end | side |
16" 25½"*

2½" → | end | side |
16" 25½"*

Design #9

Ahlgren "Humongous" Feeder

* Change to 25¾" if board is ⅞" thick.
** This length will vary if ends are not ¾" thick.
Measure after the ends are in place.

Materials:
- 48" x 48" - ¾"
  exterior plywood
- 2" x 2" - 22½"
- 2 - 1" x 3" - 41¾"

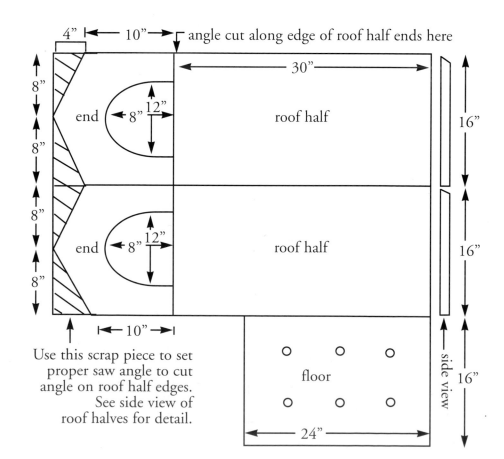

4" ← 10" → ⌐ angle cut along edge of roof half ends here

8" | end | (8" 12") | 30" roof half | 16"

8"

8" | end | (8" 12") | roof half | 16"

8"

← 10" →

side view

Use this scrap piece to set
proper saw angle to cut
angle on roof half edges.
See side view of
roof halves for detail.

floor

24"

16"

width. The techniques for cutting out this feeder are similar to those used for the medium fly-through feeder.

Ahlgren humongous feeder

This feeder design was developed by Dave Ahlgren of Stillwater, Minnesota. It is called the humongous feeder because, according to Dave, that's what people usually say when they see how large it is. It has the same floor dimensions as the medium fly-through feeder, but it is made from a half sheet of 3/4-inch thick exterior plywood. This is an extremely sturdy feeder that still provides good visibility for the birds so they can watch for approaching predators.

One advantage of this feeder is that an old cookie sheet can be set inside and periodically lifted out for easy cleaning.

This view shows the inside detail of the Ahlgren humongous feeder. The original designer, Dave Ahlgren, has redesigned the feeder by raising the 2-inch by 2-inch board so that it's tight against the roof sections. Drive screws or nails through the roof sections near the peak and into the 2 x 2 board for additional support.

The Ahlgren feeder has the same size base as a medium fly-through feeder, but the roof and end sections are all made from plywood. There are no gable pieces to cut.

SCREEN FEEDERS

Screen feeders are a relatively new type of feeder that provides an open, unobstructed field of view for the birds and a screen floor that allows wet seeds to immediately dry out from below. This reduces the chance of toxic mold developing in the seeds. It is excellent for all larger seeds like black oil sunflower seeds. White proso millet cannot be used in screen feeders; it is so small that it falls through the screen. The screen used for these feeders—1/8 by 1/8 wire screen like that used for screen doors—can be purchased at most hardware stores.

Hanging screen feeders are easy to make and well-used by birds. This feeder is being visited by a female cardinal. The advantage of this feeder is that the screen on the bottom allows the seeds to dry out faster whenever it rains or snows.

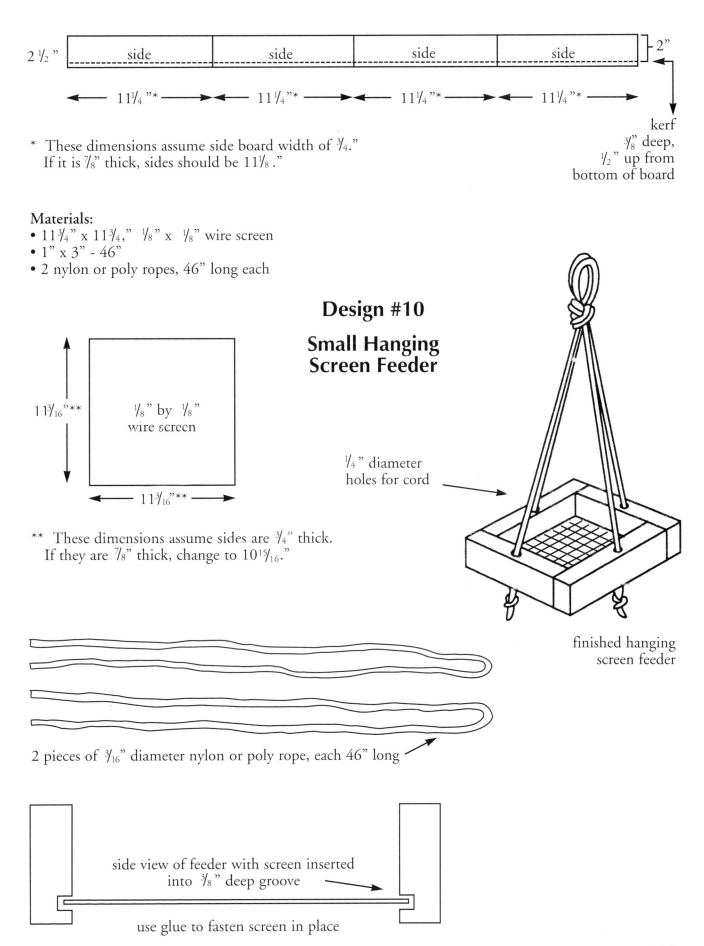

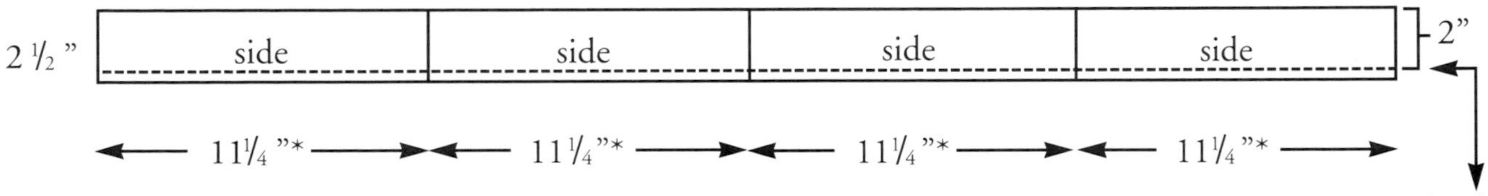
2 $\frac{1}{2}$"
side
side
side
side
2"
$11\frac{1}{4}$"*
$11\frac{1}{4}$"*
$11\frac{1}{4}$"*
$11\frac{1}{4}$"*
kerf
$\frac{3}{8}$" deep,
$\frac{1}{2}$" up from
bottom of board

* These dimensions assume side board width of $\frac{3}{4}$."
If it is $\frac{7}{8}$" thick, sides should be $11\frac{1}{8}$."

Materials:

- $11\frac{3}{4}$" x $11\frac{3}{4}$," $\frac{1}{8}$" x $\frac{1}{8}$" wire screen
- 1" x 3" - 46"
- 2 nylon or poly ropes, 46" long each

Design #10

Small Hanging Screen Feeder

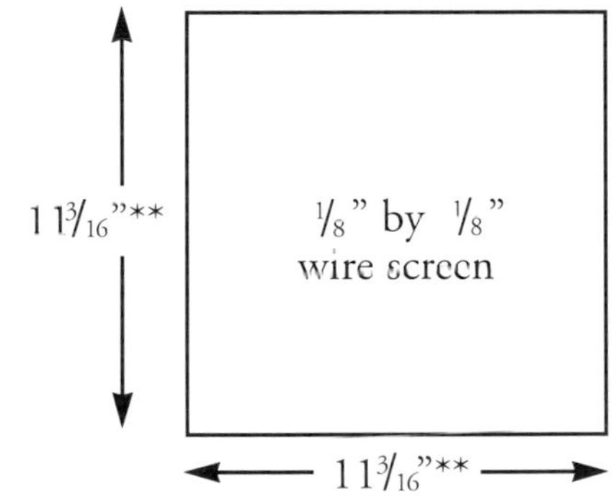
$11\frac{3}{16}$"**
$\frac{1}{8}$" by $\frac{1}{8}$"
wire screen
$11\frac{3}{16}$"**

** These dimensions assume sides are $\frac{3}{4}$" thick.
If they are $\frac{7}{8}$" thick, change to $10\frac{15}{16}$."

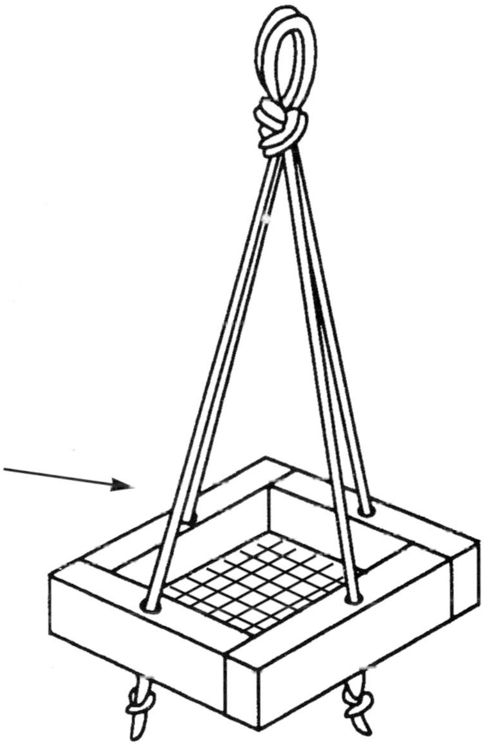
$\frac{1}{4}$" diameter
holes for cord

finished hanging screen feeder

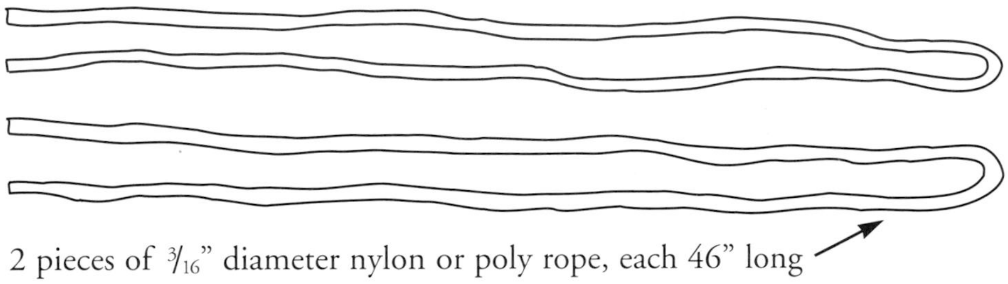

2 pieces of $\frac{3}{16}$" diameter nylon or poly rope, each 46" long

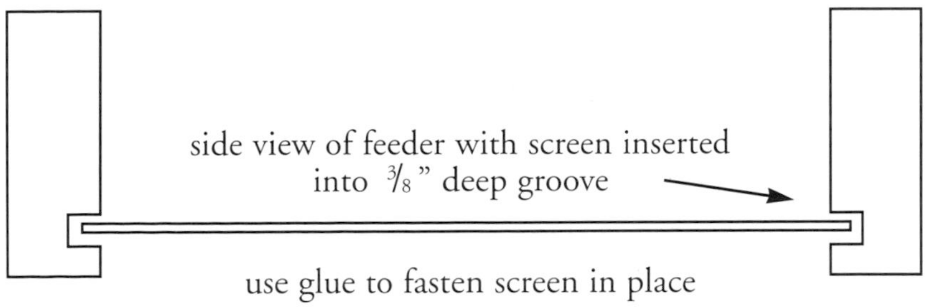
side view of feeder with screen inserted
into $\frac{3}{8}$" deep groove

use glue to fasten screen in place

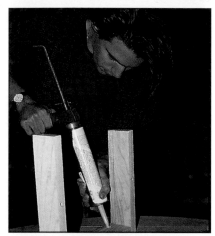

Small hanging screen feeder

The small hanging screen feeder is a simple design that would be good for young people to assemble as part of a nature or bird study. Try stocking these feeders with black oil sunflower seeds to attract a wide variety of birds. Cardinals, blue jays and chickadees quickly learn to use this feeder; they usually perch temporarily on the ropes before hopping down into this hanging feeder to eat.

This design shows a kerf groove for the wire screen. Use a caulking gun with industrial adhesive to lay a line of glue into the groove to help hold the screen in place. If you do not have a table saw to create the kerf, simply staple the wire screen to the bottom of the feeder frame. You could also cut 3/8 of an inch off the bottom of the side units, staple the wire screen to the new bottom, and then reattach what you cut off to cover the screen on the bottom of the feeder frame. Assembly steps for the small screen feeder are pictured on the left:

- Cut out the board for the sides and, if desired, make the kerf for inserting the screen. Then cut the board into its four equal parts and fasten three sides together.

- If you're using a kerf, place glue in the groove to help hold the screen in place.

- Mark the screen with a square and cut out the screen with tin snips. Remember, the screen's dimensions depend on the thickness of the wood used. If you're using a kerf, allow for a groove that is 3/8 inch deep.

- Slip the screen into the kerf groove, if you have one, or else staple the screen to the bottom of the feeder.

- Fasten the fourth side to the feeder.

- Drill a 1/4-inch diameter hole through the feeder sides, insert the rope and tie the ends.

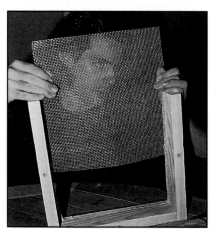

186

Ahlgren wonder trays are small screen feeders on legs that get all kinds of interesting visitors--including mallard ducks and cottontail rabbits.

Design #11

Ahlgren "Wonder Tray" Medium Screen Feeder

$12\frac{1}{4}$ "* $\frac{1}{8}$ " x $\frac{1}{8}$ " wire screen

$18\frac{3}{4}$ "

* This dimension is based on $\frac{3}{4}$ " thickness of ends and sides. Change to 12" for $\frac{7}{8}$ " thick boards.

Materials:
- $12\frac{1}{4}$ " x $18\frac{3}{4}$ " wire screen ($\frac{1}{8}$ " x $\frac{1}{8}$ ")
- 1" x 12" - 26"
- 1" x 3" - 36"
- 13" dowel, $\frac{3}{8}$ " diameter

finished wonder tray

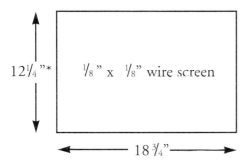

Drill $\frac{13}{32}$ " diameter hole for inserting $\frac{3}{8}$ " dowel as support under screen.

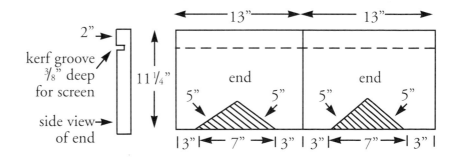

2"

kerf groove $\frac{3}{8}$ " deep for screen

side view of end

$11\frac{1}{4}$ "

13"   13"

end   end

5"   5"   5"   5"

3"   7"   3"   3"   7"   3"

$\frac{3}{8}$ " dowel

13"

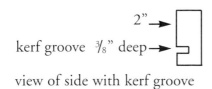

2"

kerf groove $\frac{3}{8}$ " deep

view of side with kerf groove

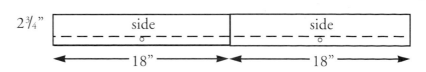

$2\frac{3}{4}$ "

side   side

18"   18"

To assemble an Ahlgren wonder tray feeder, first cut out the two end pieces and the two sides. Then run all four pieces of wood through the saw after setting the kerf groove 3/8" deep and 2 inches from the top edges of the feeder. Fit the two ends to one side.

Fill the kerf with glue to help hold the screen in place.

Right: Add the other side piece.

Above: Finally, drill a hole for a dowel just under the screen on both sides of the feeder. After the dowel is inserted, it helps keep the screen from sagging when it is filled with seed.

Design #12

Large Screen Feeder

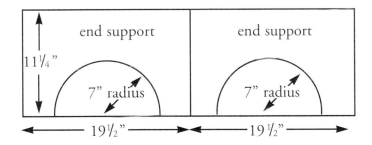

8½" space between bottom supports

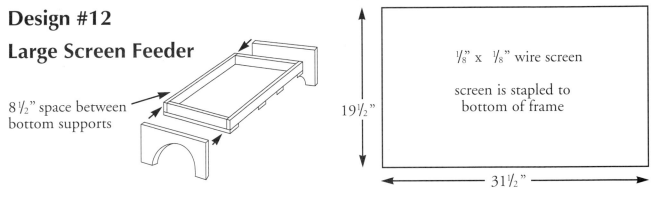

⅛" x ⅛" wire screen

screen is stapled to bottom of frame

19½"

31½"

2¾"	side	end
2¾"	side	end

31½"   18"*

* 18" for ¾" thick board; 17¾" for ⅞" thick board.

Materials:
- ¾" x 19½" - 31½" wire screen
- 2 - 1" x 3" - 60"
- 1" x 2" - 78"
- 1" x 12" - 39"

1½"	bottom support	bottom support	bottom support	bottom support
	19½"	19½"	19½"	19½"

end support	end support
7" radius	7" radius

11¼"

19½"   19½"

The large screen feeder is fitted with a 1/8" by 1/8" screen on the bottom.
The screen can be stapled directly onto the bottom if you don't have a saw that can create a kerf.
You can also rip 3/8" off the bottom of the side pieces, staple on the screen, and then replace the cut off bottoms.

189

The Perry extra large screen feeder has an extra divider across the middle to give the feeder extra strength. This feeder provides a lot of space for the feeding birds. A different seed mix can be used on each side.

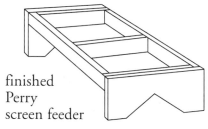

finished
Perry
screen feeder

Design #13

Perry Extra Large Screen Feeder

Materials:
- 24¾" x 48¾" wire screen (⅛" x ⅛")
- 1" x 12" - 51"
- 2 pieces of 1" x 3" - 72"
- 1" x 3" - 23¼"

⅛" x ⅛" wire screen

staple to the bottom of frame

24¾"*

48¾"

24¾"*   24¾"*

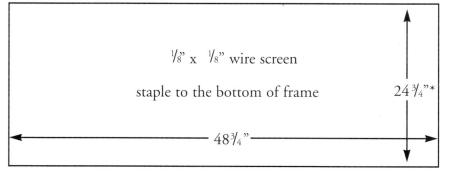

12⅜"   end support | end support   11¼"

4"   6"   6"   4"

16¾"   16¾"

* This dimension assumes side pieces are ½" thick.
Change to 24⅞" if sides are ⅞" thick.

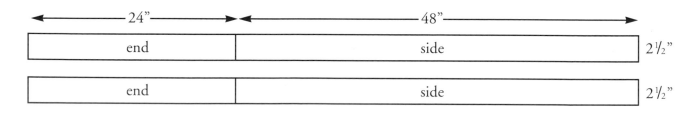

24"   48"

| end | side | 2½" |

| end | side | 2½" |

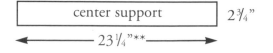

| center support | 2¾" |

23¼"**

** This dimension assumes sides are ¾" thick.
Change to 23⅛" if sides are ⅞" thick.

Ahlgren wonder tray medium screen feeder

The medium screen feeder design was also developed by Dave Ahlgren. He calls it the wonder tray because it is so successful in attracting birds that it makes you wonder what will show up next. Mallard ducks and cottontail rabbits might use this feeder when it is stocked with shelled corn. Rabbits do look a little unusual sitting in the tray, but at least you know that when they're in your bird feeder they're not eating flowers in your garden.

These feeders are lightweight and easy to make. Remember that before you insert the wire screen into the kerf grooves you should put a line of adhesive along the groove to help fasten the wire to the frame.

Staple the screen to the bottom of your Perry screen feeder's frame.

Large screen feeder

Large screen feeders provide a substantial 18 by 30-inch surface for birds to feed on. The end supports serve as legs so the feeder can be placed in an open area where birds can see approaching predators. This feeder can also be placed under a hanging feeder to catch fallen waste seed. Ground-feeding birds like mourning doves, white-throated sparrows and dark-eyed juncos do not hesitate to use this feeder.

Perry extra large screen feeder

Perry extra large screen feeders were developed by Ken and Pam Perry of Brainerd, Minnesota, to feed the wide variety of songbirds that visit their yard. This extra large feeder allows many birds to use it at one time and, because of the screen on the bottom, still keeps the feed relatively dry. The divider in the middle provides structural support and gives you the option of providing sunflower seeds on one side and perhaps shelled corn, safflower or a mixture of seeds on the other side.

The feeder is low enough that ground-feeding birds readily use it. This type of feeder is well used by dark-eyed juncos, pine siskins, blue jays, white-throated sparrows, northern cardinals, black-capped chickadees, indigo buntings, purple finches, mourning doves and ring-necked pheasants. Varied thrushes will also use this feeder.

A completed frame with the screen in place.

Wood strips are screwed onto the bottom of the screen edges to keep the edges from fraying.

A completed feeder.

191

CHALET FEEDERS

Rustad chalet feeder

The chalet feeder design was provided by Orwin Rustad of Faribault, Minnesota. This feeder has several desirable features and has worked very well. The seeds stay dry, and you can divide the feeder into sections for sunflower seeds and shelled corn. Blue jays prefer the kernels of corn.

After cutting out this feeder, you will want to prefit all the pieces. You may need to trim some of the edges before you do any nailing if your cuts were not exact.

When constructing a Rustad chalet feeder, make a 33-degree beveled cut to accommodate the sloping roof.

Before fastening all the pieces together, prefit them to make sure they fit tightly.

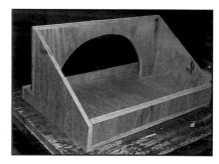

Rear view of the chalet feeder (above) and a completed feeder (below).

The Rustad chalet feeder is an attractive feeder that keeps bird food dry.

Materials:
¾" exterior plywood, pieces as follows:
- 23" x 31¾" roof
- 3¾" x 28¼" back
- 15⅞" x 29¾" front and front edge
- 19" x 28¼" floor
- 2   13¾" x 19" sides

Design #14
Rustad Chalet Feeder

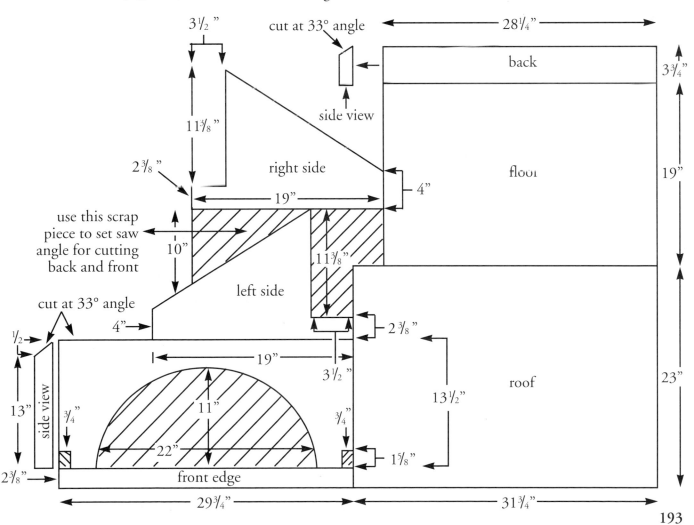

SELF FEEDERS

Self feeders, also known as hopper feeders or bin feeders, have reservoirs that can be filled periodically. The seeds flow out at the bottom of the feeder as they are removed and eaten by birds.

These feeders need to be filled only once every week or so. The best ones have Plexiglas® or glass sides that make it easy to see when you need to refill the feeder. You should check these feeders every few days because sometimes seeds jam in the feeder spout (like on the hanging pop bottle feeder) or there may be squirrel damage to repair.

If you have a choice between Plexiglas® and glass in a self-feeder, like in Designs #15 or 16, pick glass. Squirrels can easily chew through Plexiglas®, destroying the feeder in minutes. You may, however, wish to make an exception and use Plexiglas® if children are assembling the feeder because they might cut themselves while handling the glass.

Female evening grosbeaks visit a small self feeder.

Small self feeder

The small self feeder is one of the best all-around standard feeders that will be used by a great variety of songbirds. The feeder can be fastened to the railing of a deck, to the top of a pipe or post, or, if the roof section is screwed shut, suspended from a tree branch. If a squirrel baffle is placed under the feeder on a pipe or post, this feeder can be relatively squirrel-proof.

The advantage of this feeder is that the seeds are kept dry, and they continue to flow out as birds eat them.

Medium self feeder

The medium self feeder has a larger seed capacity than the small self feeder, but all its other benefits are similar. This feeder will be used by northern cardinals, tufted titmice, purple finches, house finches, goldfinches, chickadees, brown thrashers, dark-eyed juncos, nuthatches, evening grosbeaks and many other species.

Here are some steps to help you construct your self feeder. Board dimensions can be found in the next pages.

Above: Side pieces are attached to the ends of the feeder tray.

Above left: This ventral view of the roof sections shows the gables in place. The gables must have a 12-inch space between them on the small self feeder and a 16-inch space on the medium self feeder.

Left: The roof unit is designed to tilt for filling. The divider piece has been attached to the floor to force the feed to the sides. Notice the kerf grooves in the side piece for the glass.

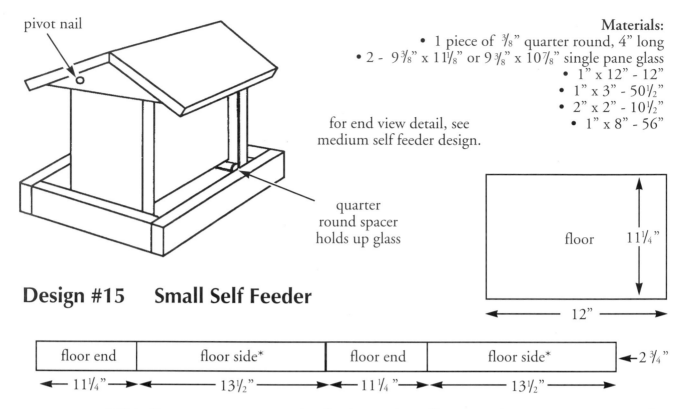

pivot nail

Materials:
- 1 piece of ⅜" quarter round, 4" long
- 2 - 9⅜" x 11⅛" or 9⅜" x 10⅞" single pane glass
- 1" x 12" - 12"
- 1" x 3" - 50½"
- 2" x 2" - 10½"
- 1" x 8" - 56"

for end view detail, see
medium self feeder design.

quarter
round spacer
holds up glass

floor   11¼"

12"

Design #15   Small Self Feeder

floor end	floor side*	floor end	floor side*

←─ 2¾"

←─ 11¼" ─→ ←──── 13½" ────→ ←─ 11¼" ─→ ←──── 13½" ────→

* This dimension assumes wood is ¾" thick. If it is ⅞" thick, floor sides should be 13¾".

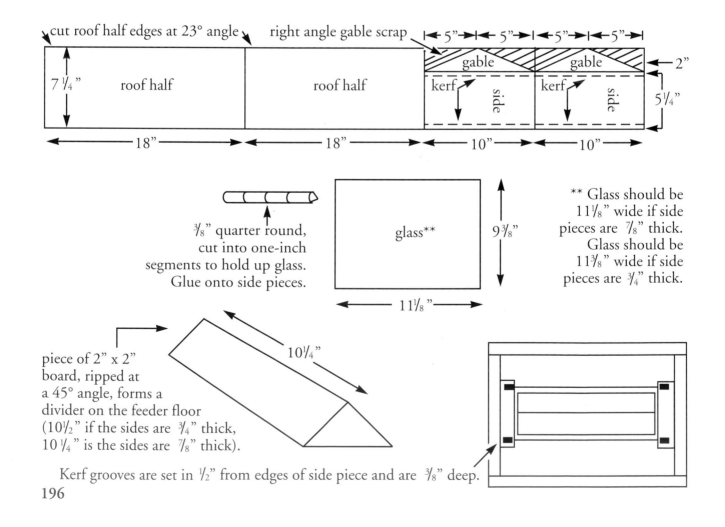

cut roof half edges at 23° angle   right angle gable scrap   ├─5"─┤├─5"─┤├─5"─┤├─5"─┤

7¼"   roof half   roof half   gable   gable   2"

                                          kerf   kerf
                                               side   side   5¼"

←──── 18" ────→ ←──── 18" ────→ ←── 10" ──→ ←── 10" ──→

⅜" quarter round,
cut into one-inch
segments to hold up glass.
Glue onto side pieces.

glass**   9⅜"

11⅛"

** Glass should be
11⅛" wide if side
pieces are ⅞" thick.
Glass should be
11⅜" wide if side
pieces are ¾" thick.

piece of 2" x 2"
board, ripped at
a 45° angle, forms a
divider on the feeder floor
(10½" if the sides are ¾" thick,
10¼" is the sides are ⅞" thick).

10¼"

Kerf grooves are set in ½" from edges of side piece and are ⅜" deep.

196

Design #16
Medium Self Feeder

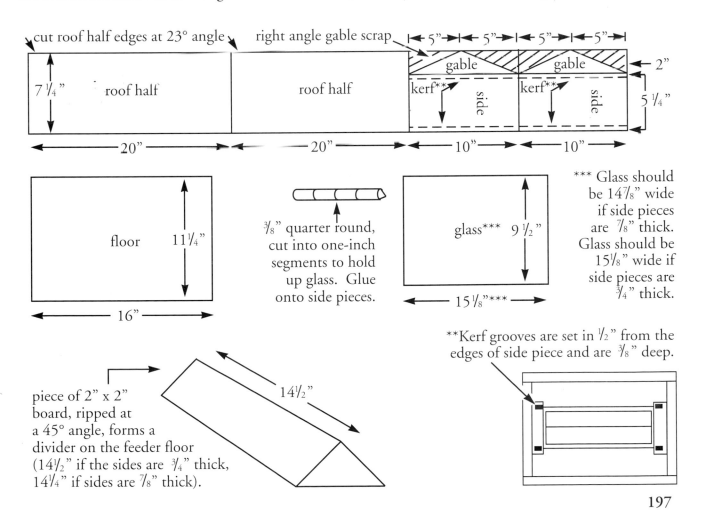

Materials:
- 1 piece of ⅜" quarter round, 4" long
- 2 - 9½" x 14⅞" or 9½" x 15⅛" single pane glass
- 1" x 12" - 16"
- 1" x 8" - 60"
- 1" x 3" - 58"
- 2" x 2" - 14½"

pivot hole for nail

end view detail (same for medium and small feeder)

⅜" above

3" from pivot hole to outer gable edge

nail and ⅜" between nail and bottom of roof

kerf grooves for glass

quarter-round for spacer

5½"

16"

10"

gable side side gable

20"

underside of roof section

| floor end | floor side* | floor end | floor side* | ← 2½" |

11¼"   17½"   11¼"   17½"

* Floor sides should be 17½" long if wood is ¾" thick, and they should be 17¾" long if wood is ⅞" thick.

cut roof half edges at 23° angle

right angle gable scrap

5" 5" 5" 5"

7¼"   roof half   roof half   gable   gable   ← 2"

kerf** side   kerf** side   5¼"

20"   20"   10"   10"

floor   11¼"

16"

⅜" quarter round, cut into one-inch segments to hold up glass. Glue onto side pieces.

glass*** 9½"

15⅛"***

*** Glass should be 14⅞" wide if side pieces are ⅞" thick. Glass should be 15⅛" wide if side pieces are ¾" thick.

piece of 2" x 2" board, ripped at a 45° angle, forms a divider on the feeder floor (14½" if the sides are ¾" thick, 14¼" if sides are ⅞" thick).

14½"

**Kerf grooves are set in ½" from the edges of side piece and are ⅜" deep.

Grackle log roller on a self feeder.

Detail of log roller parts.

Grackle log roller

The grackle log roller was developed by Dr. Bernie Daniel of Cincinnati, Ohio, as a means of reducing grackle use at his wooden self feeders. He did not mind feeding a few grackles, but wintering grackles overwhelmed his feeders and prevented smaller birds from eating.

The log roller is a 1/2-inch diameter wooden dowel that is placed 2 inches above the perching ledges of a wooden self feeder. The dowel has screws in the ends that allow it to spin like a log in water whenever a grackle lands on it. After several moments of wild wing flapping and confusion, the grackle leaves.

The log roller also deters feeder use by starlings and cowbirds, but smaller birds like finches, tufted titmice, chickadees, cardinals, blue jays and red-bellied woodpeckers can reach under the dowel and are not prevented from feeding.

To make the grackle log roller, you need two pieces of 1/2-inch diameter dowel that are the length of each side of the self feeder, four 3 1/4-inch cotter pins and four 1-inch stainless steel screws. These pieces allow you to put a grackle log roller on each side of a self feeder. Dowels need to be treated with wood preservative, or they will rot rapidly.

The cotter pins are installed on the corners of the feeder by drilling 3/32-inch diameter holes 1/2-inch deep. Each hole should be located so that the eye of the cotter pin is 2 1/4 inches above the outer edge of the feeder tray. Drive the cotter pins into the holes with a tack hammer. Cut the dowel so that it fits just inside the two cotter pins.

Drill a hole into the center of each end of the dowels with a bit that is slightly smaller than the stainless steel screws. Insert each stainless steel screw through the eye of the cotter pin and into the hole in the dowel so that the dowel spins freely and is 2 inches above the edge of the feeder where smaller birds will stand.

Rustic tree bark feeder

This commercial feeder is made from tree slab wood. The bark gives it a natural look that many people enjoy and provides birds such as chickadees with a firm base on which to crack seeds. Seeds, suet, suet mixes or even mealworms can be placed

A hairy woodpecker visits a wooden rustic tree bark feeder.

inside this feeder to attract chickadees, nuthatches, woodpeckers and other birds. Look for this type of feeder at wild bird specialty stores or craft fairs.

Cylindrical feeders

There are many types of commercially-made cylindrical feeders that have large feeding ports to accommodate sunflower and other large seeds. Most of them have clear sides so you can see how much seed is left in the feeder. They usually have multiple ports that allow more than six birds to feed at once. Some have dividers that allow several types of seed to be provided in different compartments.

Smaller birds like purple finches, goldfinches, house finches, pine siskins and redpolls readily use these feeders. Perches are usually provided below the feeder ports, but some have perches above the ports to discourage use by house finches. This is used mainly in the eastern United States where house finches are so numerous that they prevent other birds from using the feeders. The best cylindrical feeders have metal feeding ports to prevent squirrel damage.

This feeder has metal fittings to deter squirrel damage. It has multiple compartments and in this photo is being visited by house finches.

Purple finches are using this cylindrical feeder.

A white-breasted nuthatch, chickadee, female purple finch and pine siskin are visiting this feeder. Notice the yellow wing highlights on the pine siskin.

This Gilbertson PVC feeder was filled with white proso millet in the summer especially to attract indigo buntings.

The Gilbertson PVC cylindrical feeder has proven to be an effective almost-squirrel-proof bird feeder used by a wide variety of songbirds. The perches are made of spring-steel, and they flop down whenever a squirrel tries to feed at either of the two feeder ports. Squirrels have so much momentum when they jump onto a feeder placed at least 5 feet out from the trunk of a tree, and on a wire at least 3 feet long, that they can't hold on to the perches.

Cylindrical feeders can also be suspended from wagon wheel supports on top of posts or pipes that are at least 10 feet high. When the support post or pipe has squirrel baffles installed, it will protect all the feeders suspended from the wagon wheel support. See the feeders on page 245.

Goldfinches use a thistle feeder during the winter.

The Craigmile PVC feeder, left, comes with feeder ports either for larger seeds or Niger thistle. Photo by Art Craigmile.

The Gilberston PVC feeder, below, is durable and usually squirrel-proof.

Thistle feeders are popular with goldfinches all year long.

Niger thistle feeder

Thistle seed feeders are an essential component of any bird feeding operation. A feeder stocked with Niger thistle seed will attract goldfinches all year long. It will also attract pine siskins, redpolls and an occasional indigo bunting.

Niger thistle feeders have very small slits that prevent birds with larger bills from removing the feed. Sunflower chips can also be used in these feeders, alone or mixed with thistle seed. However, the sunflower chips take on moisture more readily than thistle seed, so you will need to check the feeder more frequently to ensure that condensation inside the feeder is not causing mold. The best thistle feeders have multiple ports and some have metal fittings to discourage chewing by squirrels.

In eastern regions, house finches have been known to overwhelm thistle feeders and prevent other birds from using them. If this becomes a problem, shorten the perches. Use a hacksaw to cut the perches to 5/8 inch long. House finches find it difficult to use such short perches.

Thistle feeders can also be made from 2-liter pop bottles, but it is important to cut the feeder holes small enough that the seed does not spill out. A heated wire or the heated tip of a screwdriver can be used to burn feeder holes in the plastic pop bottles.

Instructions for making 2-liter pop bottle feeders can be found on pages 202 through 204.

Window stick-on feeder

Window stick-on feeders are small clear plastic feeders with suction cups that allow you to watch birds close up while they pick at the sunflower seeds. Wet the rubber suction cups before attaching them so you get a better seal.

Some of the feeders have small, hopper-fed reservoirs for seeds and others simply have a small seed compartment. These feeders don't hold much seed, but they are surprisingly effective for attracting chickadees, goldfinches, house finches and even cardinals, rose-breasted grosbeaks, nuthatches and indigo buntings.

These feeders are great for children to place on the windows of their rooms. They are also excellent for large picture windows because they help reduce the chance of birds flying into them. Try placing one or two stick-on feeders on windows where bird-strikes are a problem. When the birds see the feeders they are alerted that the window is present and they may fly to the feeder instead of flying into the glass.

Make sure these feeders are placed in the center of the window to make it difficult for squirrels or raccoons to reach. If the feeders are too close to the lower sill of the window or too close to either side, the squirrels will jump up, eat all the seeds, and probably chew up the feeder.

Window ledge feeder

A window ledge feeder can bring many birds right up to your window. You can use 8, 10 or 12-inch wide lumber to construct a frame that is fastened outside the window you select for viewing the birds. Dimensions will vary depending on the size of the window.

Trays with screen bottoms can be fitted to the inside of the frame to provide feeding surfaces.

Hanging 2-liter pop bottle feeder

Hanging 2-liter pop bottle feeders are very economical and effective feeders for many kinds of birds. Plastic or cast metal ports can be purchased and screwed onto the neck of an empty 2-liter plastic pop bottle. When the bottle is hung upside down, birds can eat the seeds that flow through the spout.

To fill this feeder, make a refilling funnel from another 2-liter pop bottle. Cut the bottle in half, making a funnel from the top half. Place your index finger over the spout, fill the funnel with seeds, match up the spouts of the two bottles and remove your finger.

This simple feeder has been a most heavily-used bird feeder. It is visited by cardinals, blue jays,

Small stick-on feeders can help decrease the number of birds flying into large windows.

Window ledge feeders allow you to see birds at close range.

Note the dowel placement and the feeder hole on a pop bottle feeder.

This is a homemade pop bottle feeder that hangs upside down. A small dowel provides a perch for the birds. A feeder hole is cut about two inches above each dowel.

Even larger birds like blue jays, cardinals and red-winged blackbirds will use these pop bottle feeders.

red-winged blackbirds and lots of house finches. You can stock your pop bottle feeder with black oil sunflower seeds, millet mixes, sunflower chips or peanut hearts.

Bottle feeders can also be made by drilling a 3/8-inch diameter hole through the neck area or cap of a plastic 2-liter pop bottle. Insert a 3/8-inch dowel through the hole so it extends out on both sides of the feeder about 4 inches. Depending on what size seeds you plan to use in the bottle, either cut, drill or burn it with a heated nail, screwdriver tip or large wire to create feeder port holes. They should be about 1-1/2 to 2 inches above the perches.

To use Niger thistle mixed with sunflower chips and peanut hearts, make feeder holes about 3/16 inch in diameter. If you're supplying black oil sunflower seeds, the feeder holes should be about 5/16 inch in diameter.

Using this feeder with the cap end down allows moisture to accumulate inside the cap. Seeds may germinate inside the cap, and they

You can buy a metal feeder fitting at most wild bird stores. This feeder is being visited by a red-breasted nuthatch.

This feeder has a hook screwed into the cap. A dowel fits through the base and there is a 3/8″-diameter hole about 2 inches above each dowel.

This female rose-breasted grosbeak uses a counter-weighted feeder that closes when a squirrel stands on the front.

may also mold. Be sure to frequently take your feeder down and check the cap area to keep it free of moldy or germinating seeds.

According to Peggy Jones of East Bethel, Minnesota, these feeders make great children's gifts, and also work well for nature classes. She uses a mixture of half Niger thistle and half sunflower chips in these feeders to attract goldfinches, pine siskins and redpolls.

Counter-weighted feeder

Counter-weighted feeders have feeding troughs in the front and counter-weighted balances in the back. Originally marketed with the trade name "Hi-larious bird feeder®," they can be adjusted to close in front when a heavy animal like a squirrel stands on the perch. There are now other feeders on the market that use the same principle.

The feeders are made of metal to prevent damage by gnawing squirrels. They cost about $40 to $50, but will save a considerable amount of money in the long run because squirrels won't eat or waste the bird feed. This feeder is not raccoon-proof, however. Dr. Walter Breckenridge of Minneapolis has had a raccoon lay on top of the feeder with its hind legs holding the counterweight up while it eats seeds from the front.

Blue jays, rose-breasted grosbeaks, black-capped chickadees and northern cardinals adapt readily to this feeder.

204

Woven wire fence pheasant feeder

If you have access to ear corn from a farmer or a feed store you can use an extremely simple and effective cylinder of woven wire fence to feed pheasants during the winter. All you need is a 3 1/2 to 4-foot long section of woven wire fence or a section of 2 by 4-inch welded wire garden fence. Both should be 3 feet high. You don't need new fencing to make this feeder; you can use old woven wire farm fencing that has been discarded.

Roll the wire into a cylinder that is 12 to 16 inches in diameter and fasten the cylinder with wire. Set the cylinder on a pallet on the downwind (southeast) side of good winter cover as described for the Olson barrel feeder. Fill the cylinder with ear corn. You may need to put wire over the top to keep squirrels from removing entire ears.

Woven wire fence feeders were designed for use with ear corn. The feeders should be placed near winter cover used by pheasants.

Michael and Andrew Henderson of Zearing, Iowa, had to refill their pheasant feeder three times one winter because of the high number of visiting pheasants. Photo by Don Henderson.

205

Olson barrel feeder

Olson barrel feeders were developed in 1975 by Minnesota DNR heavy equipment operator Art Olson of Milan, Minnesota. They were intended as an efficient way to feed deer in state parks and wildlife management areas where shelled corn, rather than ear corn, was available. The feeder has proven very successful and is readily used by pheasants and wild turkeys as well as deer. This feeder uses two 55-gallon metal barrels that can hold large supplies of shelled corn to feed wildlife during the winter.

Select two 55-gallon barrels that have not been used for storage of flammable materials. Cutting barrels that have held flammable materials could cause the barrels to explode! Cut one barrel in half with an acetylene torch. The two halves will be used as tops for two feeders.

Cut an 8 by 10-inch hole in the end of each barrel half. These holes are used fill the feeders with shelled corn. A 1 by 10 by 12-inch board can be used to cover the holes. The bottom edge of each barrel half should be bent out with a hammer to make them easy to slip over the other barrel. When you are finished, set the tops aside.

Cut the top out of the second barrel and cut a 4-inch diameter circular hole in the center of that top. This will be pushed down to the folded-in rim just above the feeder openings and be used as a feeder plate. Take a 1-pound coffee can that is 4 inches in diameter and cut down 1 inch from one end to form tabs that will hold the can in place once it's in the feeder plate. Attach the tabs to the feeder plate with a couple small bolts and set the lid aside.

Cut three feeder holes in the bottom of the main barrel. The lower edge should be 3 1/2 inches above the bottom of the barrel. The holes should be 12 1/4 inches wide and 7 1/4 inches high. Extend the vertical cuts upward one extra inch to the center of the expanded rim of the barrel. Then fold in this rim above each feeder hole. The rim will hold the feeder plate in place. The feeder holes should be 10 1/4 inches apart.

Make drain holes in the bottom of the barrel. Then force the feeder plate down to the rims above the feeder holes. Place the top barrel section over the main barrel and push it down onto the barrel so there is at least 1/2-inch overlap. Bronze these barrels together in at least four places.

Set the barrel on concrete blocks or on a pallet to facilitate drainage. Set the barrel on the downwind side (usually the southeast side) of good winter cover, like a patch of switchgrass, sudex or corn, in a woodlot or on the edge of a farm grove or shelterbelt.

12"
10" board

8"
8"
18"
bend out this edge

feeder plate
6"
4"

bend in this edge

fold in
12 1/4 "
7 1/4 "
3 1/2 "
10 1/4 "
3 1/2 "
from bottom of barrel to lower edge of feeding hole.

drawing by Janice Orr

A double layer of half-inch mesh hardware cloth can be used to feed pheasants in the same manner as a woven wire pheasant feeder. This hardware cloth feeder is filled with shelled corn.

New hardware cloth feeder.

Hardware cloth pheasant feeder

Another simple feeder that works well to feed pheasants and wild turkeys during the winter is a cylinder of 1/2-inch mesh hardware cloth rolled to create a double thickness of wire. A single layer of this wire mesh allows the corn kernels to flow out too freely.

To make this feeder, purchase a piece of 1/2-inch mesh hardware cloth that is 65 to 75 inches long and 3 feet wide. Roll the wire into a cylinder that is approximately 10 to 12 inches in diameter. Keep rolling the wire to create a double thickness, and then fasten the roll with small wire fasteners or hog rings.

Since this roll could be easily tipped over, use a square piece of scrap exterior plywood, at least 24 inches on a side, to make a base for the feeder. Place the cylinder in the center of the board and draw an outline of the circle created by the wire. Temporarily remove the wire and drill several pairs of holes about 1/2-inch apart, bracketing the line that was drawn. Then you can wire the cylinder of hardware cloth onto the base through those holes. Place the plywood on four bricks to discourage mice and voles from living underneath.

207

SUET FEEDERS

Suet dispensers are very simple containers—wire cages, dowel containers or string bags— that hold suet for the birds. They will be used regularly by woodpeckers, nuthatches, chickadees and many other species. Since some animals will try to carry suet away from the feeder, it's a good idea to have it secured in the feeder.

A wire cage, string bag or dowel feeder is easy for birds to use but may eventually be overwhelmed by starling use. Some suet dispensers have been adapted to prevent starling visits. Design #17 provides a simple alternative: it forces birds to feed upside down. Since starlings cannot hang upside down while feeding, this feeder will only be used by chickadees, nuthatches and woodpeckers.

Wire cage feeders are easily used by woodpeckers, chickadees and nuthatches. This feeder has a shield on top to discourage use by starlings.

Wire cage feeder

Wire mesh of 1 by 1-inch chicken wire can be shaped to create a square, rectangular or cylindrical suet feeder that can be fastened to a post or suspended from a tree branch. The exposed wire may create problems for the birds by making their tongues stick to the wire in cold weather so some people eliminate potential problems by spraying the wire with an acrylic or plastic coating.

Commercially-made wire cages that hold square suet cakes are also available.

Starling-proof suet feeder

Starling-proof suet feeders have a relatively simple design that requires only one board (a 1 by 8-inch board that is 31 inches long), a piece of 1/2-inch mesh hardware cloth measuring 10 by 11 inches, a dowel and a piece of nylon or poly cord. This would be an easy feeder to make with children.

Starling-resistant suet feeders force birds to feed upside-down .

Starlings have weak feet and need to feed on suet feeders from above.

As mentioned above, starlings do not have strong leg muscles for hanging upside down like chickadees and woodpeckers do, so the suet placed in this feeder is unavailable to them. To fill the feeder, the roof section slides up on the rope.

String bag suet feeder

The simplest suet feeder is a discarded onion or potato string bag in which suet can be suspended from a tree branch. It's a very effective feeder and provides a constructive way to use kitchen waste materials. Extra bags can be given to local nature centers so they can distribute them at bird feeding classes.

Used onion or potato sacks make good suet feeders. The string bag feeder pictured is being used by a female downy woodpecker.

Assembly detail of the starling resistant feeder. The 7/8-inch dowel is inserted and glued into the holes on the end pieces and half-inch hardware cloth is stapled onto two sides of the resulting frame.

Materials:
- 11" x 10" hardware cloth ($\frac{1}{2}$" x $\frac{1}{2}$" mesh)
- 1" x 8" - 31"
- 9 $\frac{1}{2}$" dowel, $\frac{7}{8}$" diameter
- 21" nylon or poly cord

Design #17

Starling Proof Suet Feeder

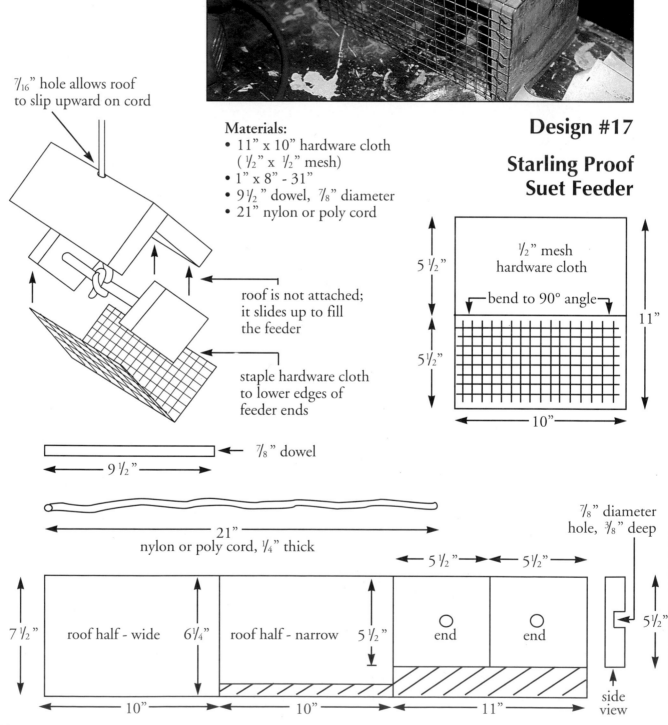

$\frac{7}{16}$" hole allows roof to slip upward on cord

roof is not attached; it slides up to fill the feeder

staple hardware cloth to lower edges of feeder ends

$\frac{7}{8}$" dowel

9 $\frac{1}{2}$"

21"
nylon or poly cord, $\frac{1}{4}$" thick

$\frac{1}{2}$" mesh hardware cloth

bend to 90° angle

5 $\frac{1}{2}$"

5 $\frac{1}{2}$"

11"

10"

$\frac{7}{8}$" diameter hole, $\frac{3}{8}$" deep

5 $\frac{1}{2}$"   5 $\frac{1}{2}$"

7 $\frac{1}{2}$"   roof half - wide   6 $\frac{1}{4}$"   roof half - narrow   5 $\frac{1}{2}$"   end   end   5 $\frac{1}{2}$"

10"   10"   11"   side view

210

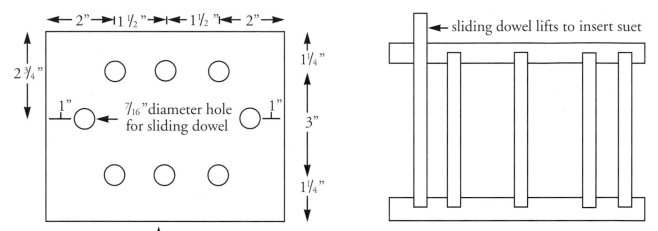

This diagram shows placement of dowel holes on the top and bottom pieces. Holes are ½" diameter and ½" deep, except that the floor hole for the sliding dowel is ½" deep, but the sliding dowel penetrates the roof and is lifted to insert suet.

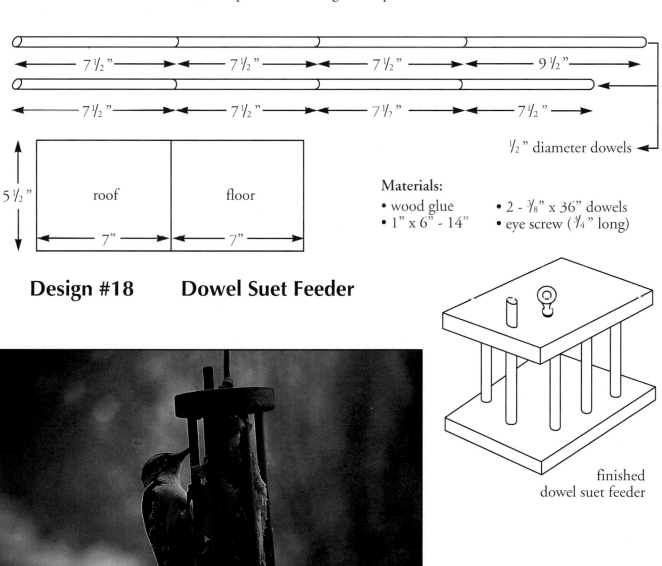

½" diameter dowels

Materials:
- wood glue
- 1" x 6" - 14"
- 2 - ⅜" x 36" dowels
- eye screw (¾" long)

Design #18   **Dowel Suet Feeder**

finished
dowel suet feeder

This feeder is being visited
by a hairy woodpecker.
Photo by Ethelle Henderson.

Dowel suet feeder

Dowel suet feeders are also easy to make. They require only a 14-inch long piece of 1 by 6-inch wood and 62 inches of 1/2-inch dowels. One dowel on the end is not glued in place, slipping upward to allow suet to be placed in the feeder. A screw eye allows the feeder to be suspended from a tree branch.

Hanging log suet feeders can be used with melted suet mixes, the Janilla suet mix, or peanut butter.

Hanging log suet feeder

This suet feeder is made from a 3 to 4-inch diameter section of a tree branch that is between 14 and 18 inches long. Look for a branch or small log with knobs or branches that can serve as perches. Drill holes above the perches with a 1 to 1 1/4-inch diameter drill bit.

Drill from 6 to 12 holes into the log, making sure each hole is about one inch deep. Place a screw eye in the end of the log to hang the feeder. Push peanut butter, suet, melted suet mix or the Janilla bluebird mix into the holes. You will be amazed at how successful and

A hairy woodpecker feeds at a hanging log suet feeder.

Design #19   Thorsnes Hanging Log Feeder

Materials:
- 1 log, 6" diameter, 16" long
- 1 screw eye
- ½" mesh hardware cloth, 12" by 12"

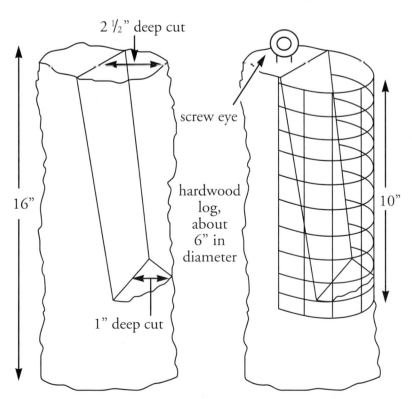

2 ½" deep cut

screw eye

16"

hardwood log, about 6" in diameter

10"

1" deep cut

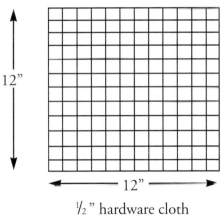

12"

12"

½ " hardware cloth

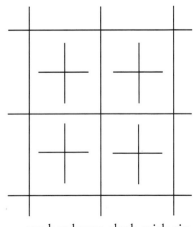

cut hardware cloth with tin snips to change to a 1" mesh

213

popular this feeder is with everything from chickadees to nuthatches and woodpeckers. This feeder is a good one to make with children, and they make nice gifts to foster people's interest in watching birds.

Thorsnes hanging log feeder

A log about 6 inches in diameter and 16 to 18 inches long can be used to make this rustic woodpecker feeder that holds large chunks of suet or deer fat. Cut a sloping vertical slice from the log that is about 2 1/2 inches back into the log and about 10 inches deep. Then cut out a piece of 1/2-inch mesh hardware cloth (at least 12 by 12 inches) that will cover the log over the cut area.

Staple the wire onto the log so that the feeder is open at the top and the wire overlaps the bark at least one inch on the sides and bottom of the cut edge. With a tin snips, cut out portions of the wire in the mesh to create a 1-inch wire mesh surface where the suet will be exposed to the birds for feeding. A large screw eye is fastened into the top of the feeder so it can be hung from a tree branch or other support.

Assembly detail for the Thorsnes hanging log suet feeder. The half-inch mesh hardware cloth has been clipped with tin snips to create a 1-inch mesh mesh over the feeding area.

A male downy woodpecker visits a Thorsnes hanging log suet feeder in the wintertime.

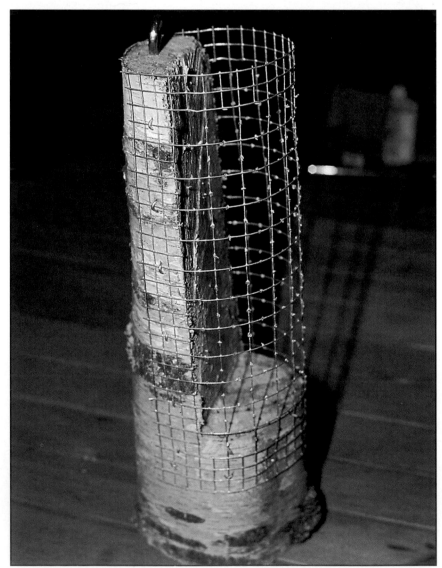

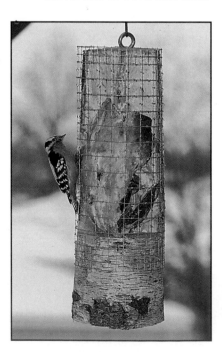

Coconut and pine cone suet feeders

Coconuts and pine cones can be used to make simple and effective suet and peanut butter feeders.

To make a coconut feeder, use a hacksaw with a 1/2-inch wide blade and 18 teeth per inch to cut a 70-degree angle slice from the upper portion of a coconut. Drill two small holes (3/32 or 1/8 inch in diameter) in the top of the coconut about 1-1/2 inches back from the cut edge. Clean out the coconut meat. Make a hook out of wire to hang the coconut feeder. Place suet, melted suet, peanut butter, Janilla bluebird suet mix or sunflower seeds in the feeder and hang it on your deck, porch or from a tree near your house. It won't be long before the first chickadee arrives.

Pine cones can be collected and used for suet feeders. Either smear peanut butter into the pine cone with a spatula, or dip the pine cone in a melted suet mix. The mix may need to be forced into the cone with a spatula. Hang the cones with string from tree branches, or arrange them into a mobile. You might want to hang them in front of a window to prevent birds from striking it.

Above left: Make a coconut feeder by cutting a 70-degree slice out of one side of a coconut and cleaning out the meat. Drill two small holes about 1 1/2 inches back from the top cut edge and insert a wire hook through the holes to hang the feeder.

Above right: Pine cones can be used to make simple bird feeders for chickadees and nuthatches. Just fill them with peanut butter or melted suet mixes.

Photos by Ethelle Henderson.

Coconut feeders can be filled with sunflower seeds, suet or suet mixes. A red-breasted nuthatch is feeding here.
Photo by Ethelle Henderson

NECTAR FEEDERS

There are many varieties of commercial hummingbird nectar feeders. Most of them have red plastic fittings and feeding ports that attract the hummingbirds.

Nectar feeders are excellent for attracting ruby-throated hummingbirds and northern orioles. Other birds that may visit nectar feeders are white-breasted nuthatches, downy woodpeckers and Tennessee warblers. Migrating warblers may visit nectar feeders that are filled in early May before the hummers return. If you have numerous hummingbirds competing for a nectar feeder, place additional feeders in nearby locations to reduce the territorial conflicts between the birds.

Commercial hummingbird feeders

Many kinds of commercial plastic and glass hummingbird feeders are available. Most have red coloring, including plastic red flowers, to attract the hummingbirds. The feeders have small holes into which the hummingbirds can insert their bills to feed on the sugar water. Sugar water is made according to the instructions given on page 149.

You might be able to increase hummingbird use by hanging a string bag of over-ripe fruit like bananas and cantaloupe near the nectar feeder to attract fruit flies. The hummingbirds will feed on both the nectar and the fruit flies. If bees become a problem, rub Avon Skin-so-soft® or Off Skintastic® onto the feeder surface by the feeder ports to repel the insects. Some feeders have bee guard grids over the ports.

In mid-summer you will need to take down the hummingbird feeder about twice a week, clean it out with a bleach solution, let it dry and refill it. If you don't do this, the sugar water will spoil and a black fungus will form. See page 249.

Hummingbird feeders can be hung on decks and porches or on trees near flower gardens for viewing enjoyment as the hummingbirds come and go. In the upper Midwest, place the feeders in late April to early May and take them down by late September. Don't worry about keeping the hummingbirds from migrating; they will go when they are ready.

The yellow grid on the upper left feeder serves as a bee guard. Oriole feeders normally have larger perches and orange fittings.

Commercial oriole nectar feeders

Commercially-made oriole nectar feeders usually have orange trim and use the same sugar-water solution as hummingbird feeders. They are hung from tree branches or deck supports. The only difference is that these feeders have larger perches for the orioles to stand on as they drink the sugar water solution.

Some feeders have springs on the perches that bend down when an oriole stands there. This opens the feeder port and allows the oriole to insert its bill. When the oriole leaves, the port closes and prevents bees from entering the hole. These feeders may also be used by white-breasted nuthatches, downy woodpeckers and ruby-throated hummingbirds. Oriole nectar feeders will also need to be cleaned frequently in warm weather to prevent fungus from growing in the sugar water.

The oriole feeder above has a spring-loaded perch and the feeder on the left has a bag of overripe fruit to attract fruit flies, which in turn attracts hummingbirds.

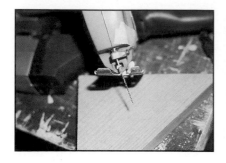
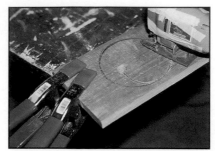

Top left: To make a hanging chick waterer oriole feeder, set your jigsaw blade to the same angle as that on the red plastic feeder base, so that the feeder will fit snugly into the base.

Top middle: Trace the feeder base outline onto the wooden base. Drill a half-inch starter hole so you can insert the saber saw. Cut out the hole.

Top right: A detail of the wooden base with the hole cut.

Lower right: Put the second base under the portion with the hole and fasten them together with glue and screws. Place screen door turnbuttons on the top to hold the red feeder base in place. Drill holes in the corners to attach the ropes.

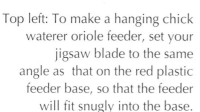

Chick-waterer oriole feeder

Most nectar feeders are commercially made, but there is one homemade design that is both easy and fun to make: the hanging chick waterer feeder for orioles. The key to making this feeder is to buy a chick watering jar (a quart jar with a plastic screw-on lid) from a farm or poultry supply store. When the jar is turned upside down, it works for watering chicks.

It works perfectly for sugar water, too. When this waterer is fitted into the hanging wooden base shown in Design #20, it will become a popular feeder for northern orioles. The pointed wooden dowels at the ends are for placement of orange halves early in the spring to attract the returning orioles. Once the orioles discover the sugar water, however, they tend to ignore the oranges. Orioles will typically land on the ropes that support this feeder, and then hop down to take a drink.

The sugar water does not need any coloring. You will need to check the sugar water frequently in warm weather and clean the bottle with a mild bleach solution whenever necessary. See page 249.

You can also make a good nectar solution for orioles by melting grape jelly and mixing it one-to-one with water. Place it in the chick waterer feeder.

218

A chick waterer can be used to make a very effective homemade oriole feeder. This feeder was regularly used by orioles.

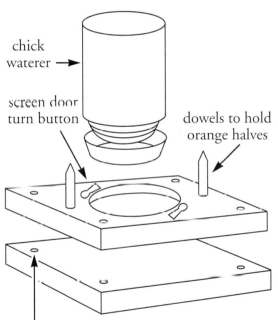

chick waterer →

screen door turn button →

← dowels to hold orange halves

Drill ⅜" diameter cord holes after fastening two boards together with glue and screws.

Design #20

Hanging Chick Waterer Oriole Feeder

Materials:
- 1" x 8" - 22"
- ½" diameter dowel, 6" long
- "S" hook to suspend feeder
- chick waterer
- 2 turn buttons to hold waterer in place
- 2 nylon or poly cords, 45" long each

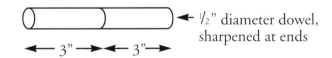

← ½" diameter dowel, sharpened at ends

← 3" → ← 3" →

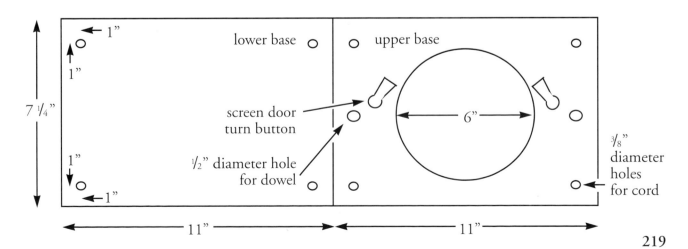

7 ¼"

1" → | 1" |

lower base ○ | ○ upper base

screen door turn button

½" diameter hole for dowel

6"

⅜" diameter holes for cord

1" | 1"

← 11" → ← 11" →

You can also make a good nectar solution for orioles by melting grape jelly and mixing it one-to-one with water. Place it in the chick waterer feeder.

MEALWORM FEEDERS

Mealworm feeders can provide a great amount of enjoyment by attracting birds, like bluebirds, that don't eat seeds. These feeders feature small, shallow, steep or vertical-sided trays that prevent mealworms from crawling out. You can use tuna cans, soup bowls, the clear plastic dishes sold in garden stores that prevent water from leaking out of flower pot bases and onto the furniture, or the clear plastic trays used in meat markets for small portions of meat. Place a rock in the center of these lightweight feeders to keep them from tipping over or blowing away.

The feeder should be placed where birds sitting on nearby trees, bushes or perches can look down and spot the moving mealworms. The movement attracts them to the feeder. Once the birds learn to visit the feeder they will return regularly for more mealworms. You will be amazed to see how many different bird species are attracted to mealworms.

Linda tray feeder

This tray is named for Linda Janilla who developed the Janilla bluebird suet mix that has been so popular with bluebirds, woodpeckers and other species that need a high protein diet. The whole feeder can be made from a 1-inch by 6-inch board that is only 3 feet long. Although it's not very large, this feeder is designed to be attached to a deck or patio support post or tree where you can get a close-up view of the birds visiting the feeder.

The Linda feeder is a small but very effective feeder to use in a porch or deck area. When filled with sunflower seeds it will attract birds ranging from redpolls (shown here) to cardinals.

220

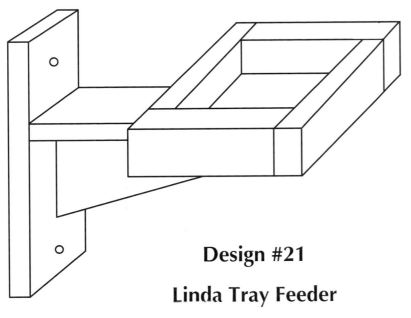

Design #21

Linda Tray Feeder

Materials:
1" x 6" - 39½"

Ethelle Henderson displays a Linda
feeder that she has just assembled.

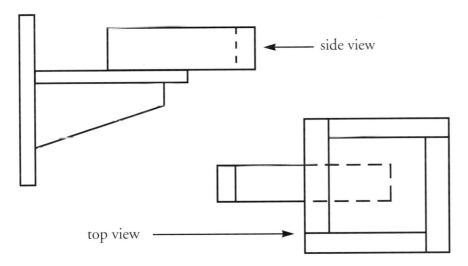

side view

top view

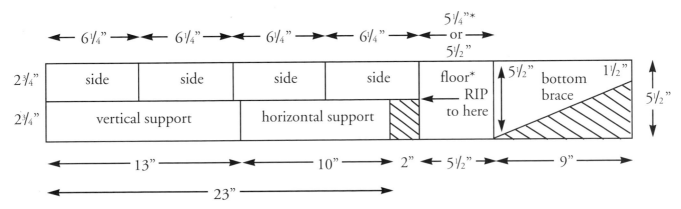

	6¼"	6¼"	6¼"	6¼"	5¼"* or 5½"		
2¾"	side	side	side	side	floor*	5½" bottom brace	1½"
2¾"	vertical support		horizontal support		RIP to here		5½"

13" 10" 2" 5½" 9"

23"

* If the board is ¾" thick, the floor must be 5½" by 5½."
  If the board is ⅞" thick, the floor must be 5¼" by 5¼" inches.

221

Assembly for the Linda feeder:
Above: Screw the sides onto
the edges of the floor unit.

Top right: After assembling
the frame for the back, set
the feeder box in place.

Right: Ventral view of
the assembled feeder

This male bluebird has just taken a mealworm from the food cavity on the top of a Peterson T-post feeder. These feeders can also be filled with grape jelly to attract orioles.

Design #22

Peterson T-post Feeder

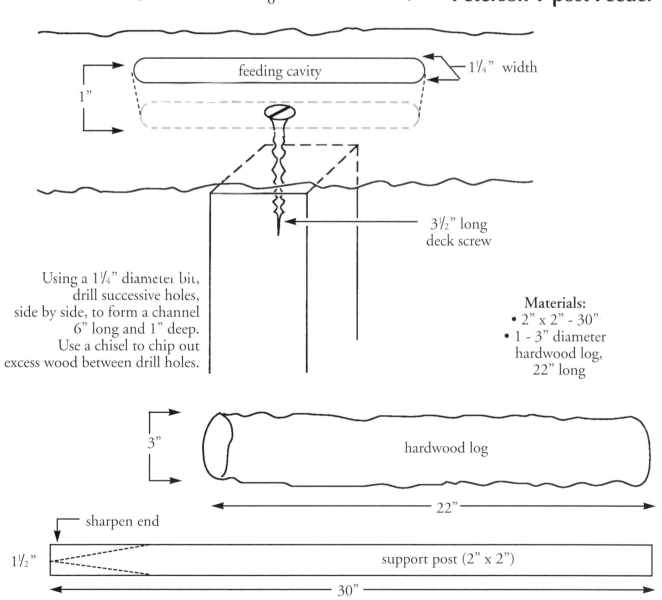

6"

feeding cavity

1¼" width

1"

3½" long
deck screw

Using a 1¼" diameter bit, drill successive holes, side by side, to form a channel 6" long and 1" deep. Use a chisel to chip out excess wood between drill holes.

Materials:
• 2" x 2" - 30"
• 1 - 3" diameter hardwood log, 22" long

3"

hardwood log

22"

sharpen end

1½"

support post (2" x 2")

30"

If you use grape jelly or mealworms in the feeder, you may wish to place a small bowl or tray inside the feeder. You can also use this feeder for sunflower seeds, Niger thistle, peanuts or other bird food items. This feeder is easy to make and is good to use as a gift for friends.

Peterson T-post feeder

Dick Peterson of Brooklyn Center, Minnesota, developed this delightful feeder as a rustic design for feeding mealworms to bluebirds. It requires only a short length of hardwood log about 3 inches in diameter, 22 to 24 inches long, and a 2 by 2-inch board about 30 inches long. This feeder does not require exact measurements. Bore a 1-1/4-inch wide channel into the center portion of the log by drilling successive 1-inch-deep holes, and chip out extra wood with a wood chisel.

The Peterson T-post feeder can attract bluebirds if it is placed near an active bluebird nest and regularly filled with mealworms.

After sharpening one end to a point, pound the 2-inch by 2-inch post into the ground with a hammer, place the log horizontally on the post and, using a cordless drill with a screwdriver bit, drill a 3-1/2-inch deck screw from the bottom of the food channel into the top of the post.

The post should be near a perching area used by bluebirds, orioles, cardinals or any other species that you are trying to attract. Place mealworms into the food channel several times a day and wait for the action.

You can also put grape jelly into this channel to feed northern orioles. To help attract the orioles, I usually drive a finishing nail into the top of the log and place orange halves there in May when the orioles begin their nesting season.

Deck railing feeder

If you have a deck or patio railing, you can take advantage of this design to bring songbirds right up to your home. This extremely simple feeder can be assembled in 15 or 20 minutes. Depending on which birds you wish to attract, you

Deck railing feeders can be equipped with shallow trays .

If the tray is filled with mealworms, deck railing feeders will attract many species of birds including robins, cardinals, catbirds and chipping sparrows.

225

Design #23

Deck Railing
Fruit and Mealworm
Feeder

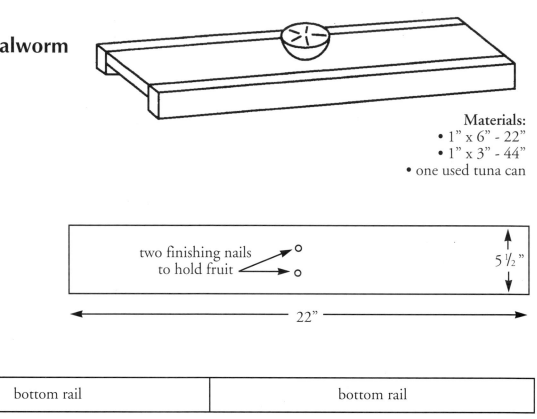

Materials:
- 1" x 6" - 22"
- 1" x 3" - 44"
- one used tuna can

two finishing nails
to hold fruit

5 ½ "

22"

2 ¾ "	bottom rail	bottom rail

22" 22"

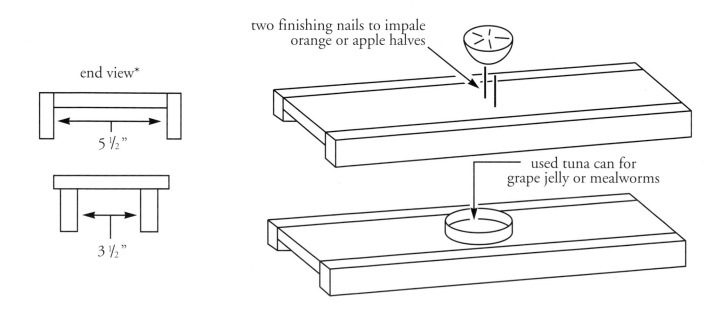

two finishing nails to impale
orange or apple halves

end view*

5 ½ "

3 ½ "

used tuna can for
grape jelly or mealworms

*If top of deck railing is 5 ½ " wide, place bottom rails on side of floor. If top is narrower (3 ½ ")
fasten the bottom rails under the floor at a width that will straddle the deck railing.

226

Enclosed bluebird feeder

Another innovation for feeding bluebirds is to create an enclosed feeder where the birds go in to obtain the mealworms or Janilla bluebird mix. This reduces the competition from other species that might try to use the feeder.

It works because the entry hole is the same size as it is for a regular bluebird house: either an oval 1 3/8 inches wide and 2 1/4 inches high or a circle 1 1/2 inches in diameter. This prevents starlings or other larger birds from entering.

Since the feeder has at least one glass side, you can still watch the birds eating inside the feeder. This design is available commercially and was adapted from plans used in bluebird wintering areas where chopped raisins and dogwood berries are placed in enclosed feeders. This provides the birds with a steady food supply in the winter.

When mealworms or Janilla bluebird mix are used, the feeder can be placed in bluebird nesting and feeding areas during the summer.

The enclosed bluebird feeder can use either mealworms or Janilla bluebird mix to attract bluebirds. They enter the small holes in the back of the feeder to eat the food, while larger birds are prevented from using the feeder.

GRAPE JELLY FEEDERS

Grape jelly feeders are similar to mealworm feeders. They hold small, shallow trays for grape jelly, an irresistible food for northern orioles and gray catbirds. You may want to place a couple of orange halves on the feeder early in the spring to attract the orioles to your feeder, but they usually ignore the orange halves after they discover the jelly. Generic brands of grape jelly are cheaper than name brands, and they're eagerly consumed by the orioles.

Linda tray

When the Linda Tray is stocked with a shallow tray of grape jelly it can work successfully as an oriole feeder.

The speckled head on this oriole shows that it is a male molting into its adult plumage. It has been attracted by the grape jelly in this feeder.

Peterson T-post feeders, filled with grape jelly, will attract northern orioles and gray catbirds.

Peterson T-post Feeder

This feeder is highly successful for feeding orioles. Stock the feeder with grape jelly in May when the orioles return from their wintering grounds. Entire oriole families may visit the feeder, bringing their young to eat the jelly after they fledge.

Deck railing feeder

As with the Linda Tray and Peterson T-post feeders, deck railing feeders are easily adapted for feeding grape jelly to orioles. All you need to do is to fasten a small shallow tray to the top of the feeder and keep it stocked with grape jelly. You may wish to place an orange half on the feeder early in the spring to help attract the orioles if they do not have a tradition of coming to your feeders.

APPLE AND ORANGE FEEDERS

Apple and orange half feeders attract orioles, robins, blue jays, catbirds and house finches as well as other songbirds.

Drive a couple 8D finishing nails into a stump, feeding platform surface or even the roof of a bird feeder. Stick apple halves or orange halves or both onto the feeders and see what comes. To keep the cost of this kind of feeding down, you can use the cheapest apples available, including those with worms.

Drive one or two headless nails into your deck railing feeder and stick orange or apple halves on them. This will attract red-bellied woodpeckers, robins and other birds.

Deck railing feeder

Deck railing feeders work well for presenting either orange halves or apple halves. Instead of placing the nails in the center, you could place the nails at the ends of the feeder with a mealworm tray in the middle.

Hanging orange half feeder

Hanging orange half feeders are designed to offer two orange halves to orioles. Two and a half inch deck screws are used to hold the orange halves in place on the feeder. This feeder can be made from a piece of 1 by 6-inch board only 20 1/4 inches long. Besides being easy to make, this feeder also makes good use of leftover wood scraps.

An orange slice can be placed on each side of this feeder for orioles.

Design #24

Hanging Orange Half Feeder

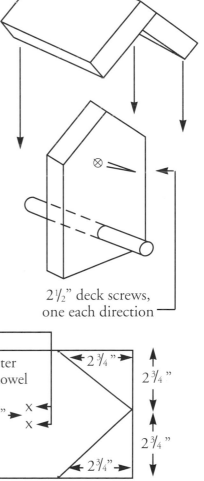

screw eye

2½" deck screws, one each direction

Materials:
- 1" x 6" - 20"
- ½" diameter dowel, 6" long
- 2 - 2½" deck screws
- 1¼" screw eye

½" diameter dowel

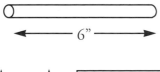

← 6" →

finished hanging orange half feeder

locations for deck screws. Drive one to face each side.

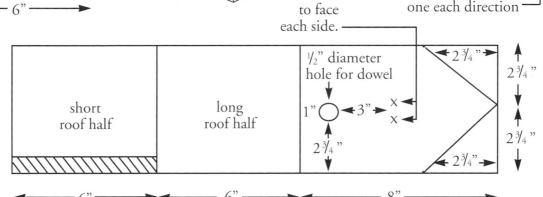

5 ½"

5"

½"

short roof half

long roof half

½" diameter hole for dowel

1" ◯ ←3"→ ×
×

2¾"

2¾"

2¾"

2¾"

2¾"

2¾"

← 6" → ← 6" → ← 8" →

231

PEANUT FEEDERS

Hardware cloth peanut feeders attract many bird species and are good alternatives to suet during the summer. Shown feeding at this peanut feeder are, from left to right, a blue jay, male downy woodpecker, and a male white-breasted nuthatch.

Hardware cloth peanut feeder

The hardware cloth peanut feeder provides an easy and effective way to dispense shelled peanuts without exposing them to exploitation by squirrels. The 1/4-inch wire mesh makes the birds peck at the peanuts through the wire so that pieces can be removed with little effort. Peanuts are very appealing to chickadees, blue jays, nuthatches, downy and hairy woodpeckers and other species. This is an excellent alternative to suet in the summertime. Peanuts do not become rancid as quickly as suet in warm weather.

Squirrels may eventually damage the wire at the bottom, causing the peanuts to flow out. If this happens, just roll up the bottom of the feeder to cover the hole. There is a hole in the top of this feeder for the hanging chain to extend through, and the top is lifted to fill the feeder.

If the peanuts are not eaten right away they may become rancid, so you should check the feeder every now and then and replace the peanuts if there is a problem. Most larger wild bird supply stores have peanuts in quantity for feeding the birds.

It's probably just as easy to make several of these feeders at once as it is to make just one. You might want to make several others at the same time to give to friends.

Materials:
- 1" x 6" - 6"
- 2" x 4" - 3"
- 8 ½" x 18" hardware cloth ¼" mesh
- small chain, 18" long

A soldering gun
and solder
are needed to
make this feeder.

¾" thick top

Cut this
from a piece
of 1" by 6."

← 5 ¼" →

← 2 ¼" →

lower portion of top,
1 ½" thick

Cut this from a
piece of 2" by 4."

Design #25

Hardware Cloth
Peanut Feeder

wire tips exposed on one side

8 ½"

¼" mesh hardware cloth

18"

Glue and nail two pieces of
top together, then drill ⅜"
diameter hole through the top.

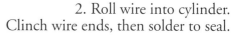

2. Roll wire into cylinder.
Clinch wire ends, then solder to seal.

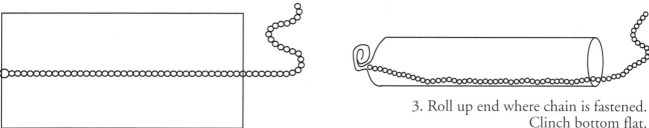

1. Lay chain on hardware cloth.
Attach chain at bottom (left end).

3. Roll up end where chain is fastened.
Clinch bottom flat.

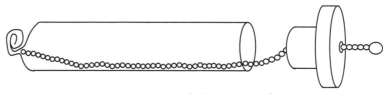

4. Insert wooden top onto chain

HOLLOW STUMP FEEDER

One of the most delightful aspects of building bird feeders is the chance to be creative and to use natural objects to create the feeders. Short sections of tree trunks work great as bird feeders. They only need to be about a foot high, and seed can be scattered on top of the stump. Two or three sections of tree trunks of different heights can be clustered to create an attractive and natural-looking feeder arrangement. They can't be damaged by squirrels and they last many years.

Another variation of this feeder involves a section of a hollow tree that has been cut into 1-foot segments. You make this feeder by placing a recessed floor in the hollow section of the stump, resting about 2 inches lower than the outer rim.

Trace the outline of the inner cavity of the stump onto a large sheet of paper. Cut around the outline and then trace it onto a piece of exterior plywood. Cut out the plywood so that it will fit inside the hollow portion of the stump.

Pound at least four nails into the inner cavity of the hollow stump about 2 inches down from the top. But don't pound the nails all the way in; make sure they extend out from the wood about 2 inches. The plywood rests on these nails. You may need to use some caulking around the edge of the plywood to seal up any gaps that would allow sunflower seeds to fall into the cavity under the plywood.

This hollow stump feeder is popular with blue jays and squirrels.

This feeder is extremely popular with blue jays, cardinals, fox sparrows, white-throated sparrows, juncos and gray squirrels. And there is nothing for squirrels to destroy! The feeder is also low enough to the ground that ground feeding birds do not hesitate to hop up and use it. You could also add to the appeal of this feeder by driving 8D finishing nails into the wooden rim of the hollow stump to feed apple halves to the robins, blue jays and catbirds.

234

You can drive finishing nails into the outer rim of your stump to feed apple halves to gray catbirds and American robins.

Other visitors to stump feeders are ground-feeding birds like white-throated sparrows.

This hollow stump feeder has a center portion of plywood added to create a feeding area. The plywood was cut with a jigsaw to match the shape of the cavity.

235

GROUND FEEDING

One of the best ways to feed many birds is with no feeder at all! Simply scatter sunflower or millet seed on a relatively bare patch of ground. Birds like mourning doves, rufous-sided towhees, dark-eyed juncos, song sparrows, chipping sparrows, white-throated sparrows, fox sparrows, cowbirds, red-winged blackbirds, brown thrashers and ring-necked pheasants are regular ground feeders.

Sunflower seeds are a good all-around choice. In spring and fall you could include white proso millet to attract the juncos and native sparrows that are migrating through the region.

You will periodically need to remove the waste grain and empty sunflower hulls from a ground feeding site to keep it relatively clean. Ground feeding can attract meadow voles, house mice and even Norway rats, so watch for signs of rodent problems. Rodents may in turn attract owls or hawks to your yard.

Art Hawkins of Hugo, MN, is shown here scattering seeds at his lean-to feeder. This feeder is very popular with cardinals and many other bird species.

236

Here are examples of birds you can attract by scattering bird food on the ground:

fox sparrow (pictured on the left) and mourning dove

white-throated sparrow,

To control rodents, follow their trails back to the shelters where they live: under a deck, foundation or wood pile. If you set snap traps for the rodents, place them adjacent to walls or other structures and lean a piece of wood against the wall so the trap is not visible or accessible to birds. Otherwise the birds could be killed in the trap.

Often a ground feeding site evolves naturally under a hanging bird feeder where birds and squirrels spill seed onto the ground. Once the birds adapt to such a site you can maintain it by keeping the grass short and occasionally scattering some extra sunflower seed or millet.

Lean-to feeders

A lean-to feeder is simply an adaptation of a ground feeding station with an added lean-to roof that keeps the seeds on the ground relatively dry and free of snow cover. It is usually a rather large but very rustic and effective feeder for many birds.

The lean-to structure can be a panel, a sheet of exterior plywood or a frame of posts or tree branches. It should be between 4 and 8 feet wide and about 6 to 8 feet long. The lower edge of the roof is anchored to the ground and the opposite side is fastened to posts or tree trunks so that it is about 4 feet above the ground. A frame of boards or branches can be covered with pine or spruce boughs to make it look more natural in the winter.

In the Midwest, the prevailing winter winds are from the northwest, so the open end of this feeder should face to the southeast. That will limit problems with drifting snow covering the seeds.

These feeders accommodate many birds at once, so scatter grain in these feeders every day or every other day.

red-breasted nuthatch,

and wild turkey.

This lean-to feeder, made of landscaping timbers, has a plywood roof.

237

BOTTLE FEEDERS

Juice bottle feeder

A simple, cheap and effective bird feeder can be made from a glass juice jar as shown in the photograph. Two straps are tightened to encircle the jar and a 6-inch piece of wood on the top. A 1/2 inch diameter screw eye is fastened into the wood to provide a convenient point of suspension, and the wood should be adjusted back and forth so that the jar hangs horizontally.

Chickadees readily enter this feeder for sunflower seeds. This design was contributed by Fritz Kuhnle of Menomonee, Michigan.

Chickadee-in-a-bottle feeder

This novel feeder is usually placed on a solid support post, but in Design #26 the base has been revised to set on a deck railing. It provides a protected site for chickadees to feed where they won't be molested by house sparrows or other larger birds, and where they are kept warm by the sun even on cold winter days.

The circle of 1/8-inch thick Masonite for the entrance replaces the ordinary liner for the jar's canning lid. The 1 1/8-inch entrance hole allows chickadees to enter the jar for sunflower seeds, but prevents larger house sparrows from entering.

This feeder is fun to make with children. Orwin Rustad, the naturalist who provided this feeder design, helps kids make them during bird feeding workshops.

The juice bottle feeder keeps seeds dry and is popular with chickadees.

A chickadee picks a sunflower seed from a Rustad chickadee feeder.

Orwin Rustad of Faribault, MN, shows how canning jars can be used to make a creative feeder that accommodates chickadees but not larger birds. The canning lid liner is replaced with a 1/8 inch thick piece of masonite with a 1 1/8-inch diameter hole.

238

The chickadee-in-a-bottle feeder is designed to sit on a deck railing.

Materials:
- 1" x 6" - 25"
- 1" x 3" - 40"
- 1" x 2" - 38"
- two one-quart canning jars with lids
- one piece of ⅛" thick masonite, 2½" x 5"
- two pieces of wire, 12" long each

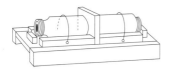

finished chickadee-in-a-bottle feeder

Design #26
Chickadee-in-a-Bottle Feeder

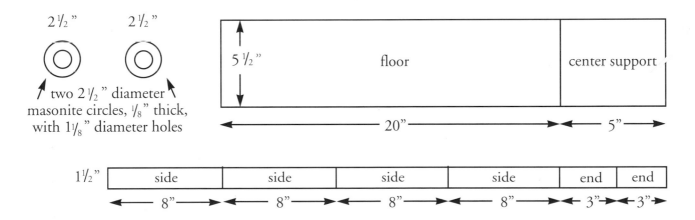

2½"   2½"

↑ two 2½" diameter masonite circles, ⅛" thick, with 1⅛" diameter holes

5½" | floor | center support
←———— 20" ————→ ←— 5" —→

1½" | side | side | side | side | end | end
←— 8" —→ ←— 8" —→ ←— 8" —→ ←— 8" —→ ←3"→←3"→

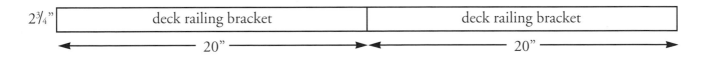

2¾" | deck railing bracket | deck railing bracket
←———— 20" ————→ ←———— 20" ————→

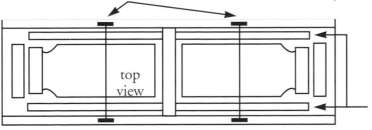

Sheet rock nails are used to fasten wire that holds the jars in place.

top view

Deck railing brackets should be placed on the edge or bottom of the floor so they will fit snugly onto the deck railing.

These boards are fitted in from the edge of the floor so the jar fits snugly in place.

SPRING WARBLER TRAY

The springtime bird migration includes the northward movement of warblers, tanagers and kinglets. These are primarily insect-eating birds, but their diets are in transition as they move north. They don't usually visit feeders during the summer, but in the spring they can be enticed to eat at large tray feeders stocked with the following array of food items: a shallow dish of finely crushed eggshells (for the calcium), a couple of orange halves, sliced bananas, a shallow bowl regularly supplied with mealworms, a variety of day-old bakery goods like doughnuts, bread and cornbread, a chick waterer oriole feeder (Design #20) filled with sugar water, suet, Janilla bluebird mix, peanut butter, chopped raisins and a 5-quart plastic ice cream bucket of overripe bananas and cantaloupe along with a culture of fruit flies.

Yellow-rumped warbler.

This unusual smorgasbord should be set out for the last ten days of April and the first ten days of May to coincide with the arrival of the migrant songbirds. You may be surprised at the interesting visitors at your feeder: perhaps orange-crowned warblers, yellow-rumped warblers and kinglets.

Feeders that work well for this purpose include the large tray feeder (Design #3), the large deck railing feeder (Design #5), the large fly-through feeder (Design #8) or the large or extra large screen feeders (Designs #12 and 13).

To establish the colony of fruit flies, put a variety of overripe bananas, cantaloupe and orange halves in an ice cream bucket in early April. Set it in a garage or outbuilding to attract free-living fruit flies. The flies should be there by April 20, in time to set up the warbler tray.

You could also consider ordering a commercial culture of fruit flies. A culture of wingless fruit flies, a variety that can't escape from the feeder, is available from the Carolina Biological Supply Company at 1-800-334-5551. Ask for item #17-2900. They should cost under $5 before the shipping fee. If you want to raise your own fruit fly culture with a kit from Carolina biological supply, ask them for item #17-2910.

The Minnesota DNR would be interested to learn the results of your warbler tray efforts. Write to the Nongame Wildlife Program at the Minnesota DNR, 500 Lafayette Rd, St. Paul, MN 55155-4007.

HOW TO ATTACH BIRD FEEDERS TO POSTS OR PIPES

Small to medium-sized bird feeders can be placed on posts or pipes purchased at local lumber yards, garden centers or hardware stores. Make sure your post will be strong enough to support the feeder. You must also think about how to make your feeder cat and squirrel-proof. A feeder should be at least 5 feet above the ground to prevent cats from jumping directly onto it. The feeder should also be far enough from nearby buildings and trees to prevent squirrels from jumping onto the feeder from above.

A good way to attach a smaller feeder like the small or medium self feeder (Designs #15 and 16) is to use a 1-inch diameter metal plumbing pipe that is 8 feet long. Place it in a 2 1/2 foot hole dug in the ground and then pour a small amount of concrete into the hole, letting it flow around the pipe to provide a solid anchor for the feeder. You can buy small quantities of concrete (known by trade names like "Quickcrete®") at hardware stores and lumber yards.

Fasten a floor flange fitting for plumbing pipe to the bottom of the feeder using 3/16-inch stove bolts. Then the floor flange can be screwed directly onto the threads of the plumbing pipe. You can smear the pipe with lithium grease to discourage climbing by squirrels, raccoons and cats, or you can install a baffle under the feeder to keep these mammals from it.

Larger feeders may need support from two or three posts to prevent them from bending, breaking or blowing over in high winds. Feeders can also be placed on top of wooden fence posts or cut-off tree trunks by drilling several holes in the bottom of the feeder and securing it to the tree stump with lag screws. It would probably also help to also use several L-shaped shelf brackets to anchor the bottom of the feeder to the sides of the fence post or tree trunk.

Floor flange attached to the bottom of a feeder.

Plumbing pipe screwed into a floor flange.

This feeder arrangement has been secured to a post.

241